Help!

If you think there's anything that ought to be in this guide that's not, do the world a favour and let me know about it. If it's important and no one else has told me about it already, you'll receive a free copy of the next edition.

PO 177 Potts Point NSW Australia
dands@magna.com.au

Dirk Flinthart

Coasting

Dirk Flinthart

D
S

Published in 1996 by Duffy & Snellgrove
PO 177 Potts Point NSW 2011 Australia
dands@magna.com.au

Distributed by Tower Books Australia 02 9975 5566

Cover and illustrations by Russell Tate
Designed by Maggie Cooper
Maps by Maggie Cooper and Shannon Kerr
Printed by Griffin Paperbacks

ISBN 1 875989 06 4

Contents

Introduction

Congratulations on buying the Dirk Flinthart Guide to Australia's East Coast! (You did buy it, didn't you? You're not just standing down the back of the bookstore having a surreptitious peek between the covers, are you? Swine! Stop it at once!) You have made an excellent decision in choosing the Flinthart Guide to aid and assist you on your perilous journey.

Why? Well, for one thing, this is the only guidebook dedicated specifically to the East Coast of Australia. After all, most of the action in Australia is on the coast, and the best of the tropical coast is on the east, by the Barrier Reef. That being true, this book is specifically dedicated to the extremely interesting and entertaining strip of land between Sydney and Cooktown inclusive and that's it. No chapters about the endless desert. Nothing at all about Western Australia, or Melbourne or Canberra – just the bit you really wanted to know about. Keeps it nice and light to carry.

The next thing that makes the Flinthart Guide a unique and valuable publication is that, unlike most guide-books, it's not completely, mind-numbingly, brain-staggeringly tedious. Not only has the publisher given us permission to exercise a sense of humour, but we're even allowed to tell the rude, brutal truth about places you don't want to go. For instance: *Do Not Go To Weipa. It Is Boring. It Is Difficult To Get To. It Is Ugly. There Is An Enormous Bauxite Mine There And Not Much Else. It Is A Waste Of Time And Money For Travellers.*

See how useful this can be? Already you know more about Australia than you did – and it's good, solid, useful stuff, not more obnoxious facts about fish exports, iron production, or dung beetles. Think about it: when you're faced with a stretch of land nearly 3000km long, with every separate hamlet along the way vying for your hard-earned cash, knowing what places are a complete loss can be much more helpful than being told how great the other places are. So – no Pollyanna bullshit from the Flinthart Guide. If a place is dead boring, you'll be told.

And if an activity is the sort of thing that will only interest one per cent of readers, we've left it out. Most guide books cram in everything, which can be very confusing because any one reader will have time for only a fraction of the activities suggested – and no way of knowing which ones are essential. I've taken the opposite approach and *left out* almost everything. As you can tell from the weight of this book, there's still enough to keep you busy. And if you do everything I suggest, you'll have seen and done everything that, according to most of the travellers I've talked to, is essential.

Another thing: The Flinthart Guide is dedicated to the poor but hardy travellers of the world. It may be true that you can drink all the Moët & Chandon you like for the all-inclusive price of $500 or so per night at the resort on Bedarra Island, but who cares? If you could afford that kind of life, you wouldn't be buying this book anyway. From us, you'll hear about hostels and campsites, cheap meals, good deals and where the most fun for the least money lives.

So there you have it. In one fell swoop, you've acquired an invaluable, comprehensive, interesting guide to the most travel-friendly area of

Australia. Complete with maps, commentaries, anecdotes from the people who've been there before you, illuminating historical and social information and a discreet smattering of absolute bullshit. So what are you waiting for? Take the book down to the cash register and pony up the bucks: it may well be the best investment you'll ever make …

Now, let's answer some tough questions.

Where Am I Going And Why?

It's a long way from Sydney to Cairns. About 2,800km, more or less. If that's a little difficult to picture, think of it as being about three times the length of the UK. Or thereabouts, anyway. Biggest city in Australia is Sydney, with a population of about three and a half million. Biggest in Queensland is Brisbane, with a population of about a million and a half. Most cities in Australia, however, don't even reach the 100,000 mark. Be careful when you're navigating: unlike Europe and the USA, a big dot on the map with a reassuring name attached may not be even a village – it may be a farmhouse, or even a water tank.

The point is that this is not a journey to be carelessly tackled. Personally, I think the best direction to do the trek is from South to North, for a number of reasons. The first is simple: if you're visiting from overseas, chances are Australia is considerably hotter than your home country. If that's the case, you should certainly take a little time to acclimatise down south before moving up into the tropical regions. It's not like the sudden change in climate will really damage you – but I can assure you that if you come straight from a Northern Hemisphere temperate autumn, or even winter, you will not enjoy your first two weeks in Far North Queensland. Not even a little.

Another reason for going northwards is transport. Far and away the best way to attack this journey is to buy an old car and drive for yourself. Up in the Deep North, cars tend to be badly savaged by salt water and persistent rain, whereas down south, they're usually a little better maintained. Furthermore, the much, much larger population base in Sydney means that there's a much wider range of vehicles available for purchase.

Still another reason is the scuba diving, which is something you really ought to do. The very best diving in the entire world is found on the Great Barrier Reef and on that reef, the very best of the diving is to be had in the Deep North. On the other hand, dive courses up in Cairns, the Whitsundays and Mackay tend to be savagely expensive and if you learn to dive up there, you might not have time to accumulate the experience necessary to do any really interesting dives independently. Therefore, the best thing to do is surf your way up the coast to about Bundaberg, where the surf stops, take a cheap dive course and dive your way up the Reef to Cairns.

Then there're matters of safety. There are hazards peculiar to Australia, mostly to do with its size and the lack of water. Better that you learn about the place and get used to taking precautions down south, where there are plenty of towns and people about if you get into trouble, than if you plunge straight into the Deep North and get in over your head. Civilisation wears a bit thin in the strange north and west country of Queensland. There are stretches of country where it's possible to travel three or four hundred kilometres without seeing a sign of humanity. Start with the South. See what Australia has to offer in terms of art and culture, history and cuisine. Learn about the country and then take the plunge. You'll be much better prepared to enjoy it.

The trip itself can take as long as you like. I guess if you were determined only to hit the high points and to cut sleep to an absolute minimum, you could possibly see the dozen or so best points of the journey within two weeks. Not if you were driving, of course; the sheer effort of all that travel would shag you before you got halfway done. And if you did do the whole thing in a fortnight, you'd be seeing only the barest minimum of sites, without the opportunity to meet Australians and get the flavour of the place.

Most of the people I spoke with allocated about two months to the trip from Sydney up to Cairns. Not only that, but most of them wound up losing the plot; they'd get somewhere they really liked, such as Airlie Beach, get a job with a hostel and wind up staying two months in the one place. The East Coast can do that to you. There are some absolutely magical places along that stretch of the world – and if you're from practically any other nation on the planet, the laid-back and relaxed approach to life in Australia is going to be very, very tempting. (Trust me on this one. You may think you're homesick for a week or so – but just wait. This place grows on you faster than fungus under a fullback's jockstrap.)

Still, if you are pressed for time, here's a list of the ten most absolutely primo, top-hole excellent things to see and do along the way, with the best at the top. Try not to miss any of them – they're all world-beaters.

Dirk's Dozen

(You'll notice there are rarely twelve choices in these lists, which are scattered through the book. Alliteration has won out over logic).

1. Whitsunday Islands, Queensland. Easy first choice. Practically defining the term 'tropical paradise', with fantastic sailing, diving, fishing, swimming, snorkelling, walking, camping, climbing. Three, four weeks if you have the time.

2. The Great Barrier Reef, Queensland. Has to be considered a destination in itself. Finest diving and fishing anywhere. Could be revisited as often as you could afford it. Two weeks, easy. Try camping on some of the deserted national park islands.

3. Fraser Island/Sand Islands of south-east Queensland. These islands are unlike anything else in the world – giant islands of blown sand, with forests, lakes, swamps, heaths and fantastic beaches. Fraser is getting a little too popular for me these days, but Moreton Island is still very lightly visited and even North Stradbroke has a lot going for it. A week or more, walking and camping.

4. Hinchinbrook Island, Queensland. A thirty-plus kilometre walking track through dense rainforest, sliced with crystal creeks and waterfalls, next to strips of golden beach. Much of the island is practically unexplored. The flora and fauna are utterly amazing and the strenuous nature of the walk means you're unlikely to encounter many others there at all.

Three tough days. Take your time, do it in five, and stick around the Cardwell area for World Heritage-listed rainforests.

5. The Big Scrub. In the far north-east of New South Wales about three million years or so ago, a total monster of a volcano arose. The caldera which remains is about sixty kilometres across and as a result of the uplifting, plus freaky climactic conditions, fairly large areas of rainforest have been preserved which are practically straight out of Gondwanaland. Much has been cleared, but enough remains to totally blow your mind. Two weeks, walking, camping and visiting the little villages around Murwillumbah.

6. North Coast, New South Wales. There's a whole stretch of coastline from about Port Macquarie up to Tweed Heads, where if you can just get off the highway and down to the shore, you can stake out your own chunk of completely deserted surf beach. Broad white sands, glass-clear waters with excellent waves and the dolphins and seabirds your only companions. If you've never had the chance to walk five kilometres along a million-dollar beach without seeing another human being – not even so much as a footprint – this just has to be. Two weeks, broken up – take two or three days any time you need to chill out.

7. Cairns and the Atherton Tableland, north Queensland. More fantastic World Heritage rainforests, access to some of the very best of the reef, an astounding local artistic, cultural (and food!) scene, plus one of the biggest backpacker-friendly setups in the world. The city of Cairns has practically given the keys away to the backpackers. Three to four weeks without any trouble at all.

8. Undara Lava Tubes. Unique lava caves way the frag out the back of nowhere behind Cardwell and Tully, also in northern Queensland. These are the largest, most extensive lava caves known on the planet and they are unlike anything you've ever seen before. Country's a bit dry and savage, though, so this is only a two-day site.

9. Hunter Valley, just north of Sydney. Pretty, accessible and the best possible introduction to Australian winemaking. Although the best of the Australian wines are the internationally-famous heavy reds, the Hunter Valley has been turning out quality white wines for years. No visit to this country is complete without diving into the wine scene and a tasting excursion through the Hunter Valley is next door to heaven, as far as I'm concerned. Two or

three days for the tasting, but you'll want to break them up so as not to destroy yourself, so call it a week for wine buffs.

10. Sydney! Definitely a world-class destination in its own right. It possesses a sufficiency of unique architecture and monuments to equal most cities of the world and although it lacks the history-laden atmosphere of the European cities, it makes up for that with a brilliant sunny energy that easily outclasses those older, greyer places. I could spend a month in Sydney without ever doing the same thing twice.

Thanks ... but all I really wanted was a few statistics on population centres and things like that.
Sorry. I got carried away.

Yeah, well maybe you can tell me a bit about the stuff I'm likely to see. Animals and plants and things. Only keep it short, will you?

Nature

Australia is the oldest continent. The shield rocks in Western Australia go back to the earliest days of life on earth. Since Australia separated from the ancient mega-continent of Gondwanaland quite a long time before everything else did, its isolated ecosystem retained a variety of species seen nowhere else in the world

Most noticeable amongst these are the marsupials. These differ from the rest of the mammalian world by giving birth to extremely undeveloped offspring, who are then carried and nurtured in a pouch. Outside Australia, marsupials are found only in Papua New Guinea and as a single species of opossum in the Americas. As placental mammals (mammals which nurture their young inside the body for a lot longer, with the aid of a disposable organ called the placenta) did not arise on the Australian continent, the marsupials achieved a diversity never seen anywhere else on earth. Right up until the turn of the century, there existed a large marsupial predator, a wolf-like species called the Tasmanian Tiger. They're extinct now, it seems likely. Australia's record for that kind of thing is utterly appalling.

Despite the occasional hiccup, there still remains a fascinating range of marsupials on the Australian continent. From the great Red Kangaroo, which can stand nearly two metres tall, down to the tiny marsupial mice which can easily sit in a teaspoon, they are found in nearly every possible environmental niche. Treetops to desert floor, there are marsupials all over this country.

The strangest animals in Australia are without doubt the monotremes. This group of mammals is represented by only two species, the Platypus and the Echidna. Both of these are notable for the fact that unlike every other mammal on the planet, they lay eggs. Leathery ones. They're definitely mammals, though: hairy, warm-blooded creatures which feed their young on milk. Of course, the fact that the platypus is mostly aquatic, with webbed feet and a duck-like bill for grubbing up worms off the river bottoms, doesn't really help convince you. At least the Echidna, or Spiny Anteater, has the good grace to resemble a large, square hedgehog. These days, due to destruction of habitat and competition from feral species, both the platypus and the echidna are rare enough to be considered under threat. If you are fortunate enough to spot either species in the wild, please leave the poor bastards alone.

Actually, the whole of the Australian environment is kind of alien to the rest of the world. There's the bird life, for instance, with its plethora of multi-coloured parrots and the big, flightless cassowaries and emus. Australian birds don't sing in quite the same manner as well-bred European and American birds – they screech, howl, whoop, whip-crack and even laugh. The famous signature call of the Laughing Kookaburra – the largest kingfisher in the world – is certain to wake you at dawn at least once during your stay, so be prepared.

Then there's the reptiles – huge monitor lizards called 'goannas', enormous killer crocodiles and more snakes than anybody knows what to do with. Check out the section on Monsters towards the end of this introduction for a better idea of this kind of thing.

One thing you'll notice on your trip is a long range of mountains and cliffs running from the bottom of the east coast right up to the top. It's called the Great Dividing Range and, while it's neither great nor a range, it does divide the rivers that flow east into the Pacific Ocean from those which flow west into the Darling and Murray Rivers, which end up entering the sea over a thousand kilometres away down in South Australia. This is one of the largest river systems in the world, even though the rivers themselves are not much to write home about. The Darling has been robbed of most of its water by farmers wanting to irrigate their properties and is now, thanks in part to chemical runoff from cotton farms, something between a sewer and an industrial drain. It has provided some colourful – and toxic – blue-green algae 'blooms' in recent summers.

The Great Dividing Range, which is only 2,228 metres at its highest point (Mount Kosciusko, Australia's tallest mountain, in southern NSW), runs up the coast of NSW about 100km in from the sea and includes the impressive Blue Mountains west of Sydney and some rugged east-facing cliffs further north. You will be travelling up the strip of lush coastal land between these mountains and the sea. In Queensland the range veers inland for several hundred kilometres and dwindles in size until it ceases to be a meaningful feature of the landscape. The typical formation for much of the range is not the mountain but the plateau, as the peaks have been weathered over the years. Lots of years.

Regarding plants and stuff, the most interesting two aspects are that the ever-present Eucalypt or Gum Tree (of which there are hundreds of species all over the continent) loses its bark, not its leaves, and that most Australian native plants have flowers that are incredibly small by European standards. It gets pretty complicated after that, so if you want to know more, visit the bookshop at the Sydney Botanic Gardens.

Fair enough, I guess. What about this Barrier Reef thing I keep hearing about?

The Great Barrier Reef

The Great Barrier Reef, off the eastern coast of Queensland, is the largest built structure on the planet. It is best described as a gigantic colony organism some 2000km long. The Barrier Reef proper gets started at about the level of the Tropic of Capricorn, but it really firms up about 500km north, off Mackay. From that point on, it becomes almost literally a barrier, a long line of connected coral reefs which pose one hell of a hazard to navigation. This also means there is no surf on the beaches behind the Reef.

Coral reefs are made up of the limestone skeletons of millions of tiny organisms closely related to jellyfish. These organisms live together in vast colonies, filtering tiny plankton and the like out of the marine waters to feed on. These large colonies, or reefs, act as food source and shelter to literally thousands upon thousands of other species, including fish, molluscs, echinoderms and worms. With variation in sea level over geological periods of time, some reefs can even form islands, which eventually trap sand and acquire plant life. Although coral ecosystems occur in warm marine waters all over the world, the Great Barrier Reef is by far the most complex and diverse such system anywhere on the planet. There are more species of creature on the Barrier Reef than there are on any other coral reef.

This makes the Barrier Reef something of a paradise for divers, as well as a magnet for visitors from all over the planet. Access to the reef is available up and down the coast of Queensland and it is possible to visit many of the numerous isles of the reef. In actual fact, there are three kinds of island offshore from Queensland. Most common are normal, everyday islands formed from continental, mainland rock, such as Dunk Island, the Whitsunday Islands and Lizard Island. Then there are the coral cays, formed directly on the reef itself. Coral cays tend to be rather smaller than the continental islands, usually only a couple of square kilometres in size at best. Among the best-known of the coral cays are Lady Musgrave Island, Lady Eliot Island and Green Island. The last group of islands are the sand islands, found off the south-east Queensland coast, more of which will be said later.

Unfortunately, the popularity of the Barrier Reef may yet prove to be its undoing. Although it is World Heritage listed and has mostly been protected by status as a marine park, the increase in agriculture on shore, with resultant chemical runoff from rivers, combined with the stress caused by visiting tourists is leading to a definite decline in the general health of the reef as a whole.

Yeah, I've heard of this World Heritage thing. What should I know about it?

World Heritage Areas

World Heritage listing is conferred by an international body which deems certain places or things to be of irreplaceable natural or cultural value to the world. In Queensland, the World Heritage sites are the Wet Tropics around Cairns and Cardwell, the Great Barrier Reef and Fraser Island. In New South Wales, the rainforest parks in the North-East are listed, as is the Lord Howe Island group. Other places round the world include the

Taj Mahal, the Grand Canyon, the Serengeti National Park and the Great Pyramid.

Actually, Heritage listing doesn't mean anything except that some international body thought the place in question was really cool. It doesn't obligate governments to protect them in any way. It does, however, focus international attention on the area and increase the awareness of the site as a tourist point. Generally, this leads to the governments passing legislation to protect their World Heritage sites and that has been the case in Australia.

On the whole, however, the Australian environmental record is not good. Over three quarters of all the original forest on the continent has been cut down in the last two hundred years – three out of every four trees. Even the World Heritage forests of northern New South Wales might have become woodchips and lumber, if not for the action of a dedicated group of conservationists in 1979, who went literally head-to-head with loggers until the government stepped in. As a matter of fact, much of what is now World Heritage region was set for clear-felling, as things stood at the time. Australia's native forests, despite some moves to protect them, are still in great danger. For some bizarre reason, the logging industry has not yet acknowledged that full-fledged native forests don't spring back overnight when you cut them down. They are still baying for conservationist blood and slavering at the shoulder of the Conservative government in an effort to get a bigger share of the rapidly-dwindling forests, so they can turn them into woodchips and send them off to Japan. Then, of course, we can buy back our irreplaceable forests, at a much higher price than we sold them, in the form of toilet paper.

Then there's the introduction of exotic species. Ecology being a non-concept back in the 1780s, the consequences of bringing outside animals into a closed environment like Australia never occurred to the Poms. James Cook started it all, dumping a couple of pigs on Cape York, to breed up and act as a food supply for future visitors. This seemed like such a cunning plan that half the coastal islands had goats introduced in order to feed potential shipwreckees. You would not believe what a population of goats can do to an island's plant-life.

Of course, the British aren't British without foxes to hunt, so they were introduced. And cats – gotta have cats to fondle. And what about rabbits? Ooh, good idea, Blenkinsop – let's bring a few rabbits into the bally country.

Even the agriculture is a major environmental mistake. Take sheep, for example: they crop the grasses down low, in a manner the native species never evolved to survive. And with their sharp hooves, they tear at the roots which hold the soil together. The results? Australia has a topsoil erosion problem which is beyond belief. It's so bad that in New Zealand, the snowy mountaintops are sometimes stained orange-pink when the Westerlies blow, carrying Australian topsoil all the way across the Tasman.

Of course, the one disaster everybody knows best is the Cane Toad. Introduced to Queensland from South America in 1935, they completely failed to control the Grey-backed Cane Beetle and have since gone on to become one of the most widely recognised and repugnant features of the Queensland landscape. Join the rest of us: aim to run the bastards over

14

when you're on our highways. They make a wonderful crunchy pop when you get them square under the wheels.

The Weather

The hot part of the year, summer, occurs from November through February. The temperatures are generally higher inland, reaching 40 degrees Centigrade quite frequently. In summer, the average maximum temperatures in coastal areas relieved by the sea breeze usually stay in the high twenties in Sydney and the low thirties in Cairns. (Brisbane sits between the two). January and February are the hottest months. The humidity is more consistent in the north than the south and lasts a month or two longer. Summer is the period when most of the rain falls. Monsoon rains can be quite dramatic for those of you who may not be used to a three-week constant downpour, so when you are out in the country, always remember to check local road conditions. And never, ever, camp in a dry riverbed.

During summer, throughout most of Australia, the heaviest clothing you'll need will be perhaps a pair of jeans and a sweater – and that only for the mountain regions, or for unusually cool nights on the coast. A raincoat is essential, however, and make it a damned good one.

Winter isn't too rough. There will be no snow where you'll be going and in July, the coldest month, the average daily maximum temperature is 16 in Sydney and twenty-five in Cairns. It can qet quite chilly at nights, though – a warm jacket, good socks and heavy jeans recommended.

What all this means is, if you don't like temperatures of much over thirty degrees, you might think about starting your trip in March in Sydney, when it's pleasant and move up the coast so that by the time you reach Cairns in a month or two the temperature has cooled down and the jellyfish have moved away, allowing swimming. It will still be pretty warm in northern Queensland.

The most important garments for Australia are a good, broad hat to keep the killing sun off your face and good solid boots for walking. You're probably better off to buy both of those here in Australia. It won't necessarily be cheap, but they'll be right for local conditions.

You may find the heat and humidity quite distressing initially and it will take your body some time to adjust to your new water requirements. Try to make certain that you drink at least two litres per day in inactive conditions – and up to five or more if you are walking, exercising or the like.

Currently, large areas of Australia are in the grip of a crippling drought. This includes areas of inland New South Wales and Queensland, some of which have literally not seen rain for eight years. Pay attention to any instructions regarding the lighting of fires and to rules regarding water conservation. Most importantly, remember that water for washing and water for drinking may not be the same thing out in the country.

Monsters

Dinosaurs are not extinct. In the Deep North of Queensland and in the Northern Territory, the salt water Crocodile lurks like a sort of lazy, horizontal Tyrannosaurus Rex. This is not a joke. We lose a tourist or two every couple of years to these babies.

When I was in the US, the locals in Louisiana tried to frighten me off the bayou paddling trip with tales of alligators that sometime reached 17ft in length. Gosh! Five whole metres! The really big salties up in the North get to ten metres. And a bit more. You could be forgiven for mistaking them for small islands, I tell you.

The trick is this: NEVER SWIM OR WADE IN ESTUARINE WATERS IN NORTHERN AUSTRALIA. Actually, in the far, far North, on the Gulf of Carpentaria, it doesn't pay to visit the beach, either ... but what are you going to do?

Now since crocodiles have been a protected species for the last 25 years or so, they've undergone something of a population boom. And good for them, I reckon. I like the bastards. The thing is, you shouldn't assume you're safe just because you're near cities or towns. Don't mess with estuarine waters and talk to the locals before you swim practically anywhere!

While we're on the topic of monsters, in the rainforest you may find feral pigs. These are not cute little talking porkers with a yen for sheep, oh no. These bastards are big as a small rhinoceros, twice as tough and equipped with a vile temperament. If you do run across feral piggies in the bush, leave them well alone. Give them lots of space, especially the females with piglets. They are quite capable of disembowelling you with those tusks if you give them reason – and for a pig, 'reason' can include 'breathing'. Worst comes to worst, remember: most pigs can't climb trees.

Now, aside from the crocs, another purely Northern hazard is the Stinging Tree. This is a small tree with large, heart-shaped leaves which grows in disturbed areas of the rainforest – ie, anywhere that a path has been cut through and you might want to walk. Stinging Tree leaves are covered in fine silicaceous hairs which are coated in one savage motherfucker of an irritant poison. All you have to do is brush against the suckers and it's like getting an electric shock, followed by the kind of burning itch that makes most people think longingly of the pleasant times they had under the Spanish Inquisition. You can also get a bit of a fever and some immune reaction. Mostly, though, it's just the unrelenting pain of the fuckin' stuff that makes it such a delight.

If you're stung, you won't sleep the first night. The worst of the pain will go within a couple of hours, but the sensation won't vanish for at least a day. And the first time you get it wet, it will come back just as savagely as the first moment. Not only that, but you'll feel it every time you get it wet for the next three months.

Now, this is important: every bloody North Queenslander has a cure for Stinging Tree rash and they're all different. Some will tell you to douse the area with cider vinegar. Others will suggest you use sticky tape to pull the residual needles away from the skin. Still others swear by an all-purpose commercial alleviating agent called 'Stingose'. Then there's the lot who insist that for every rainforest poison, an opposing agent must always be growing miraculously nearby. These people will tell you to rub the sap of a Cunjevoi over the affected area.

Horse-shit. All of it. I've tried each and every fraggin' one and they didn't do me any bloody good at all. And some of them may even be hazardous. Who knows what's in the sap of a Cunjevoi? Not fuckin' me. Take several aspirin or paracetamol and when you need to sleep, get good and bloody drunk. There's bugger-all else you can do except wait it out.

Obviously, the best option is not to get stung. To that end, when you get to the rainforest regions of North Queensland, try to collar a ranger, or a relatively sober local. Ask them to point out a Stinging Tree to you and look it over carefully. Then all you have to do is avoid touching them.

Another interesting rainforest menace is the Cassowary, a rare giant flightless bird, standing about 1.6m tall. There has been only one recorded fatality from the kick of the cassowary, in Mossman (north of Cairns) about seventy years ago. Nonetheless, they are large, powerful creatures with a dirty big fighting claw on their feet and being birds, they are dense as a block of wood. Leave them alone if you're lucky enough to see them; who knows what gets a bird cranky?

Once you've left the rainforest and the rivers, the coast and the reef also pose a few hazards. If you're doing any diving or swimming, the iron-clad rule is: look but DON'T TOUCH. There's a surprising number of seriously venomous critters out there.

Consider the Cone Shells, for example. Conical, patterned shellfish ranging in size from 2cm to 12cm. They look very pretty and are a perfect size to be picked up and souvenired. Unfortunately, they also pack an extremely fatal sting. Normally, this is used to allow the Cone Shell to paralyse the fish upon which it feeds, but it will have no difficulties paralysing you instead. As in complete paralysis: no breathing, no heartbeat. Of course, if you've got someone handy who is able and prepared to manage a few hours of complete cardio-pulmonary resuscitation, you'll be fine.

Stonefish, which dwell both inshore and on the reef, look exactly like ugly lumps of greenish-grey rock until you stand on them. At that moment, you will discover that the stonefish has a venomous, exceptionally painful dorsal sting. Note that word 'exceptionally'. Any fatalities associated with Stonefish envenomation are likely to be from shock. If necessary, immerse the stung portion of the body into water which has been heated just as high as you can stand it. The poison is more sensitive to heat than you are. By the way, there's a freshwater version of the stonefish as well. It's quite uncommon, but it's as well to be careful when you're wading in those enticing rainforest rock pools.

The stonefish has a much more attractive cousin, variously called the lionfish, scorpionfish, or butterfly cod. They're slow-moving, very beautiful white-and-red striped fish that live on the reef. The spines are prominent and easy to see, so if you simply avoid antagonising the lionfish, chances are you won't have to worry about it.

In the rock pools and along the coast all the way down to Sydney lives the Blue-Ringed Octopus. Looks like a cute little piece of animated calamari, no more than the size of your hand at most – but get it cranky and electric blue rings appear all over its squidgy body. The bite of the Blue-Ringed Octopus delivers a remarkably efficient and fatal neurotoxin. By the way: there may be a Deep North variation of the species which doesn't show the blue rings; leave ALL the octopods alone, okay?

One of the most serious marine dangers in northern Queensland is the infamous marine stinger – any one of several species of highly venomous jellyfish. Most dangerous of these, the Box Jellyfish can become quite large, (up to 4 metres long, including the tentacles) and is found in inshore marine waters (especially estuaries, but including beaches) from about Gladstone northwards, between October and April. The sting of a box jellyfish is horrifically painful and has been fatal on a number of occasions. If someone is stung, the area should be washed liberally with household vinegar. DO NOT TOUCH THE TENTACLES, THE STING, OR ANYTHING ELSE. Get the victim to a doctor. Artificial respiration may be necessary in the meantime.

Avoiding the Box Jellyfish is easy. Don't swim in the ocean at the coast between October and April, or restrict your swimming to appropriately netted enclosures. Sorry.

Sharks? Forget it. Hardly anybody in Australia gets done by sharks. Mind you, I wouldn't be swimming in any tidal river systems on the change of the tide … not long ago a guy way up in Parramatta in Sydney had a bite taken out of one of his thighs, including a chunk of his wedding tackle, because he decided to go jumping off the wharf by night.

More likely, you'll be the one eating shark. They call it 'flake' when they feed it to you at the fish'n'chip shops, but it's shark all the same. Not bad, either. A sight better than some of the fish around – at least sharks aren't known for carrying Ciguatoxin.

What's Ciguatoxin? Another poison. This time, it's a toxin which accumulates in the flesh of certain fish which have been eating other fish which like to eat the wrong kind of algae. Very debilitating and potentially fatal. It's not particularly common, and the species of fish prone to it are fairly well known, so the answer is to avoid eating the wrong kind of fish. If you do go fishing, get one of those excellent Identification Charts which are freely available at most of the National Parks and Wildlife outlets.

So much for the marine life. Next, we consider the insects and the like. First of all, there's the infamous Sydney Funnel-Web Spider. (*Atrax robustus*. Love those Latin names). It's a big, black, hairy, ground-dwelling spider with a shiny back and a serious attitude. They peter out up around the NSW-Qld border, so you can rest easy from there on. Funnel-webs are quite toxic. If you're bitten, treat as for snake-bite (see below), with a pressure bandage, and get medical attention immediately.

The other spider worth worrying about is the Red-back. A relative of the famous Black Widow, the Red-back is a small, spindly-legged, glossy spider, usually black, with a trademark red stripe on the back and a red hourglass shape underneath. Quite attractive, really. They make straggly webs and are often found around human dwellings, so keep an eye open.

They're not usually fatal, but they'll make you sick as all hell and if you're bitten, you should go straight to the nearest medical facility.

Then there's the ticks. You know about ticks, don't you? Little multilegged crab-like bastards about the size of a big pinhead. They like to crawl up your trouser legs and bite you on the warm, moist bits.

Normally, this isn't a problem. You lose a bit of blood, the tick drops off, fat, bloated and happy and everyone continues on their merry way. Trouble is, there's at least one species of tick in Queensland and northern New South Wales which is distinctly toxic.

Symptoms of attack by the Shellback or Paralysis Tick include: headache, mild fever, impaired balance, apparent 'drunkenness', slurring of speech and nausea. The really irritating thing is that there may not be a tick visible on the victim. For starters, the creatures like to head for places like skin folds, or up above the hairline. More worrying is their tendency to leave their mouthparts behind in the victim's flesh if they are plucked off by hand. The mouthparts and salivary glands can go on poisoning a victim quite efficiently, altogether without a tick attached.

It is a good idea to check yourself very thoroughly for ticks after you have been bushwalking. Consider getting somebody else to check the bits you can't see too well. Should you find a tick attached to you, DON'T PULL IT OFF. Douse it with kerosene, or methylated spirits. That usually sorts the little bastards out. If that doesn't work, consult a doctor.

What else? Ants, I think. Australia has a number of species of stinging ant. Most of them are just painful. Bull Ants, which are over 2.5cm long and savagely aggressive, are downright dangerous. Every bit as fatal as wasps or bees, as a matter of fact, although fortunately, Bull Ants are not at all common along the coastal strip. Watch where you step and for fuck's sake, check the ground where you propose to camp.

Caterpillars can be a bastard in Australia too. There's a couple of species – nothing special to look at, just a little 2cm blackish-grey furbooger – which are covered with stinging, irritant hairs. These are completely non-fatal, but they itch like a bastard and come up in dirty great welts. If you're unlucky enough to meet one, just wash the affected area with methylated spirits, alcohol, kerosene or the like and try not to scratch. Scratching is the fastest possible way I know to spread the welts. It's absolutely fascinating watching someone turn from a normal human being into a sort of lumpy Michelin Man in the space of ten minutes …

Getting near the end of the list now. Have you bought insect repellent? If not, get ahold of some as soon as possible. Although there's no Malaria or Yellow Fever, Queensland has at least two mosquito-borne diseases, one of which is all its own. Both are insidious, nasty, debilitating painful things and the more brutal form of Dengue (pronounced 'Denggie'), known as Dengue Haemorrhagic Fever, can be fatal. No fatalities reported in Australia yet; good hospital care will usually get you through.

Both illnesses are carried by the bite of the *Aedes aegypti* Salt-Marsh Mosquito. Not nearly as much is known about how the illnesses work as should be. Dengue is usually associated with a rash, strong, diffuse pain in various parts and a fever, often very high. Dengue usually has a short critical period of about a week of illness, but may have lasting aftereffects, especially in terms of muscle loss, lack of energy and debilitation, as a result of the high fever.

Ross River Fever, while not usually so critical as Dengue, often lasts much longer. The predominant feature of Ross River Fever is extremely strong joint pain, which may even call for hospitalisation. On the other hand, mild cases may go unnoticed, to be remarked on as nothing more than a bad hangover, or stress, or lack of sleep. Mild or strong, however, the virus is frequently associated with a long-term problem sometimes called post-viral syndrome. This is characterised by depression and a deep lack of energy and motivation, without any readily identifiable medical symptoms. This can last years, and has wrecked quite a number of lives, especially as it is often thought that the sufferers are simply malingering.

There has been substantial work on a vaccine for Ross River Fever, but to date, human trials have not been undertaken. This is simply because nobody wants to put up the money. Since the virus affects only a limited area of the world and is not particularly critical, the pharmaceutical companies don't see that there would be sufficient profit to be generated from the expensive research they would have to undertake. Perhaps as the East Coast becomes more popular with travellers, this attitude will change – but until then, you are very well advised to use insect repellent almost everywhere along coastal Queensland.

I've saved the best for last. You'll hear tell about dangerous snakes all over the world, of course. (Except Ireland, where the snakes only come after a bottle or two of whiskey). In Australia, though, they are genuinely very dangerous. This country boasts seven of the ten most poisonous species of snake on the planet – and the top three are all ours. How poisonous are they? Well, the bite of the famous US rattlesnake takes several hours to really have an effect and you'll probably survive even with minimal treatment. An Australian Taipan, though, will totally fuck you up in a matter of minutes. Terminal within an hour, unless you get serious treatment.

Now on the whole, snakes are not really a problem. The rule is: you leave them alone, they'll leave you alone. If you have to walk in the bush at night, carry a light and watch where you put your feet. If you have to gather firewood, be very careful about turning over logs and the like. Give any snakes you see a very wide berth. Stay out of their way. Don't poke them with sticks. Don't photograph them. Don't try to feed them. Don't chase them away from your campsite – move your campsite instead. Get the picture?

Should you have the misfortune to be bitten, don't panic. With treatment, your chances of survival are excellent, and they will be much improved if you keep a cool head and follow simple first aid procedures. Don't wash the wound, or cut it, or suck at it, or any of those other stupid cowboy remedies. They don't help and they can make things an awful lot worse. Apply a pressure bandage to the immediate area of the bite, if it is on a limb. Wind the bandage tightly, working from the site of the bite to the base of the limb and back down. Do not wrap the bandage so tightly as to prevent the flow of blood through the limb; a good, firm, immobilising bandage is what you're after. Splint the limb as well. The venom travels through the lymphatic system and muscular action just helps pump it along. This treatment will delay the onset of symptoms for many hours, if done correctly. If the victim has been bitten on the body or head, lie them down and keep them calm. If they're lucky, the snake was non-venomous, or didn't really cut loose with the poison. In many cases, a snake will 'dry-bite' to drive off potential predators. After all, the venom is there to help the snake get dinner — and you're far too big to qualify.

Now get help. Fast. It will help if you can identify the snake that bit you, so the right anti-venom can be administered.

Although there's a positive glut of the bastards, three snakes in particular deserve individual mention. First amongst these is the Taipan. Uncle Taipan is a Queensland snake, who can grow up to three metres in length. He's normally a reasonable enough sort, but unfortunately, during the spring mating, he can get just a little tetchy. He's monumentally poisonous, too — one good bite can dose you with enough venom to knock off about a hundred healthy horses. Taipans favour dry, open scrubland and nice long grass. Stick to the trail, in other words. And if you should see one of these suckers, see if you can tell which way he wants to go. Then go the other direction, just as fast as you possibly can.

Then there's the Tiger Snake. Not so poisonous as Uncle Taipan, he lives a little further south, but still favours the dry, open country. Tigers get downright nasty in the mating season. Mess with their love life and the bastards will actively chase you. This is a real problem, as they're a fair bit faster than humans over the short sprint. Tigers are so named because they're often striped, or banded. Unfortunately, so are a lot of other Australian snakes. Leave them all alone.

The last of the big three is the Death Adder, a creature who lives in the northern part of Queensland. The real problem with these is that unlike most snakes, they don't actively hunt. Instead, they lurk and wait for potential prey to come to them. This means that whereas most snakes will piss off when they feel the vibrations of your footsteps, Brother Death Adder will just stay still. Very still. You may even tread on him and then you're in deep, deep shit. Brother Death Adder is almost entirely nocturnal. The simple answer is, if you do any walking by night (even leaving the tent to take a piss in the trees) you should carry a light and watch carefully where you place your feet. And remember that the black road surface often holds the sun's warmth until fairly late in the evening. Cold-blooded sorts just love slithering around on nice warm roads ...

Does that cover it? Pretty much, I think. Leeches aren't worth the effort; all they do is suck a little blood. I've left out Fire Coral and Toadfish, but we've got to get on with the book sooner or later and hey — there's got to be some surprises left for you, right? Let's get one thing straight, though: THERE IS NO SUCH THING AS A DROP-BEAR. That hoary piece of mythology has been around since the Diggers were taking the piss out of the GI's in World War II!

Thanks a bunch. I feel much better now. Can we get on with this trip before I lose my nerve altogether?

Of course! Glad to be of assistance. Welcome to Australia, mate!

Err – yeah. Maybe you could acquaint me with this Australia thing first.

History

Nothing simpler! Australia is a democratically governed nation of about seventeen million souls, scattered thinly around the edge of a whacking great continent in the Southern Hemisphere. It is a member of the British Commonwealth of Nations and as a former British colony, the titular head of government is a Governor-General, who supposedly acts for the English monarch. (In practice, ever since 1975 when Governor-General Sir John Kerr assisted Malcolm Fraser of the Liberal party in ousting the sitting Labor government of Gough Whitlam, a succession of Prime Ministers has kept a firm hand and a wary eye on the position of Governor-General. Other than that, though, everyone ignores the G-G.) The government consists of a parliament with an upper and lower house, led by a prime minister and a cabinet full of dummies.

The principal (read 'only') language is English, but due to a lot of immigration since the last big war you may expect to hear languages from all over the world, if you listen hard enough. Or catch public transport in Sydney. The original inhabitants of the continent are a dark-skinned people, originally of a hunter-gatherer society. At the time of the European invasion in the late eighteenth century, it appears that the Aborigines had been continuously inhabiting the land for a bare minimum of forty thousand years. It took less than a hundred years for the British colonists to reduce the Aboriginal culture to a complete wreck.

The country is broken up into states, each with their own annoying government. There are six of these, plus another self-determining region out in the never-never called the Northern Territory. The largest cities in Australia are Sydney, Melbourne, Brisbane, Adelaide, Perth and some others which nobody really cares much about anyway.

For the purposes of this book, we're concerning ourselves only with the northern two states on the East Coast: New South Wales (referred to as NSW), whose capital is Sydney, and Queensland, whose capital is either Brisbane or Castlemaine Fourex, depending on who you ask. New South Wales is big – approximately three times the land mass of the United Kingdom. Queensland is enormous; big enough to give much of Europe an inferiority complex. Most of the civilisation in both states occurs along the coast; we're mostly concerned with the areas which can be reached from the coastal highway.

New South Wales is the oldest of the states and the site of the first British colony was at Sydney Cove. It was originally going to be in Botany Bay, where explorer James Cook made his first landing in 1770; but Cook was a sailor and a navigator, not a colonist. When Captain Arthur Phillip arrived with a load of convicts in 1788, he took one look at Cook's proposed colony site and spat the dummy.

England kept pumping convicts into the new colony until 1848 – it was either that, or weight them with chains and throw them in the Thames, and the Thames was getting a little too full. The first few decades were a typical clusterfuck. The English seemed to regard New South Wales simply as a place to send people and forget about them, so rather than sending desperately-needed supplies and equipment, so that the colony could become self-sufficient in the difficult conditions of this new land, they just kept sending more convicts. The Second Fleet apparently had about a 25 per cent death rate and that was only on the way across …

Nobody had made any useful plans for development and expansion. Furthermore, nobody had given consideration to things like land ownership, or the legal standing of free-born children of convict transportees. Things looked bad. Actually, they looked a lot like mass starvation.

Then they got worse. Arthur Phillip, who'd been trying to attract free settlers and generally make the place look like something other than a savage penal death camp, went back to Britain. His successor, Major Grose of the New South Wales Corps, was a right bastard who established a tradition which holds even today, by giving all the best bits of land to his mates in the Corps and ensuring they had plenty of convicts to work the land for them. Once the officers had become fat corporate bastards, paying the convict labour in rum and reaping the rewards of low overheads, New South Wales looked more of a brothel than ever. Then some bright spark back in Blighty decided that the right thing to do was to send in William Bligh as Governor, to sort them all out. Bligh – does that name ring any bells? That's right, same twit who managed to have both Marlon Brando and Mel Gibson mutiny under him when he captained the *Bounty*.

No prizes for guessing what happened next. There was a mutiny and the officers – now known as the Rum Corps – organised a Rum Rebellion to turf Bligh out. England finally got wise and sent out one of the prototype SAS officers, Colonel Lachlan Macquarie, with a slightly rusted Swiss Army knife, to take control of the colony. It was all he needed. Ten minutes after he'd arrived, the Rum Rebellion was nothing more than a hangover and most of New South Wales had been renamed 'Macquarie'. Everything went well for a while, until people realised that under Macquarie, the place was less of a prison and more of a rapidly-growing Club Med and health farm. Exit Macquarie, back to England to answer some questions from the Board In Charge Of Sending The Irish To Really Shitty Places …

By then, the colonists were tired of Sydney and in any case all the places around had been named Macquarie. In an effort to get out, they did some poking around and discovered the Blue Mountains, which presented them with a real problem. Matthew Flinders tried to sail round the Blue Mountains in 1802, but accidentally went right around Australia instead. Fortunately, he kept extensive notes. Then some enterprising chap named Evans managed to cross the mountains, where two rivers were found which, in a burst of imagination, were promptly named 'Macquarie' and 'Lachlan'.

Something had to be done. In response to the growing Macquarie crisis, a series of explorers began finding places and carefully not naming them Macquarie. This included Tasmania in 1825, South Australia in 1834 and Victoria in 1850. This was something of a triumph – not a

Macquarie amongst them. However, enlightened minds realised that something still wasn't right, so in 1822, John Oxley was sent off to discover Queensland. He did, and everyone immediately felt much better, but it wasn't until 1859 when England actually had a Queen that they felt quite right about naming the place.

New South Wales went on to discover a lot of gold and the other states promptly followed suit. So much gold was found right up into the 1880s that by 1901, Australia managed for the first and only time to pay off its foreign debt and become a nation in its own right.

Not long after that, World War I broke out for artistic reasons (see the section on Art and Culture) and a lot of promising Australian Art students went to Europe and didn't come back. Then there was a Great Depression and Sydney got really crowded. Then they built the Harbour Bridge in 1932 and everybody felt a lot better again.

Things speeded up a lot, without changing much, right through World War II. After that one, the name of the enemy was changed to 'Communists' and people went on doing pretty much what they always had. Vietnam stirred things up in the 1970s, though, and led to an invasion of Hippies who went north and established Nimbin. Flared trousers came and went. The 1980s happened.

By then the police had come to quite like being paid twice as much to do half the work and they'd become very good indeed at looking the other way from almost anything: shonky real estate deals, Aborigines dying mysteriously in custody, flared trousers, drugs, more drugs and quite a lot of paedophilia. After the very fashionable Fitzgerald Inquiry in Queensland managed to put a dent in a century-old system of political butt-sniffing, it was felt that New South Wales was falling behind the times, so they declared a sort of perpetual ongoing Judicial Commission into Everything, officially called the Independent Commission Against Corruption. Traditionalists, at first shaken, have taken heart at the fact that the Commission has been almost a complete failure where police corruption is concerned. We now know that in the 1980s members of the NSW police force regularly commissioned criminals to do armed holdups for them and engaged in a wide range of other entrepreneurial activities such as the licensing of pickpockets on racecourses. There's a royal commission looking into the force at the moment.

Queensland, on the other hand, got off to a much better sort of start back in the nineteenth century. Moreton Bay never became the kind of summer-camp that Macquarie made of Sydney; Dread Captain Logan of the Lash made certain of that. In fact, he was so good at his job of keeping convicts in line that Queensland didn't manage to become a place until 1859!

In the 1840s however, a number of bright persons noticed that quite a lot of Queensland was still completely unknown to anyone except the Aborigines and they clearly weren't using it. There followed a number of exceedingly hamfisted attempts at exploration; Ludwig 'Mad Ludwig' Leichhardt – disappeared somewhere over the Darling Downs. Burke & Wills – walked across Australia in search of Queensland. Found the Gulf of Carpentaria by mistake, walked back and starved to death at Coopers Creek. Edmund Kennedy – looking for a new Club Med site in the Deep North of Queensland, found a lot of mangroves instead and got speared

to death by Aborigines. Major Thomas Mitchell – managed to name a species of galah after himself while trying to find inland Queensland, but forgot his pooky-bear and had to go home again.

Happily for the future of the world, a couple of cool-headed chaps managed to find gold in Queensland and we were all saved. The gold was in all kinds of places and managed to bring a sizeable population all the way up to Cooktown. A lot of Chinese came to Queensland for the gold, but many of them were eaten by Aborigines (thus establishing the custom of the 'Chinese Take-away') and most of the rest had such a rotten time that they went home again. The sudden expansion of Queensland to fill its borders, the end of the supply of convicts, and the exodus of the remaining Chinese meant that while there were any number of rich bastards prepared to be land-owning farmers, there was practically nobody left who was actually prepared to do a day's work. Besides, everybody knew that it was quite impossible for delicate Europeans to do hard manual work in the punishing Queensland summer sun.

This lack of workers made being a rich landowning farmer bastard very difficult. As a result, Robert Towns (another man who wanted to be Macquarie – Townsville is named for him – and he deserves it!) responded by sending out ships to the nearby Pacific Islands to acquire labour. Towns was a very decent chap who promised his Solomon Island labourers (who came to be known as Kanakas) all the dirt they could eat and a free pebble up the nose if they'd come and work in the canefields for a year or so. Initially, the islanders jumped at this generous offer, though later they claimed that they were jumping to avoid the whips being swung in their direction.

By the 1880s, there were upwards of 14,000 Kanakas working more or less voluntarily in Queensland. Despite complaints that land values were being depressed by the influx of coloured persons, the coercion of South Sea Island labour continued right up until 1901. Shortly after that, in a fit of pique, the White Australia immigration policy was passed in 1906 and of all the Islanders who had genuinely come to see Queensland as their home, only about 1,500 were permitted to stay.

By this stage, however, there had been a really big Shearers' Strike in Queensland, which the government put down with guns and dogs. It was too late, though – the far-thinking Queenslanders had thrown a big Labor Party and even managed to overthrow the government for six days in 1899. This was the famous Dawson Labor Government – the first Labor Government anywhere in the world, which just goes to show how far ahead Queenslanders were thinking. (They spelt the word 'Labor' because they had more respect for the American Labor movement than its pallied British equivalent.) Unfortunately, having decided that Labor government was a good idea, they elected another one. This Labor Government promptly rewrote the electoral system so that one Labor vote counted for roughly two and a half Conservative votes. Labor supporters argued that this was more than fair – one Labor man was worth at least three Conservatives on the open market. Despite protests from the now savagely outnumbered Conservatives, the Labor Government of Queensland bought the police department outright and governed for the next sixty years, or thereabouts.

Then, in the 1960s, along came a middle-aged peanut farmer from Kingaroy. All over the state, Queenslanders decided, 'Yes! Joh Bjelke-Petersen is the man for me! Love those boots!' and suddenly, just before 1970, there was no more Queensland Labor Government. Queenslanders had got quite used to the system, however so they didn't much mind when Joh rewrote the rule books in favour of his National-Liberal coalition. One farmer's vote was now equal to approximately three businessman's votes, or roughly five hundred and twelve Labor votes.

Joh did an enormous amount for Queensland during his twenty years of iron-fisted rule. He abolished the Environment, making it possible for developers of all nations, but especially those with lots of hard, loose currency like Japan, to build enormous golf courses and holiday resorts on otherwise useless tracts of pristine coastline and rainforest. He took away the arduous moral responsibility of protesting against things like apartheid in South Africa by making street marches illegal. He established a very large, well-funded Special Branch of the police force in order to prevent terrorism by beating the living shit out of anyone who went on an illegal street march. And he encouraged the economic growth of the state by ensuring that certain people got the biggest and most valuable pieces of real estate.

In the early 1990s, Queenslanders finally realised that Bjelke-Petersen wasn't really a kindly, funny old peanut farmer at all, but a senile dictator in an Akubra hat. The National Party threw him out and tried a couple of new leaders, but it was all in vain. A Royal Commission was needed and so it was that Saint Anthony Fitzgerald QC spoke from on high. He examined the state of the State and found that like nearly everywhere else, it was mostly corrupt. Fitzgerald then created the Criminal Justice Commission (CJC), gave them orders to arrest everyone and himself ascended to the heavens in a blaze of glory.

The CJC tried hard, but only managed to imprison a couple of minor ministers and the State Police Commissioner Terry Lewis. Lewis, despite having kept extensive coded diary notes, couldn't seem to recall anybody who had ever done anything illegal in the history of Queensland, so they locked him up in disgust.

Meanwhile, there was an election and Queensland had a Labor Government again. Unfortunately, Wayne Goss and his team promptly rewrote the electoral laws to favour nobody at all; which so deeply shocked Queensland after nearly a century of gerrymandered elections that as soon as his four years were up, they elected another National-Liberal Coalition. If you listen closely, you can still hear the faint gurgles as the new Queensland government flounders in a mire of blatant jingoism and mindless stupidity ...

Whoa! Sorry I asked. Do I dare ask about the Aboriginal culture of this country?

You'll be sorry you did.

Aboriginal History

The Aborigines probably migrated to Australia from South-East Asia over forty thousand years ago. Sea levels were lower then. They may even have been able to walk the whole way. They developed a technologically simple hunter-gatherer culture, based on extended family units. Despite the fact that their culture had a minimum of tools and technology, their culture was highly complex in the sense of their religion and their oral mytho-history. This much is clear simply from the fact that even today, though they are fast fading out, more than two hundred separate and distinct Aboriginal languages remain – mostly in the Northern Territory. So effective was their oral history transmission that the Fraser Island Aborigines retained a clear understanding and recollection of the sighting of Cook and the *Endeavour* in their songs and stories 150 years after the event.

The English Navy explorer James Cook was not the first European captain to find Australia (the Dutch had been 'finding' the north-west corner by mistake for hundreds of years after overshooting the Dutch Indies, now Indonesia) but he's had the best PR. When Cook arrived at Botany Bay in 1770, he found a small group of slightly cranky warriors awaiting him on the shore. A few volleys of musket fire sent them packing, however and he hoisted the Union Jack and claimed the land for King George (the mad one) under the legal doctrine of *terra nullius*. Essentially, since the locals didn't shoot back, nobody really lived here and it was first in, best dressed.

Unfortunately, the loosely-knit clan structure of the Aboriginal peoples didn't lend itself to a large and organised resistance. They tended to put up a fuss whenever their own personal territories were encroached upon, but by and large this had very little effect. Other than making the Europeans regard them as dangerous savages, of course. European reprisals were thoroughgoing and often very nasty. They ranged from training native troopers, and taking them away from their home territory to help hunt and kill Aborigines to whom they had no relationship of kin, through putting strychnine in flour and poisoning waterholes.

Later, in the early 1900s, 'legal' means were employed to shift inconvenient Aborigines to places where the new white Australians were prepared to have them live. Nominally, these laws were enacted to protect the Aborigines themselves, but in reality they served only to herd them into convenient reserves and missions. In the twentieth

century, things didn't get a lot better for the remaining Aborigines on reserves and missions and dwelling in the parts of the country the whites didn't want. Some Aborigines, of course, were at least partially integrated into Australian society. They could hold jobs on the distant cattle and sheep stations and the famous black-trackers continued to assist police in the bush until well into this century.

In 1967, the Australian nation voted to allow Aborigines and Torres Strait Islanders full citizenship in what had once been their own land. There is now an increasing awareness that perhaps all is not well with our history. Aboriginal art, stories and culture are beginning to assume an important place within the mainstream of 'multicultural Australia' and in 1992, after a High Court case against the concept of *terra nullius* organised by a Torres Strait Islander named Eddy Mabo, it was conceded that perhaps the Aboriginal peoples do indeed retain some rights to their lands. What exactly those rights may be is still being argued about.

It's a bit late, though, don't you think?

Wow. Umm – moving right along … I've got to get along in this country for a while. Can you tell me why Australians talk so funny?

Culture

Look, mate – don't come the raw prawn with me. We Australians don't talk funny. It's all you flaming galahs from overseas – all you Pommies and Seppos and everyone else. Just so's you don't get your knickers in a knot, though, I'll give you a crash course in Speaking Downunda.

A few stubbies shy of a carton – not possessing one's full wits. Mad or stupid. Also, *A kangaroo loose in the top paddock* and *A few snags short of a barbie.*
Blowies – blowflies
Bludger – lazy, malingering person, who *wouldn't work in an iron lung.*

28

Blue – a fight; also the verbs *to blue,* or *to have a blue.*

Bonza – extremely satisfactory; also *Beaut* or *Beauty!* or even, in moments of extreme excitement, *You Beauty!*

Bottle-oh – a bottleshop or liquor store.

Bucket bong – device for the inhalation of marijuana probably unique to Queensland; for full description see John Birmingham's hilarious book about shared housing, *He Died with a Felafel in his Hand.*

Bush – the uncultivated wild lands of Australia. To *go bush* is to disappear into the outback.

BYO – Bring Your Own (alcohol to a restaurant).

Chook – chicken.

Chunder, To – to vomit.

Crook – below standard. Of a person, meaning ill or unwell.

Cuppa – cup of tea.

Dag – clump of shit-caked wool on a sheep's arse. Used to refer to socially inept persons.

Dam – a pond on a farm.

Dekko, To Have A – to take a look at something.

Digger – general term of affection, also an old soldier.

Drongo – foolish person.

Fair Dinkum – really, truly.

Flat out like a lizard drinking – hard at work.

Dunny – toilet. Originally outdoors. Hence, *As much use as a glass door on a dunny.*

Ethnic – immigrant of non-English-speaking background (derogatory).

Fair go! (uttered in plaintive voice) – give me a break.

Football, or *footy* – Rugby League, in Qld and in NSW. In Victoria, it refers to Aussie Rules.

G'day – standard non-committal greeting.

G'day, mate – greeting to someone you've met at least once before, or have just been introduced to.

G'day you old bastard! How's it hanging – friendly and enthusiastic greeting to somebody you know well enough to buy you a beer ie, almost anyone.

Give it a burl – try to do something.

Good on yer – well done, old chap.

He's so generous he'd lend you his arsehole and shit through his ribs – this was actually heard in Newcastle in 1988.

He wouldn't know the time if the town hall clock fell on him – lacking in intelligence.

Mate – term of address used by one man to another; less often in inter-sexual communication. While it is acceptable to address almost everyone from the derelict in the park right up to the Prime Minister as *mate,* there are a great many possible interpretations of the word. While a deep understanding of the full nuances of the term cannot be gained from reading any book, no matter how well written, it is important that you realise one thing. If at any stage anyone you don't know quite well addresses you with the words *Listen, mate,* there is a good chance you are about to be punched on the nose.

New Australian – immigrant.

No wuckas – from *No wuckin' furries,* or *No worries.* See *She'll be right, mate.*

Piss, To Be On The – to drink alcohol, usually beer (as in 'I went out on the piss last night').

Pissed as a fart – this does not mean one is angry. This means one is drunk.

Point Percy At The Porcelain, To – for a male to urinate (as the source is Barry Humphries, this might be apocryphal, alas).

Pollies – politicians.

Pommies, or Poms – Englishmen. Possibly from an acronym of convict days: Prisoners Of His Majesty.

Ratbag – term of abuse. Usually friendly, except when used in Parliament.

Redback – either a dangerous spider, a twenty dollar note, or a brand of excellent Western Australian beer, depending on the circumstances.

Rego – car registration.

Seppo – rhyming slang. Seppo = Septic Tank = Yank = American.

Sheila – woman.

She'll be right, mate – I do not anticipate any major catastrophes within the next few minutes.

She's got the painters in – a woman is menstruating.

Sickie (as in *I'm taking a sickie*) – paid sick leave from one's place of employment, taken in the absence of genuine illness; sick leave was given to the world by Australia in 1951.

Slab – cardboard carton containing twenty-four cans of beer.

Stinker – an overly hot day.

Stoned – this is not 'drunk'. This is 'high'.

Tinnie – can of beer.

Two-pot screamer – two beers, and they're on the floor.

Whack-o the diddle-o! – nobody says this. Barry Humphries invented it in the 1960s to torment the Pommies.

Whingeing Pom – the kind of Pom who would complain at the slightest thing, such as finding a redback spider under the dunny paper.

Your shout – buy everyone in the immediate vicinity a beer, or suffer the consequences. *My shout* – you are unlikely to hear this phrase.

Thanks, mate. That was bonza. This is obviously a deeply cultured country.

Art

Culture? We've got it streaming out of our arses, mate. Why, in the arts alone, Australia bestrides the world like a veritable colossus of gentility and learning. Or so you'd think if you believed the self-promoting arts pages of the Australian press. Actually, there was quite a lot of art already in the country when the Brits arrived. True, it was painted with ochre on rocks, but hey – you've got to respect Art that's been around longer than the rest of the world has even had History. Nonetheless, when the Pommies moved in to learn how to become Aussies, they started doing the Art thing.

At first it was mostly scientific. Young Joe Banks brought a couple of artists with him on the Endeavour to draw the new things found by the expedition. Some of the earliest artists in Australia were convicts, notably the forgers. (Makes sense, doesn't it)? So there's a lot of early engraving work, particularly of bank notes and letters of credit. Out of hours, the early engravers stuck to the scientific tradition of drawing plants, animals and Noble Savage Aborigines for a while, then tried their hands at the landscape.

Sadly, for anyone trained in the European schools of art, the Australian landscape was just too fraggin' big, too intimidating and they couldn't handle the strong light and colour of the place. The early landscape work of artists like William Westall, Thomas Watling, John Lewin and Joseph Lycett is mostly of huge, dark, brooding landscapes which totally overwhelm the one or two hapless human figures stuck way down in the corner. Says a lot about the way they perceived the new land, doesn't it?

Once they got over the initial fear, though, they started in on the social sort of life. Paintings of hunting, camping, felling wood and other commonplace activities such as being speared by Aborigines started to appear. The style was still very stiff and European however, and the landscape remained the primary feature. A new generation of painters of huge, brooding landscapes and tiny, frightened figures appeared on the scene: men like Chevalier, Piguenit and Von Guerard.

Despite all this, there was a serious danger of a real Art developing in Australia. In the 1880s, a bunch of Art Students by the name of Tom Roberts, Arthur Streeton and Charles Conder clubbed together and began the grand tradition of shitty share-housing. Lacking the money to buy both beer and decent paint, the boys did what any decent Australian would do and said, "Screw the paint, let's get on the piss."

As a result, they began to produce paintings without a lot of expensive heavy colours in them, sticking to cheap, shoddy washes and light splotches. When it was pointed out that a lot of their pictures didn't really look like the original subjects at all, Roberts and the lads retorted that their Art was about feeling, not representing, and anyway, they were following the path of the French Impressionists, so there. Then they threw the empty beer bottles at the questioners.

Critics hated them. The stuff sold, though. They called it the Heidelberg school, and it was quite a success. In fact, Streeton went on painting his light, splotchy landscapes for the next hundred years or so. May still be turning them out, for all I know.

Things couldn't last, what with Art doing so well, and in fact, the Victorian Era intervened. (*Didn't it come first? Ed*) Smiling became illegal. (As a matter of fact, bathing in the open surf really was illegal until 1902 …) Sex became illegal. Even discussing underpants became illegal. By this time, the Heidelbergers and the artists of Australia were on a roll. They responded to the Victorian Era in truly Australian fashion by reviving The Nude. Not like the demure, Elysian nudes of England, though, oh no. Australians painted Nudes on practically everything. (To this day, the practise of painting Nudes on panel-vans is honoured in certain suburbs of Sydney, Melbourne and Brisbane.) The Great Nude Art Uprising really culminated with Norman Lindsay, the man known and revered the world over for being the first person to convince Elle Macpherson to get her gear off in public. Lindsay read Nietzsche at an early age and never recovered. Though he did manage some scantily clothed work for the *Bulletin* magazine in his formative years, in later life, tragically, he could no longer paint anything at all which wasn't nude. This made his still lifes particularly interesting.

Meanwhile news of the Great Australian Nude Art Uprising had finally reached Europe and in order to preserve the morals of the world, a plot was hatched to start World War I. This was duly done on pretext of a minor assassination in Sarajevo and shortly afterwards, the Australians were invited to join. During the course of the senseless war, nearly sixty thousand promising young Australian art students were killed and Mel Gibson conquered Gallipoli single-handed. (*You've been watching too many films again. Ed*)

It was a blow from which Australian Art is still recovering.

In the years following the war, Modernism took the rest of the art world by storm. Back in Australia, however, the Nude Painters were getting on in years, becoming crotchety and conservative. Furthermore, they'd discovered they quite liked painting Nudes and didn't want to bother trying to find Cubist models. Desperate for a new direction, some such as Heysen began to paint nude trees – especially gum trees. In 1937, Robert Menzies, later to become famous for selling scrap-iron to the Japanese to turn into warplanes and for being Australia's longest-serving prime minister, presided over the establishment of the Australian Art Academy. This was done in a bid to bring the growing Modernist movement under control, which in turn led directly to the modern-day Australia (Arts) Council system of giving money only to writers and painters who have been lobotomised and are prepared to Toe The Line.

Fortunately, the formation of the repressive Art Academy was just what the Modernists needed and in a replica of the Nude Uprising, a wave of Modernist Rebellion swept the nation. The 1940s and 1950s were really the heyday of it all. William Dobell got going, and Sidney Nolan discovered how to paint Ned Kelly. This was so successful that he decided never to paint anything else, and continued to paint Ned Kellys on everything until the end of his days.

This was also the time of Russell Drysdale. Born in Bognor Regis, Drysdale spent the rest of his life trying to atone for that fact by painting skinny, depressed, lumpy, lonely people in the bleak and desolate outback of Australia. The rumour that he could not actually paint trees is blatantly false; he was, in fact, allergic to the colour green. Meanwhile, Ian Fairweather, perhaps Australia's greatest painter, was living in solitude on an island near Brisbane and drawing on influences from Indonesia, China, Malaysia and Aboriginal art for his own work. The Queensland Art Museum in Brisbane has a magnificent collection of his paintings, most of which were done on cardboard or other dodgy surfaces. See them before they disintegrate.

Books

Of course, Art's not all we've got. There's literature too. In mid-1996 David Malouf won the first IMPAC Dublin Prize, A$212,000, for his novel *Remembering Babylon*. Malouf is an old Brisbane boy, whose fine, short novel *Johnno* gives a glimpse of Australia during the War years. Then there was Patrick White. They gave him the Nobel Prize, so he must be good, right? Hmm. For an introduction, ignore the 'great' novels and head straight for his collection of short stories *The Burned Ones*. One of our literary claims to fame is that novelist David Foster who, with *Plumbum*, has produced the world's finest novel about rock music. Also recommended is his *Moonlite*, about the gold rush days of the mid-nineteenth century. Helen Garner's fine *Monkey Grip* was the first Australian grunge novel, years before the term became fashionable. Garner is married to Murray Bail, whose *Holden's Performance* is one of the best Australian novels. Apart from these you should also try Simon Leys' *The Death of Napoleon*. Leys, a Sinologist whose real name is Pierre Ryckmans, comes from Belgium and writes like no one else.

For non-fiction the best work of general popular history is Geoffrey Blainey's *A Land Half Won*. The best work on the white man's effect on the environment is Eric Rolls' *They All Ran Wild* and his *A Million Wild Acres*. The best introduction to the fate of the Aboriginal people is Henry Reynolds' *The Other Side of the Frontier*.

The genre at which Australian writers have done best is perhaps poetry. The best poet is the late Kenneth Slessor and there are at least three very good living poets: Judith Wright, Les Murray and Robert Gray. Back in the 1970s, Robert Graves said Australia had the best poets currently writing in English, and these were the people he was talking about.

For popular fiction about Australia try Thomas Keneally's *The Chant of Jimmy Blacksmith*, which is about Aborigines in the nineteenth century; Gabrielle Lord's thrillers; Colleen McCullough's *The Thornbirds* and the *Bony* detective novels of Arthur Upfield. These are set in the bush and concern the adventures of a part-Aboriginal detective. They have some superb descriptions of the outback landscape and climate. Read *Madman's Bend* and *Bony Buys a Wife* – you might have to try secondhand bookshops, as at the time of writing these excellent books were out of print. For a look at the seamy and corrupt side of modern Australian life, you might care to try the Autopsy Press slim volumes *Final Cut* by B. Selkie (Sydney property developers), *The Search for Savage Henry* by Harrison Biscuit (Queensland political corruption), *Body Parts* by Anna Blonski (NSW police corruption), and *Brotherly Love* by my own self, Dirk Flinthart (paedophilia and the Christian Brothers). These books are published by the publisher of this guide book, but don't let that stop you.

The best general bookshops in Sydney city are Angus & Robertson found underground in the Imperial Arcade, 168 Pitt St (there is a selection of foreign language books at the back) and Dymocks at 430 George St. Literary and foreign language books can also be had at Abbey's at 131 York St in the city, near Town Hall Station. Other good literary stores are Gleebooks at 49 Glebe Point Rd, Glebe, Ariel at 42 Oxford St, Paddington and the small but perfectly formed Clay's at 103 Macleay St, Potts Point, close by Kings Cross.

Films

Australians tend to rave about their films, but there is no escaping the fact that some of the best of them are actually by a New Zealander, Jane Campion, who directed *The Piano*. If you can find a screening, the 1955 film *Jedda*, about an Aboriginal girl raised by a white family, is very good. Frank Schepisi's 1978 film of Keneally's book *The Chant of Jimmy Black-smith* is also a fine and sympathetic look at the plight of an Aboriginal person who turns axe murderer. Director Gillian Armstrong and Australia's best screen actress, Judy Davis, worked together on the magnificent woman's film *High Tide*. Peter Weir, before he went Hollywood, made the bizarre cult film *The Cars That Ate Paris*, the good *Picnic At Hanging Rock* and the atrocious but popular English-basher,*Gallipoli*. A frightening view of the barbarism of some of the outback's white inhabitants is to be found in *Wake In Fright*. The best Australian film is *Breaker Morant*, by director Bruce Beresford, about two Australian soldiers executed by the English for committing atrocities during the Boer War.

Some of you might also have heard of the *Crocodile Dundee* and *Mad Max* films.

Yeah, that's nice, but have you actually got any culture?
Okay. It's true. We've only been here two hundred years. Apart from the above, you could try the Sydney Dance Company, world class modern dance, or listen to old rock recordings by 1960s funsters *The Easybeats*, 1970s premier punk band *The Saints* (*Prehistoric Sounds* is the most under-rated record in rock history) or the still contemporary Mr Nick Cave and his *Bad Seeds*. And then there's the wine. Yeast is a culture, right? But mostly a trip to Australia is going to be about beer, kangaroos and beaches.

Did you say 'wine?'
Ah.

Wine

The 1995 London International Wine Show was topped by none other than a Penfolds Grange Hermitage. Australia turns out some fantastic heavy, full-bodied reds; anything under the Penfolds label will be a win. Also, look for the name of Henschke and if you get the chance, St Halletts – especially their Old Block Shiraz.

The whites aren't quite so magnificent yet; a lot of vines got planted in places which were a little too hot for them and subtlety isn't exactly their strong point. Give Australian sparkling wines a wide swerve. Still, the powerful sticky-sweet wines of the De Bortoli cellars and the semillons of the Hunter Valley are worth the effort. See the section on the Hunter Valley in the main text. In the meantime, just wait until the cooler Tasmanian vintages start to come out.

Food in Australia is starting to become a real event as well. For nearly two hundred years, we laboured under the near-fatal influence of British Cooking and in the country areas, you're still likely to sit down to vast meals of steak, vegetables and mashed potatoes. Lately, however, the influence of all the different migrant cultures in the country has begun to assert itself. These days, in the larger cities, you can get not only a wide variety of cuisines from all over the world, but a new kind of cooking is growing up. Australian chefs are now fearlessly combining spices, techniques and flavours from Europe, Asia and the Mediterranean to produce a fresh-tasting, delicious fusion cuisine. The key, of course, is fresh local ingredients of tip-top quality. When you add in a smattering of uniquely Australian ingredients like wattleseed and Burdekin plum, plus unusual game meats such as crocodile and emu, as well as some of the best

seafood on the planet, you can get a really decent meal in this country. Pay particular attention to seafood of all sorts and to the wide range of tropical fruits available.

And for the Americans, we have both kinds: McDonalds and Pizza Hut.

I thought you lot only drank beer.

Well, we do drink beer. Mostly. In fact, there's a distinct etiquette to drinking beer in this country. There's the 'shout', for example – when you're drinking with a group, you may find it is expected that each member of the group will buy one round ('shout the group a drink') in turn. Leaving before your shout is a killing offence in some pubs.

Then there's the question of what beer to drink. Possibly the best of all Australian beers is the Tasmanian Cascade Lager. However, export-quality Eumundi Lager out of Queensland has real charm. On tap, go for Coopers Ale or Tooheys Old, if you can get it. Two good boutique beers are Hahn (Sydney) and Redback (Western Australia). A wonderful New Zealand drop called Steinlager is also widely available, in bottles.

For the sake of safety, in Queensland you should always express a preference for Fourex if asked. In New South Wales, that would be Tooheys. And remember: nobody in Australia actually drinks Fosters Lager voluntarily. It's for emergencies and medicinal use only.

Scuba Diving

The East Coast of Australia has the very best diving in the world, flat. No competition. Before you go head-over-tits into a dive course, you ought to try a preliminary dive, under supervision, just to find out if you like it. This can be done for a cost of $30 to $80, and two very good locations are the Solitary Islands Marine Reserve, through Coffs Harbour and Julian

Rocks, at Byron Bay, both in northern NSW.

Chances are very good that you are going to like diving. It's brilliant. Like flying, only better in some ways. And you do it well off the coast up north, where the jellyfish, which prevent swimming on the beaches in summer, won't bother you. Anyway, if you decide you want to do a bit more diving – up around the Whitsundays and off Cairns, and you're mad if you don't – you should think about doing a dive course.

A dive course which leads to open water certification through either PADI or NAUI (the two main world-wide divers' associations) should last about five days and will usually cost between $300 and $500. You will need to get a doctor's certificate before you can take a course – there will be a thorough check of your heart, lungs, ears and general fitness. The medical certificate itself will cost you about $35, although some schools include it in the price of the course.

Your diving course should be run by a fully-qualified and insured instructor, with all the appropriate equipment to be supplied by the instructor in good working order. Most courses include a mixture of dives in swimming pools, followed by one or more open-water dives. You should be certain you are taught about navigation, air consumption, snorkelling, emergency features, equipment handling, buoyancy control, ascents, depressurisation, rescues and first aid, at the very minimum.

Without an open-water certificate, you can only undertake simple, shallow dives under the direct supervision of a qualified dive master. With an open-water certificate, you can hire equipment and dive anywhere in the world. You will be required to keep a log-book of your dives, depths and hours, and there are some dives which require minimum levels of experience before you can attempt them without a senior diver but in essence, the open-water certificate is your ticket to scuba freedom.

The cheapest dive courses on the East Coast are in Bundaberg, in Queensland. Bundaberg is a town with limited tourist potential, and the price tag of $150 for full certification has come about through competition between a couple of local schools. It can't possibly last, but while it's on, you should definitely take advantage of it. Bundaberg is an excellent place to learn to dive. It is near the very southern end of the Barrier Reef, so there are a few coral isles in the vicinity. South of Bundaberg, there is no Barrier Reef and you won't miss much if you just stick to the fantastic surf beaches. On the other hand, not far north of Bundaberg, the surf turns to beach-break crap, so you'll be more interested in diving anyhow.

Dates & Events

School Holidays – Take Cover & Beware. Mid-December to late January, early April, late June to mid-July and late September to early October. Also, beware Easter, when the roads in and out of the cities become unpassable.

Australia Day – 26 January. Commemorates the First Fleet landing and the foundation of Australia. Not popular with Aborigines.

Sydney Gay & Lesbian Mardi Gras – Early February. Major festival and parade, attracting upwards of half a million spectators, plus participants from all over the world.

Hunter Valley Vintage Festival – March. Grape-stomping, grape-picking and an enormous piss-up.

Byron Bay Blues Festival – Eastertime.

Maleny-Woodford Folk Festival – New Year.

Chinese New Year – Mid-February, usually. Try to get to a large Chinese restaurant for lion dances, feasts and firecrackers.

Melbourne Cup Day – First Tuesday in November. Everything stops across the nation at about two o'clock in the afternoon. Don't try to fight it; get a bet on, join the sweepstakes at your hostel or local pub and get pissed with the rest of the country.

ANZAC Day – 25 April. Commemorates the combined Australian and New Zealand forces getting the shit knocked out of them in Gallipoli in WWI. There's a public holiday, parades, speeches and much drinking. As cartoonist Larry Pickering once noted: wonder what they'd have done if we won?

Transport

Despite the risk of hitching, it's still a pretty good way to get around Australia. The problem with travelling in Australia is that it's spread out. Domestic air-travel tends to be very expensive. There are seasonal variations and special deals which will sometimes bring fares down, so it's worth your while ringing the airlines and asking – but don't get your hopes up. Travelling from city to city in Australia by air will usually set you back at least $300 and that's only one way. It can be cheaper if you book at least seven days in advance. The two main airlines are Qantas (phone 131313) and Ansett (phone 131300).

Coming in from overseas, though, is a different matter. If you talk to your travel agent at home, you'll find you can score flights at a much, much better rate than is possible by booking in Australia. We're talking 50 per cent cheaper – sometimes more. The drawback is, of course, that it ties down your itinerary to a degree. It means that you'll have to be in specific places at specific times to pick up your flight. Still, this option is

definitely worth considering, especially if your time in Australia is limited. You could skip big boring chunks of the country that way – places like Rockhampton, for example and the central coast of Queensland.

Assuming you've prearranged your flights, you are still left with the question of how you intend to get around on the ground. Going up the coast from Sydney leaves you with two choices of public transport: train, or bus. The XPT train, which runs Sydney to Brisbane in jig time for about $95, is an excellent choice. It stops at all kinds of good places on the way, too. In Queensland, the train which runs from Brisbane to Cairns is called The Sunlander. It is hideously overpriced (about $120 for an economy sitter, one way), deadly slow, and misses half the best spots on the coast. In fact, even the most hardened train-fanatic would have to admit that a journey on The Sunlander is not unlike slow, suffocating death.

Which leaves buses. These are faster than the train, cost significantly less and generally go to places the train ignores. And they're pretty safe, too, for those of you from the States. (Travelling by Greyhound in the USA I would recommend only to the most jaded and world-weary of wanderers …)

Don't get the idea I'm recommending buses, though. I hate 'em. There's not enough space, the air-conditioning never works, the videos are mind-numbing, the seats are arse-numbing and somebody always brings a screaming baby aboard. Plus, you invariably arrive wherever it is you want to be at 2am.

No, if it were me taking this trip (and I did), I'd be getting together with another traveller and laying out about $500 – $1500 for a shitbox of a car. For that kind of price, you won't be getting any Jags or Bentleys, but if you shop around a bit, you'll probably lay hands on something that will make the trip. And you won't feel too bad about thrashing it over the rough patches, either. Sure, the car option will cost you in petrol – but with a vehicle of your own, your itinerary is your own. It's that spread-out thing again, you see. On the whole, Australia's towns are dull. Boring. You want cities and culture, go somewhere else where the places are more than 100 years old. If you're doing the East Coast of Australia, you want surf, sun, the bush – all the stuff you don't get in the towns. So even if you do take a bus to, say, Cairns, you're still going to be laying out a bucket of money once you get there just so that you can get out and see what's worth seeing. A car makes sense. You buy one through the classified advertisements in Saturday's *Sydney Morning Herald* or a weekly Sydney magazine called the *Trading Post*. There are also motor markets and you should ask the people running your hostel for their current locations.

Of course, if you're a total Green Commando, unfeasibly fit and with a pain threshold that makes dentists spasm with delight, you might want to try doing it all by bicycle.

Good luck.

Driving

This is done on the LEFT HAND SIDE OF THE ROAD. If you wish to drive in Australia, it is necessary to carry a driver's licence with you while driving. If you are in the country for three months or less, a valid driver's licence from your own country is adequate. If you are staying longer, it is advisable to apply for an international driver's licence. This should be done in your home country.

The national speed limit is 100kph on the highways – although some stretches are now signed at 110kph – and 60kph in the cities. Near schools, this lower limit becomes 40kph. Wearing of seatbelts is compulsory and fines may be levied for non-compliance. Maximum permissible blood alcohol content in New South Wales and Queensland alike is .05 per cent. That's about three drinks in an hour for a man and two for a woman. There are stiff penalties for driving with a higher blood alcohol level, and it's a stupid idea anyway. Don't drive if you've been drinking. The police often stop drivers at random to test their blood alcohol levels.

Particular hazards to driving in Australia include dirt and gravel roads. Drive these very carefully. Many roads can also become flooded during the wet season. Watch for signs indicating flood zones. In many areas, unfenced stock can wander onto the road. Be especially careful at night; hitting a cow at 100kph will be almost as bad for you as it is for the cow. Also, kangaroos are frequently found on country roads by night. Kangaroos are definitely big enough to curtail your holiday should you hit one at speed.

By the way: if you're a member of an Automobile Club or motoring organisation at home, make sure you get a letter of introduction or proof of membership. It may very well give you reciprocal rights with the local Automobile Clubs, including maps and breakdown services. This can be extraordinarily valuable in a country as large as Australia. Otherwise, you should join the NRMA in Sydney (phone 132132, branches all over the place) or the RACQ in Queensland (main office 07 3361 2444).

Local transport within cities is variable. In the capital cities, the train and bus services are usually rather good – with the exception of Brisbane. Brisbane is extremely spread-out, with only a small 'Inner City'. As a result, public transport in Brisbane is crap.

Cabs tend to be expensive. Flagfall is about $1.50 in most places, with a radio surcharge of about 60c if you've telephoned the cab rather than picked it up off the street. There's a complicated time-distance tariff as well. Basically, if you think in terms of about a dollar a minute in ordinary city traffic, you'll be close enough. Sometimes, therefore, cabs can be a very good short-distance solution to a particular problem – like getting from the bus stop to the hostel in pouring monsoon rain.

Local train systems are pretty much non-existent outside the capital cities and once you get below the 100,000 population mark, even the buses become infrequent and somewhat unreliable. Australia is a very large country; most people find they require a private vehicle sooner or later. I'd strongly suggest you do the same.

Accommodation and Camping

This guide focuses on backpacker hostels and camping grounds. Another cheap source of accomodation is the country pub – there are lots of them, but the quality, particularly of the food, can be pretty rough. Often you could be the only people staying there. There are motels all over the place, and these are usually all right, but far more expensive than hostels.

Most hostels are not part of the Youth Hostel Association. But some are, and for them it's good to have an international YHA card, from your own country or from the Australian branch at 10 Mallett St, Camperdown, Sydney (9565 1325). Some hostels, like the YHA ones, require you to have your own sheets if you don't have a sleeping bag.

There are many excellent campsites in some of the more obscure and remote locations of this country. In the national parks, although you need a permit, this is easily obtainable from the local National Parks and Wildlife offices, or often at the campsite proper. These permits usually cost no more than $3 per night and as the money they provide goes towards maintaining the campsites, it's a good investment. On the other hand, camping in the (usually unimproved) state forest reserves is legal and completely free. Both options frequently provide access to some of the most beautiful scenery and countryside that there is. The problem for you is that 'camping rough' in Australia is a slightly different proposition to what it is in most countries. Read the list of suggested equipment closely and pay heed.

Notice, too, that some of the national parks are larger than small European countries and quite wild. If you plan any extended excursions into such areas, you would be well advised to tell somebody your itinerary first. That way, if you don't turn up on time, they can send out the search parties. National Parks and Wildlife offices or ranger stations are ideal places to leave such a travel plan or itinerary.

Suggested Equipment

Shelter: Much of Australia is tropical and may seem idyllically warm and comfortable to someone from a temperate climate. Don't be fooled. Even in the warm and tropical regions, sudden downpours can make camping a cold, wet misery. If you're going to sleep under the stars, be certain of the weather forecast. Otherwise, carry a good-quality, well-sealed, thoroughly waterproof tent.

First Aid Kit: This gets ignored by a lot of people. Don't be one of them. You should carry, at a minimum, any of the standard kits available from most chemists and be absolutely certain you have a couple of nice, long pressure bandages, and plenty of painkillers. Antibiotics too, if you are prepared to use them correctly.

Sunscreen. We've discussed this already, but if you forget it, you're an idiot.

Drinking water: this may not be available in many of the more remote places. You'll want about 5 litres per person, per day. THIS IS VITAL.

Camp stove: Australia gets to be very dry, in between the rains. An Australian bushfire is bad news – Death On Wheels. In many areas, campfires are forbidden, and with good cause. Get yourself a lightweight camp stove and use it.

Maps & Compasses: Do I really have to tell you this?

Toilet paper and trowel: Make sure you go well away from trails and watercourses. And bury it properly, for Christ's sake. That's what the trowel is for.

Insect Repellent: You'll have a really rotten time without it.

Communications

Australia has an excellent telephone system and is one of the fastest-growing Internet populations in the world. Public telephones accept coins – at 40c a local call – and some accept credit and phone cards. The phone system can reach all parts of the continent, as do radio and some television broadcasts, courtesy of satellite technology. There is even a system of solar-powered emergency telephones along some of the roads and railways in the Outback. Electricity is 240 volts by 20 amps.

The media in Australia are reasonably effective, despite concentrations of ownership, mainly in the hands of Mr Rupert Murdoch, although the Fairfax Press owns three of the four best newspapers, Melbourne's *Age, The Sydney Morning Herald* and the national *Australian Financial Review.* For opinion and international news, the national *Australian* is the best of the newspapers. Brisbane's *Courier Mail* is a particularly bad newspaper. There are two weekly magazines, the local edition of *Time* and the *Bulletin.* Many larger newsagencies stock international newspapers and magazines. In Sydney the Kings Cross newsagency, next to the entrance to the railway station in Darlinghurst Road, has a particularly good range.

Most cities and even small towns have a post office, including a *poste restante* facility and faxes which can be used by the public. The Australian postal service is actually very efficient. Despite the size of the country, mail will usually reach even the most remote areas within five days. Within a city, delivery is usually overnight.

Money

Comes in different colours here. Different sizes, too. And they make the notes out of plastic, which is kind of ugly, but lasts longer than paper and is apparently much harder to forge. Plastic money is an Australian invention. You can judge for yourself whether or not it's a success.

Basic unit is the dollar, divided into 100 cents. These days, the 1c and 2c piece are no longer part of the game. They've been taken out of circulation and costs at the cash register are rounded to the nearest 5c – the 5c coin now being the smallest in circulation.

The Aussie dollar is worth about 50p British usually, but it buys roughly the same amount of goods and services here in Australia that a pound does in England. It's only worth about US 75c, though – and doesn't buy as much here as the US dollar does in America.

There are banks in most towns and they'll handle traveller's cheques if you need it. Visa, MasterCard and Diner's Club are spoken widely. Foreign currency isn't accepted – although in a really odd situation, you might find US dollars accepted at a totally ruinous rate of exchange. If you get yourself into that kind of situation, it serves you right. Australia is adopting EFTPOS technology at a rate you might not believe. Auto-banking machines are all over the place and most supermarkets and petrol stations accept both credit cards and bank-account linked cards. Business hours are generally from about 9am to about 5pm for all kinds of services.

Religion

Take it or leave it. Nobody will give you a hard time unless you want to take to the streets and try to convert us. Australia is largely a Christian country, but immigration has introduced significant populations of Muslims, Buddhists, Jews and Sikhs, to name a few.

Work

Visitors from several nations may be eligible for a 'working holiday' visa which entitles you to work three months out of twelve. It is necessary to apply for such a visa in your home country, before the trip commences.

Australia suffers from unemployment of over 8 per cent. You will find, however, that there may be jobs in the service industry – bar staff, waiters and the like – for young people on a casual basis. Most commonly, you will be able to find seasonal work as a fruit picker.

Best areas to look for such work are in the agricultural basins, of course. In the region of New South Wales covered by this book, try the Hunter Valley for grape picking around February. In Queensland, there is picking work near Bundaberg and Childers and at Cardwell most of the year round. Contact the local Commonwealth Employment Service, or simply ask at the hostels. Many hostels can help you arrange work with farmers. The average wage for a picker is about $10 an hour and how much you earn depends on how much you can pick. Picking is hot, brutal labour and in the Australian sun, it can wipe you out very quickly, so be careful and don't overdo it.

Aside from a working holiday visa, you will need a tax file number. Application forms can be had from most post offices and should be submitted to the nearest tax office. If you have not yet received your tax file number by the time you find work, most places will accept a tax office receipt which shows you have applied for a number.

Also useful is a local bank account. If you open such an account within the first six weeks of your stay, your passport alone will be sufficient identification. If you wait longer, you may be called upon to supply things like a birth certificate and driver's licence as well. The bank will want you to supply a local address; your hostel is usually sufficient.

A useful contact is International Travellers Advisory Service: (02) 262 5011. They operate out of Level 6, 38 York St, Sydney and are very good at helping international travellers find work and accommodation.

Consulates

In Brisbane – British Consulate (07) 3236 2575
– United States Consulate (07) 3831 3330
– French Consulate (07) 3229 8201
– German Consulate (07) 3221 7819

In Sydney – British Consulate (02) 9247 7521
– United States Consulate (02) 9373 9200
– French Consulate (02) 261 95779
– German Consulate (02) 928 7733

The embassies are all down in Canberra, an ugly and purpose-built inland capital city. There is absolutely no need for you or anyone else to visit it.

Weights & Measures

Australia operates under the metric system. This is a rational, logical way of going about things and it's a wonder that the Pommies and Seppos haven't worked it out yet.

Sex, Drugs, Law & Order

Well, there's only one drinking age in this country. If you're eighteen you're legal to get rotten. Being drunk in public is frowned on, and might get you a night in the cooler if you're particularly noisy and obstreperous. Drinking in public isn't strictly legal, but The Barbie In The Park is the cultural right of every Australian and if the cops tried to stop people drinking in places like that, there'd be a very short, very bloody revolution. (Though they've just started to try, in Queensland.)

Recreational drugs other than alcohol are illegal. How illegal depends on where you are. In Queensland, they're more illegal than in NSW – but there's more smokers per capita. In any case, no matter where you are, it won't get you a death penalty. Small amounts of marijuana for personal use (a couple of joints, or a stick) will generally only get you a judiciary slap on the wrist – but the time spent fragging around with the cops and the courts will really put the bite on your holiday.

Harder stuff is more illegal. It can be found, but it's a lot more trouble if you're found with it.

Australia's AIDS infection rate is extremely low, in comparison with most countries of the world. We'd like to keep it that way, thanks, so if you're going to do the Wild Thing, use a bloody condom. You can get them from most any chemist or convenience store. The age of consent is 16 (although it's been a while since I set my sights that low). Homosexuality is legal, more or less (except in Tasmania – but they're still just getting used to the electric light down there, so they don't count). One thing though: in the country towns, they tend to be a little more conservative than in Sydney and there's still a fair bit of the old 'Poofter-bashing' idea around. If you swing a little off-centre, you might want to keep a relatively low profile in such areas.

Violent crime is relatively rare in Australia, where you should take the same level of precautions you would adopt in Vancouver, London or Oslo. Hitch-hiking by women is not recommended. It is not necessary to carry identification papers with you to travel in Australia. However, it is advisable to carry some form of identification and at least a minimal amount of cash – the oldest means in the book for police officers to lock someone up for the night is to cite the vagrancy laws.

Snapshots

Conan the Librarian: I'd been picking fruit in the Hunter Valley and the work finished up, so I decided to move on. I didn't really have far to go – the next place offering work was only about ten klicks down the road – but it was hot as all fuck and I'd been picking in the sun for most of the day. The prospect of toting my damned pack all that way did not appeal to me in the least, and I decided to try my luck hitching.

I'd barely stuck out my thumb when this ute came rattling to a stop about ten metres in front of me. A guy with a big, country-boy hat stuck his head out and asked me where I was going. I told him, and he smiled and waved. 'Just toss your pack in the tray,' he said. Like a complete dickhead, I did. The last I saw of two weeks of dirty laundry, my old duffel bag and a really nice Nikon camera was a dust-cloud disappearing over the horizon.

Health

No vaccinations are necessary for entering Australia. In fact, Australia is one of the least diseased countries in the world. Tap water is properly treated and may be drunk without fear in all of the cities and towns. Even the waters of creeks and rivers may be drunk in most of the mountainous areas, although naturally, drinking downstream from human dwellings is a very poor idea.

The Australian medical system is well-organised and efficient and if there is an emergency you will receive competent treatment regardless of your ability to pay – although that will be discussed at a later time, depending on the degree of treatment required. If you have a visa which lasts more than three months, it would be a good idea for you to apply for a Medicare card. Most towns have a Medicare office where applications can be lodged. (Medicare is the government health system.) You get free care at public hospitals and the government pays two-thirds of doctors' fees. Only citizens of Britain, New Zealand, Italy, Sweden and the Netherlands need apply, as these countries have reciprocal agreements with Australia.

Emergencies

The nationwide emergency telephone number is 000. This is a free call which can be made from any phone. You will be placed in contact with the police service, the ambulance service, or the fire brigade, depending on what you ask for.

Survival

1. Hitch-hiking. Australia is no longer – if it ever was – the Hitcher's Paradise. People do get killed here, sometimes in the same sick and twisted way the Americans have been pioneering for decades. It doesn't happen often and it scares hell out of the whole nation when it does happen, but the fact remains: if you hitch, you run a degree of risk. It's not that long since seven backpackers were murdered in the Belanglo Forest area in southern NSW.

On the other hand, there's an awful lot of Australia to cover and transport costs will quickly eat into the budget of most backpackers. Hitching does work in Australia, and rather well. It pays to be vigilant and careful, though and to follow a few simple rules. I'm not suggesting you should be hitching around the country – but if that's the way you decide to travel, do it like this.

a) Do it in pairs. It's harder to get a lift, but it's a lot safer.
b) Shower, Shave and Smile: More people will pick you up if you look like a fresh young traveller, and not Charles Manson with cheese in his armpits.
c) Obey the local laws concerning hitching. Generally, these will keep you off the major expressways and forbid you hitching anywhere but on the shoulder of the road.
d) Pick a destination: Know where you're trying to go. You might even carry a little sign.
e) Tell someone else where you're going: Keep somebody you know

up to date with your travel plans and contact them when you arrive at your destination. That way, if you do happen to disappear, at least somebody will know where and when to start looking for you.

2. Walking. I don't care whether you're from Scunthorpe or the Snowies; tooling around the Australian countryside calls for a few precautions that most people don't consider.

For a civilised, industrialised country, cities and roads can be remarkably few and far between in Australia. In most countries, if you set out to hitchhike from one city to the next, it's no big deal: maybe fifty, a hundred kilometres. And there's rest stops and villages, stuff like that.

That is not the case in Australia. There are stretches of the main East Coast Highway in the North where you can travel two hundred kilometres and see no man-made structure. And if you happen to get off the highway …

The point is, you could be spending a long time getting from one place to the next. If you're not travelling with enough water, you're asking for serious trouble. This is a hot country, by and large. Very fucking hot. Wandering around with a twenty-kilo pack without due precaution can put you in the hospital faster than a roadside curry in Calcutta.

If you have any brains, you'll get yourself some basic protective gear and keep it with you. It should include:

a)   at least three or four litres of drinking water
b)   a broad-brimmed sun-proof hat
c)   a container of 15+ sunscreen (unless you happen to be blessed with as much melanin as the original inhabitants of this country)
d)   a decent first-aid kit, including a full-length pressure bandage
e)   damn good shoes or boots.

This is good stuff to have, even if you are going to be travelling by car or bus. You won't be too discomfited by the extra weight and when the time comes when you really need these things, you'll be extremely glad you carried them.

3. The Sun. Australians can probably skip this bit. The rest of you, listen up. If you want a tan, go to a tanning booth. If you want the most savage sunburn of your life, with all the pain and discomfort and the concomitant risk of skin cancer, spend an hour unprotected on a Queensland beach at noon.

This point can't be hit hard enough. Even exposures as short as fifteen minutes can be painful and dangerous. Cloudy conditions are no protection; it may cool things down, but it does nothing to cut the UV radiation. The sun kills people in this country. Melanoma is one of the leading killers of children in Queensland; it would be doing the same for adults as well if they weren't too busy dying of heart attacks instead.

Get a nice, broad-brimmed hat. (There's a reason Crocodile Dundee wore a hat, and it wasn't just to hide his bald spot.) Buy some 15+ sunscreen at any pharmacy and slather it on when you go outdoors. Don't miss any spots: after a day of sailing, a friend of mine developed the most attractive set of matched blisters below each kneecap, where she'd missed with the sunscreen. Wear a long-sleeved shirt if you're going to be in the

46

sun for any length of time. Don't be afraid to wear a T-shirt into the surf, either.

Sunburn isn't the only danger from the fierce Australian sun. Heat exhaustion and heat stroke are also pretty common, especially amongst new arrivals who insist on walking about in the heat of the day with twenty-odd kilos strapped to their back. If anybody starts behaving oddly, or collapses, get them into black shade and make sure they have plenty on hand to drink. If they don't recover in reasonably short order, get them to a hospital.

Information

The two best sources of information are other travellers and the people who run hostels, who often also arrange trips and tours. A great official place in Sydney is the **NSW Travel Centre** at 19 Castlereagh St (9231 4444). Here you can stock up on brochures and maps for the whole trip up to the Queensland border. The you should go straight to the **Queensland Government Travel Centre** on the corner of Adelaide and Edward Streets (3221 6111) and do the same again. If you buy a car and join a motorists' association (in NSW the **NRMA**, in Queensland the **RACQ**) it will provide you with free maps and accomodation guides.

Everywhere you go there will be free maps, so, to keep this book short and cheap, we've gone easy on the maps. That way you can pick up what you need along the way (which, let's face it, you're going to do anyway) and throw it away when you're through.

I've also avoided even trying to tell you how to do complicated things which require their own books. For example, there is a good *Lonely Planet* book on bushwalking, if you want to do a lot of it. There are also specialist books on the Great Barrier Reef, Sydney (*Untourist Sydney* and the *Cheap Eats Guide* are useful if you plan to live there for a while) and many other aspects of Australia.

If anyone offers to sell you the Sydney Harbour Bridge, ignore them. Despite the government's wide-ranging privatisation policies, the Bridge is not for sale. Not yet, anyway.

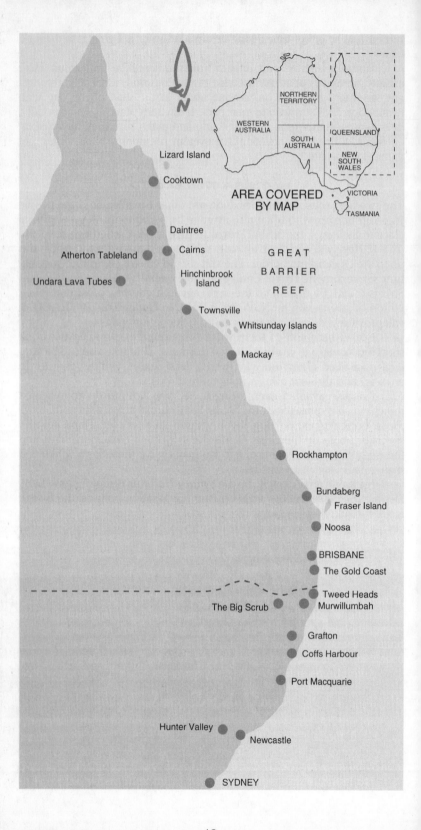

Lizard Island

Cooktown

Daintree

Atherton Tableland   Cairns

Undara Lava Tubes   Hinchinbrook
Island

GREAT

BARRIER

REEF

Townsville

Whitsunday Islands

Mackay

Rockhampton

Bundaberg
Fraser Island

Noosa

BRISBANE

The Gold Coast

Tweed Heads
The Big Scrub   Murwillumbah

Grafton

Coffs Harbour

Port Macquarie

Hunter Valley

Newcastle

SYDNEY

NORTHERN
TERRITORY

WESTERN
AUSTRALIA

SOUTH
AUSTRALIA

QUEENSLAND

NEW
SOUTH
WALES

AREA COVERED
BY MAP

VICTORIA

TASMANIA

N

Sydney

Sydney is the capital of the state of New South Wales. It was the first place in Australia to be settled by white people, when it was set up as a penal colony by the English in 1788. Today it is Australia's largest and arguably most cosmopolitan city. In its weather and lifestyle it resembles a Mediterranean city, albeit one on the Pacific. The harbour, the beaches and the climate dominate the often unfortunate architecture and urban planning. For a city founded fairly recently it has its fair share of museums, historic buildings, shops, excellent restaurants, active nightclubs, pubs and the thousand other things which make city living worthwhile. But I figure you haven't come all this way just to do what you could have done a lot closer to home, so this section will concentrate on those qualities of Sydney which are unique.

The city has over three and a half million inhabitants and, because most of them live in fairly large houses on large blocks of land, it is one of the geographically biggest cities in the world. It will take over an hour's driving to get clear of the city whether you go north, south or west. But the suburbs need not concern you because you will be staying in the inner city, or areas very close to it. Here everything you want to do or see is close and where it is not within walking distance you can use the good public transport system, which consists of buses (perhaps the most useful), trains (including an underground city circle) and ferries, for getting around the harbour. All the ferries leave from Circular Quay, in the shadow of the Harbour Bridge. There are also taxis, on both land and water. Please note that the city centre itself, which is quite small, consists largely of skyscrapers and is of little interest.

This is what you must do in Sydney. Details follow later on.

Dirk's Dozen

1.   **The Great Ferry Trip to and from Manly.** If there is only one thing you can do in Sydney, this is it.

2.   **The Great Walk,** which covers the Museum, the historical Macquarie Street, the Art Gallery, the Botanic Gardens, the Opera House, the Harbour Bridge and the nineteenth century area known as the Rocks. This is the other thing you must do in Sydney.

3.   Watch the **Sydney to Hobart Yacht Race** get under way from a harbourside park on Boxing Day.

4.   **The Gay and Lesbian Mardi Gras.** If you're in Sydney at the end of February, don't miss it. The party afterwards at the Show Ground is really something, if you can get in.

5.   The walk around the cliffs along the Pacific Ocean from **Bondi** to **Coogee**.

6. See the Australian birds and animals at **Taronga Zoo**, a short ferry ride from Circular Quay. Learn to recognise the deadly Taipan snake before you meet it in the wild.

7. Catch a bus or drive to **Watsons Bay**. Have a look at the Pacific from Sydney's premier suicide cliff, The Gap, then wander down to the Watsons Bay Hotel and have a beer and some fish and chips outdoors at sunset, looking back at the city.

8. The day trip to **Katoomba** in the Blue Mountains.

While we're on the subject of recommendations, let me advise against the following.

Dirk Dumps On

1. **Trying to drive in and around Sydney.** The place wasn't planned; it grew as a result of the wanderings of deranged convicts and savage feral cows. And there's this odd-shaped harbour in the middle of it all, surrounded by hilly bays and coves. Once off the main roads, the place can be a navigational nightmare.

2. **Sydney's beaches.** There are about seventy of them and the half of them that are on the coast (the others are on the harbour) are actually quite good. But why bother, when the coast only a few hours to the north does them so very, very much better? The only real reason to go to Manly or Bondi is to see and to be seen. Otherwise, the way I figure it, an hour spent on a Sydney beach is an hour you could have spent in paradise further north.

The generally admirable Captain James Cook must have been having an off-week when he discovered Botany Bay, a modest harbour to the south of the centre of Sydney, in 1770. First he decided it was fine agricultural land, which it was not, and which caused some consternation when the First Fleet turned up with spades and livestock eighteen years later. Cook grew up on a farm, so his mistake has never been explained. Then, on leaving Botany Bay, he proceeded to sail right past the not insignificant opening to Sydney Harbour a few miles to the north without noticing it, thereby failing to 'discover' the finest harbour in the world. Cook's confusion might perhaps be explained by a previously unguessed at use of illegal substances by those on board the *Endeavour*. This hypothesis is strengthened by a diary of Cook's journey which has just come to light. Excerpts will be presented throughout this book, this being the first time they have ever been published. The references to a Mr Banks in the diaries are to Sir Joseph Banks, a wealthy botanist of private means who paid for himself and several assistants to go along on Cook's tour. The diaries also contain certain surfing terms common in the British Navy in the late eighteenth century.

Captain's Log, James Cook 1770 World Surf Safari: 'Made landfall today. In an attempt to placate Mr Banks, I have named the place Botany Bay. I am quite certain, though, that he will never consider naming any of the plants and animals for me, as he is a selfish swine, who can barely keep a board beneath him, let alone appreciate the beauty of a two-fathom South-easterly tube.

'Approaching the shore, I discerned a number of coves with golden sand. Although there was much shore-break, there were one or two sites which appeared to be tubing up and I am eager to break out the sticks and hit the surf.

'Once we landed, there was a slight altercation with certain native dudes of a dark hue. There were quite a number of them and they did not seem altogether happy at our arrival, so I ordered the men to open fire. Once they had been driven off, I raised the flag and claimed the entire land for King George. After all, the natives were clearly not using it ... I mean, they didn't even know how to use a boogie-board, let alone a three-fin thruster.'

Phones

Most Sydney phone numbers had the number 9 added to them (at the front) by July 1996. If you have trouble calling a number, try adding 9 to it. The Sydney code when calling from other parts of Australia is 02. To reach a Sydney number from outside Australia first dial 0011 61 2. Numbers beginning with 1 800 are free.

Information

The two best sources of information are other travellers and the people who run hostels, who often also arrange trips and tours. A great official place is the NSW Travel Centre at 19 Castlereagh St (9231 4444). They're always busy and sometimes you have to be pushy to get exactly the information you want, but it's still a good idea to call in and get all the free maps and brochures you can. Make sure you get a copy of the brochure on harbour walks which the ferry service puts out. If you buy a car and join the motorists' association (see below) it will provide you with free maps and accommodation guides.

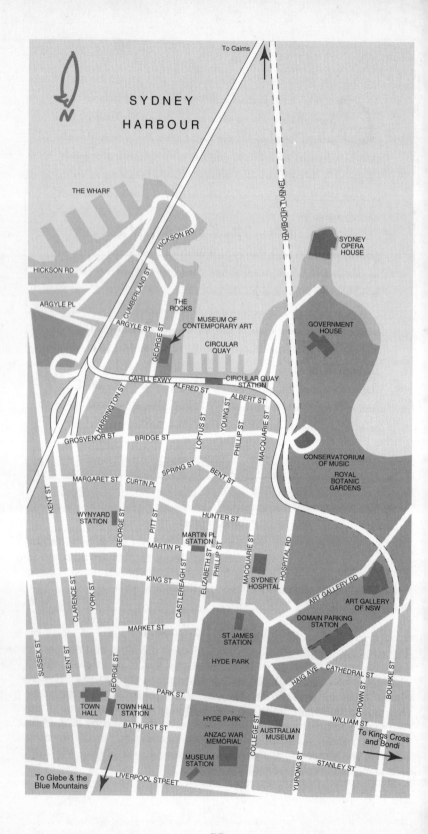

SYDNEY HARBOUR

To Cairns

THE WHARF

HICKSON RD

HICKSON RD

ARGYLE PL

CUMBERLAND ST

HARBOUR TUNNEL

SYDNEY
OPERA
HOUSE

THE
ROCKS

ARGYLE ST

GEORGE ST

MUSEUM OF
CONTEMPORARY ART

CIRCULAR
QUAY

GOVERNMENT
HOUSE

CAHILL EXWY

CIRCULAR QUAY
STATION

ALFRED ST

ALBERT ST

HARRINGTON ST

GROSVENOR ST

BRIDGE ST

LOFTUS ST

YOUNG ST

PHILLIP ST

MACQUARIE ST

CONSERVATORIUM
OF MUSIC

ROYAL
BOTANIC
GARDENS

MARGARET ST

CURTIN PL

SPRING ST

BENT ST

KENT ST

WYNYARD
STATION

GEORGE ST

PITT ST

HUNTER ST

MARTIN PL
STATION

MARTIN PL

CASTLEREAGH ST

ELIZABETH ST

PHILLIP ST

MACQUARIE ST

HOSPITAL RD

KING ST

SYDNEY
HOSPITAL

ART GALLERY RD

ART GALLERY
OF NSW

CLARENCE ST

YORK ST

MARKET ST

ST JAMES
STATION

DOMAIN PARKING
STATION

SUSSEX ST

KENT ST

GEORGE ST

HYDE PARK

HAIG AVE

CATHEDRAL ST

CROWN ST

BOURKE ST

TOWN
HALL

TOWN HALL
STATION

PARK ST

WILLIAM ST

To Kings Cross
and Bondi

BATHURST ST

HYDE PARK

ANZAC WAR
MEMORIAL

AUSTRALIAN
MUSEUM

COLLEGE ST

YURONG ST

STANLEY ST

To Glebe & the
Blue Mountains

LIVERPOOL STREET

MUSEUM
STATION

Stuff to Do

What follows is a list of the bare essentials. I estimate it would take you about five days to do them all properly and as statistics show the average backpacker spends five days sightseeing in Sydney, I'll be buggered if I'm going to confuse you by suggesting other things to do. If you don't do all these things you'll be sorry, because as you move up the coast other travellers are going to be telling you how much they enjoyed the following.

Your first step should be to buy a **Travelpass**, which gives you unlimited travel on buses, trains and ferries. There are two bus routes for tourists, the **Sydney Explorer** and the **Bondi and Bay Explorer**, which operate seven days a week from 9.30 a.m. to at least 6 p.m. Each stops at at least twenty places marked by distinctive signs and tickets can be bought on board. For details call 13 1500, but personally I'd rather do everything on the following list first.

1. The Great Ferry Trip to and from Manly: If there is only one thing you can do in Sydney, this is it. The ferries leave **Circular Quay (Wharf Three)** twice an hour between 6.00 a.m. and 11.30 p.m. The ticket will cost you less than $5. Make sure you take the big, slow ferry and not the fast commuter one, which does not provide the views or the outdoor seating of the real ferries. The trip is half an hour each way. The great thing about this trip is the ever-changing views of **Sydney Harbour**, which is still the best thing Sydney has to offer visitors.

Kenneth Slessor's 'Five Bells' is a great and moving poem about a drunk who fell off a ferry at night and was dragged down to his death by the weight of the bottles of beer he had in the pockets of his overcoat. A splendid mural by John Olsen, inspired by the poem, adorns the wall of the bar at the north end of the Opera House concert hall.

2. The Great Walk: This will take a full day and ought to be split in two if you intend spending more than half an hour at any one place. Start at **Macquarie St** at the top of **Martin Place**. Across the road you will see the **State Parliament**, a modest Georgian building which started life in 1810 as a hospital built by entrepreneurs in return for being granted a rum monopoly by Governor Macquarie. To its right is **Sydney Hospital**, which has a pleasant courtyard with a café looking onto a fountain. To the right of the hospital are the **Mint Museum** and the **Hyde Park Barracks Museum**. These have changing exhibitions and the **Hyde Park Barracks** is a good building designed by Francis Greenway, the convict forger turned Governor Macquarie's architect. Opposite, in **Queen's Square**, is Greenway's other wonderful Sydney building, **St James Church**.

At this point you have two choices. For those with a particular interest in natural history, walk down Macquarie St and into **College St** until you reach the **Australian Museum** on the corner of **William St**. This walk will take you beside **Hyde Park** and on the way you will pass **St Mary's Cathedral**, a large Catholic church of little architectural distinction. The Museum concentrates on natural history, but also has a good collection of Aboriginal artefacts. It opens every day except Christmas Day from 9.30 a.m. to 5 p.m. If you don't want to visit the Museum, go back to the hospital and walk through the central courtyard and across the park known as the **Domain** to the **Art Gallery of NSW** in **Art Gallery Road**. It's open seven days from 10 a.m. to 5 p.m., closed Christmas Day and Good Friday. Admission is free. Go in and turn left and check out the twentieth century Australian paintings. There's one restaurant upstairs and a cheaper one downstairs. Both are good for light meals.

When you leave the Art Gallery, turn right, cross the road bridge and turn left into the **Botanic Gardens**, open every day from sunrise to sunset. They're very pretty and peaceful, with lots of harbour views, a good place to have lunch when the push and shove of the city gets to be too much. Take your own lunch, as there's only an expensive restaurant and a tacky café in the gardens themselves. Have a look at the **Sydney Tropical Centre** while you're there: great big glasshouses full of tropical plants from all over the world.

After you've wandered around the gardens, leave either onto Macquarie St or lower down on the harbour and walk downhill to the **Opera House**. This was designed by Danish architect Joern Utzon following an international competition and opened in 1973. It's a mystery to me and many other people how Sydney came to choose such a good design, as almost every other building in the city less than fifty years old is pretty awful. Anyway, enjoy. The outside is a lot better than the inside, although the night view of the harbour from the north bar of the concert hall at interval is pretty good. Make sure you walk right around the building at ground level, as the view of the harbour from the promontory is fine. Ring the box office (9250 7777) if you want to catch a show. Performance information is available in the *Sydney Morning Herald* or by calling 9250 7209. For guided tours the number is 9250 7250.

From the Opera House walk around **Sydney Cove**, the bay with all the ferries, to **Circular Quay**. Rossinis has fairly cheap Italian food and drinks, but if you want something with a bit more class, detour up **Loftus St** into **Macquarie Place Park**, where you will find a good café and hotel and chairs to sit down on. This is a good cool place on hot days when the Quay can get a bit hectic. Back to the Quay, check out the buskers and keep walking around the harbour foreshore until you reach a large art deco building which contains the **Museum of Contemporary Art**. This opens every day from 11 a.m. to 6 p.m. but the collection is not up to much by international standards. Behind the Art Gallery and up towards the bridge lies the conserved area called **The Rocks**.

The Rocks is full of interesting nineteenth century buildings, including some good pubs and provides some idea of what man-made Sydney must have been like before they replaced most of it with concrete shit in the 1960s and 1970s. If, hypothetically, you decided to base your walk around the old pubs, you would start at the **Mercantile**, in George St down past the Museum of Contemporary Art. This is the centre of the action on the morning of St Patrick's Day, 17 March. (Between a quarter and a half of Australians are of Irish descent. It depends on the surname of whom you're talking to.) Then you would wander back up **George St** a bit and turn right up **Argyle St**. Halfway up here you would see the steps leading to the path across the Harbour Bridge, a walk of about two kilometres. (If you make this detour, I suggest you come back by train. **Milsons Point Station** is close and visible at the end of the pathway. The train could bring you back to **Wynyard Station**, which is only ten minutes from The Rocks.) Anyway, continue up Argyle St, detouring to the large craft centre on the right or the **Garrison Church** further up the hill, or indeed **Observatory Hill** on the left, if these take your fancy. Their attractions are self-explanatory, although it should be noted that Observatory Hill is an oasis of grass, spreading trees (the splendid Moreton Bay Fig) and calm; and nearby lies the café of the **S.H. Ervin Gallery**, in the building of the National Trust conservation society.

But the earnest seeker after truth will proceed quickly to Sydney's oldest pub, the **Lord Nelson**, at 19 Kent St, followed by a refresher at the **Hero of Waterloo**, 81 Lower Fort St, or the **Palisade**, 35 Bettington St. Between them these places offer a wide range of beers, including some house brands, in renovated but not over-gentrified surroundings. From there it is a short stagger to **The Wharf**, a large arts complex located in one of a number of finger wharves in **Walsh Bay**. At the end of the Wharf, out in the harbour, is a good and not too expensive restaurant (bookings 9250 1761) and a bar, with outdoor seating in the right weather. This is as good a place as any to watch the sun come down over Sydney. If it's late at night plan to get away by taxi or car, as it's a bit of a hike back to the city.

3. The Cliff Walk: Sydney has a host of good walks, but to my mind the other indispensable one is that from the south end of **Bondi Beach** to the north end of **Coogee Beach** (or vice versa – lots of buses run to both places from the city and along **Oxford St**, through **Darlinghurst**). What you get here, apart from a great deal of exercise (allow about two hours) are vast ocean panoramas and a lot of interesting views of the sandstone cliffs which occur along the coast around Sydney. There's also a very decent and vast old graveyard right on the cliffs at **Waverley**, if you're into that sort of thing. (No more vacancies.) Halfway along the walk is **Bronte Beach**, which has a few cafés and lots of grass for picnics.

4. Three Special Events: If you're in Sydney on Boxing Day, watch the **Sydney to Hobart Yacht Race** get under way from a harbourside park. The daily newspapers will give you the times and the best vantage points. Basically you have to be near the entrance to the harbour (the **Heads**), where you will see hundreds of craft jockeying for positions, whether as contestants or spectators.

On **New Year's Eve** there are spectacular fireworks over the harbour. Again, check the daily papers for details. Often they have particularly good displays on the Harbour Bridge, so make sure you have a good view. The Rocks and **Kings Cross** are big party areas for New Year's Eve. Allow lots of time to get home afterwards, as public transport can be very crowded.

The Gay and Lesbian Mardi Gras. If you're in Sydney at the end of February, don't miss it. The party afterwards at the **Show Ground** is really something, if you can get in. (There have been calls by homosexuals to keep heterosexuals out.) Over a hundred thousand people line the streets to watch the parade go by. If you want to watch, check the newspapers for details. If you want to be involved, call 9557 4332.

5. Watsons Bay: Catch a bus or drive to **Watsons Bay**, which is almost on the southern of the two heads which guard the entrance to the harbour. (The 325 bus goes along **Elizabeth St** in the city and down William Street and through Kings Cross.) Have a look at the Pacific from Sydney's premier suicide cliff, **The Gap**, then wander down to the **Watsons Bay Hotel** and have a beer and some fish and chips outdoors at dusk, looking back at the city, which will be backlit by the sunset. The trip out to Watsons Bay, through the salubrious **Eastern Suburbs**, should take half an hour by bus and fifteen minutes by car, except at rush hour (4.30 p.m. to 6 p.m.) when it could take at least twice that. There's an expensive fish restaurant (over $20 for most mains) called **Doyles**, where you can sit outside if you can afford it.

6. The day trip to Katoomba in the Blue Mountains: West of Sydney, these dramatic mountains are so named for the blue haze of eucalypt oil which diffracts the sunlight in the area. By car, you can take the **M4** to the **Great Western Highway**, which runs through **Penrith** to **Katoomba**, the central township of the Blue Mountains region. It's only a couple of hours drive and about the same by train from **Central Station** to Katoomba. The train costs about $9 one way and leaves at least once an hour. From Katoomba, an **Explorer** bus can be caught literally from the steps of the railway station. The bus does an hour long round trip, with many stops on the way, and it operates on weekends and public holidays as well. If you're driving, follow the well-signposted **Cliffs Drive** along the cliffs looking out over the great mountain valleys. Both the bus and the drive will take you to Katoomba's **Echo Point** lookout, several kilometres from the station. From here you see vast valleys and huge plateaus standing on lines of orange and gold sandstone cliffs. You are on the edge of a large national park, so all the valleys are full of natural bush. To your left is the strange rock formation called the **Three Sisters**. This is the centre of any visit to the Blue Mountains, closely followed by a viewing of the **IMAX** large screen film of the mountains at a cinema called **The Edge**, about two hundred metres before the railway station on the road up from Sydney.

Don't expect the Blue Mountains to be, like, *tall*. Nothing in Australia is tall by the standards of any other continent. When the late travel writer and legend Bruce Chatwin was taken to the Three Sisters lookout, he stared at the view in silence for a while and then asked what day it was. When told, he sighed and said, "Just think, this time next week I'll be at the base camp on Everest."

Mind you, this says as much about Bruce Chatwin as it does about the Blue Mountains.

Flinthart's Diary

Ever woken up in an alleyway in somebody else's underpants, with a five-star hangover and a nagging feeling that you've done something really, really stupid? I don't recommend it. Especially if it happens to be the day after the Sydney Gay and Lesbian Mardi Gras.

Stagger to a nearby pub. Must be Darlinghurst: nobody is staring at my new gold lame G-string. In fact, compared to some of the other inhabitants, I look positively normal. Funny, everybody in here has the same disaster-struck expression. Is it just the city-wide hangover?

Sit down. Leap up again - the bar stool is damned cold on the buttocks. Where the hell are my trousers? Aha - at least my wallet is still in the knapsack. Order a beer. What the hell did I do last night? Why do I have this foreboding feeling in the back of my mind? Think back, Flinthart …

Let's see. After lunch, about four or five, I ducked into a bar on Victoria St. Watched queers from all over the world assembling for the big moment. Lots of camaraderie and fellow feeling … many rounds of drinks purchased. Grenadine. Grenadine?

Very drunk … watching the parade. Lots of sequins. Oh yes - I remember now. Explained to this utterly beautiful woman that I was clearly a lesbian, since I was hopelessly attracted to beautiful women. She said I was dressed wrong and we traded underpants … she looked great in my silk boxers with little clocks on them, but I found the G-string chilly … Then what?

Oh my God.
I think I remember.

The other activity recommended in the mountains is bushwalking, but for this you need maps, expert advice and time. The starting point is the **National Parks and Wildlife Service**, whose Blue Mountains offices can be contacted on (047) 39 2950 (for general information) or (047) 87 8877 (for those wanting to do the demanding – and rewarding – trips of a day or more down into the **Grose Valley**). A good camping shop in Sydney for books on hiking in the Blue Mountains and equipment is **Paddy Palin** (9264 2685).

It is possible to go rafting through some of the canyon rivers of the Blue Mountains. Some of these canyons are very narrow and impossibly deep. Riding on a small inflatable raft or lilo, all by yourself in the wilderness, is a remarkable and beautiful experience. For information call the above numbers or the **NSW Travel Centre** (9231 4444).

If you want to hire a car to get to the Blue Mountains try **Avis**, William St, Kings Cross (9357 2000) or any of the other rental places down William St between the Cross and the city.

In and Out

Kingsford Smith Airport is a $20 cab ride from the city, but for about $5 you can catch the distinctive yellow-and-green buses which go to both the domestic and international terminals and the parts of the city you'll want to get to. These come every twenty minutes or so and take half an hour to do the trip from the city (No. 300, 5.30 a.m. to 9.30 p.m.) and Kings Cross (No. 350, 4.50 a.m. to 9.50 p.m.). Some of the hostels will permit you to deduct the airport-city cabfare from your bill if you are going to stay with them for a few days. Ring ahead and find out. There are no trains to the airport. If you're flying overseas from Kingsford Smith, there's a $20 departure tax.

There are a couple of train services that run up along the coast to Brisbane, which offer good value at about $100 for economy seats. All the trains run through **Central Station**, at the southern end of the city, so if you ring the **Central Reservation Centre** (9217 8812) you'll be able to manage bookings and timetabling without trouble. Of interest is the regular commuter service which runs up the coast as far as **Newcastle**, one way about $14. If you're planning to hitch-hike, I would most certainly take the train to Newcastle and start from there. The views of the **Hawkesbury River** from the train are spectacular.

The main **Sydney Coach Terminal** (9281 9366) is outside Central Station, on **Eddy Avenue**. From here you can get buses to – well, practically anywhere. If you go straight up the highway, the journey from Sydney to Brisbane is about 1,000km and in a bus will take you something over twelve hours. The fare will be approximately $70.

When the time comes to drive north out of Sydney, you take the **Pacific Highway** to the north. Take the **Harbour Bridge** or tunnel and follow the signs to **Hornsby**, **Newcastle**, or the **North Coast**. Try to get across the harbour before or after the morning rush hour (7.30 a.m. to 9.30 a.m.)

Shelter

There's practically nothing for the budget traveller in the city centre itself. The 'packers places cluster around Kings Cross, **Glebe**, Bondi Beach and the two adjoining inner city suburbs of **Surry Hills** and **Darlinghurst**. There are also a few hostels in other areas such as Manly and Coogee. Those listed here certainly don't exhaust the range of possibilities and if it should happen that hostel accommodation doesn't suit you, try any of the various inner city pubs and hotels, as they also often have cheap, clean places to stay.

Kings Cross

Located just east of the innermost city, the Cross is Australia's Sleaze Centre. This doesn't really mean much if you compare it with cities like New York, LA and Amsterdam. Actually, it's reasonably tame. I wouldn't advise lone women to walk the area by night, but on the whole, it provides a necessary service as an official meeting place for crooked cops and politicians and all those others who are described in the press as 'prominent Sydney identities' or, even worse, 'colourful racing identities'. Due to the rather down-market image of the Cross, a lot of cheap, comfortable places have sprung up here and there's quite an international flavour to the streets. I liked it. Probably the best area for accommodation in all of Sydney.

If you stay at the Cross, ask for directions to **Rushcutters Bay Park**, next to which is the marina from which they run the Sydney to Hobart Yacht Race. It's a pleasant ten minute walk from the Cross and is a very peaceful place. Two other good walks from the Cross are to the city via **Woolloomooloo** (about thirty minutes; lots of scenery and views of the city and harbour) and to **Taylor Square/Oxford Street** along **Darlinghurst Road** (about twenty minutes; lots of cafés and grunge charm). The Cross has frequent buses to the city and Watsons Bay and an underground rail station in Darlinghurst Road (access also from **Victoria St**) which will get you to the city or **Bondi Junction** (from which the beach is another ten minutes by bus).

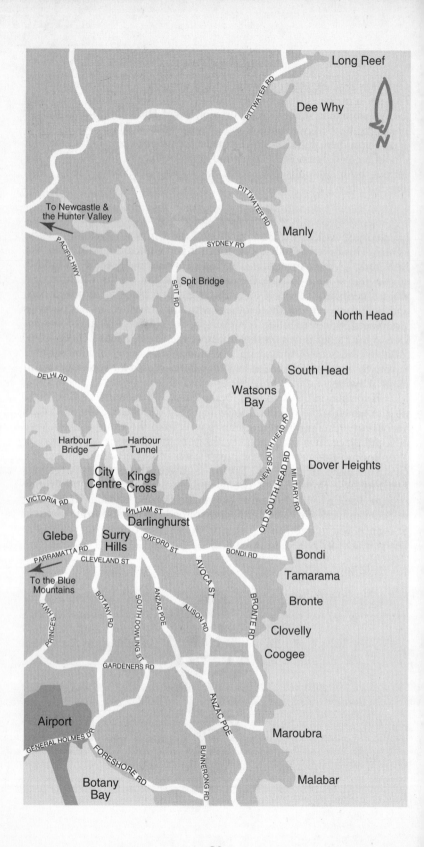

Long Reef

Dee Why

N

PITTWATER RD

To Newcastle &
the Hunter Valley

PITTWATER RD

PACIFIC HWY

SYDNEY RD

Manly

Spit Bridge

SPIT RD

North Head

DELHI RD

South Head

Watsons
Bay

NEW SOUTH HEAD RD

Harbour
Bridge

Harbour
Tunnel

MILITARY RD

Dover Heights

City
Centre

Kings
Cross

VICTORIA RD

WILLIAM ST

Darlinghurst

OLD SOUTH HEAD RD

Glebe

Surry
Hills

OXFORD ST

PARRAMATTA RD

CLEVELAND ST

BONDI RD

Bondi

To the Blue
Mountains

AVOCA ST

Tamarama

BOTANY RD

SOUTH DOWLING ST

ANZAC PDE

ALISON RD

BRONTE RD

Bronte

PRINCES HWY

Clovelly

Coogee

GARDENERS RD

ANZAC PDE

Airport

GENERAL HOLMES DR

BUNNERONG RD

Maroubra

FORESHORE RD

Malabar

Botany
Bay

60

Eva's Backpacker's (9358 2185) 6-8 Orwell St, Kings Cross. Clean and very friendly, with a rooftop barbeque. Excellent, very comfortable place, well located with topnotch facilities.

Backpacker's Connection (9358 4844) 2 Roslyn St, Kings Cross. Typical Cross backpackers, busy, crowded, open all hours, friendly, with very good facilities and service. About $15.

The Astoria (Free call 1 800 806 082) 9 Darlinghurst Rd, Kings Cross. Getting to where the action is, the Astoria is cheap (starts at $10) and cheerful, although somewhat crowded and lacking the facilities of some places. It does have laundry and kitchen facilities, though, as well as a common room with television and all that. They also claim to be able to handle the Dutch and German Languages (Spreken Hollands! Sprechen Deutsch!)

Jolly Swagman Backpacker's (9368 1332) 144 Victoria St, Kings Cross. Another very central place, busy and crowded, from about $15. There's a couple of other Jolly Swagman hostels in this Kings Cross 'chain', so if the first one is full, they may still be able to help you find accommodation in one of the others.

The Pink House (9358 1689) 6-8 Barncleuth Square, Kings Cross. Very popular place with reasonable rates – under $12 at last check. This is a big and interesting old building, with all the usual facilities, plus charming courtyards and the occasional log fire in winter. Also, despite being quite close to the centre of things, it's actually in a fairly quiet little street – although the party spirit thrives here.

Backpacker's Headquarters (9331 6180) 79 Bayswater Rd, Kings Cross. Big and clean and recently refurbished, with all mod cons and close access to the city centre. Rates are good too, with a base of about $12.

Traveller's Rest Hostel (9358 4606) 156 Victoria St, Kings Cross. Clean, well-equipped, lots of bathrooms, lots of televisions! and the airport buses stop just opposite. All this in a big 19th century building. What more could you want for a minimum of $14 per night?

Plane Tree Lodge (9356 4551) 174 Victoria St, Kings Cross. Big, comfortable place, with a variety of different rooms at different rates. Starts at about $14. Not as flash as some of the newer places, but still quite serviceable.

Glebe

A nice, relaxed, sprawling suburb full of academics, students and weirdness. Lots of coffee shops and good ethnic restaurants, most of which are strung out along **Glebe Point Rd**. Excellent place to walk off a hangover, near enough to the city to make it a very good choice for accommodation. Slightly more expensive than the Cross. The food and bookshops are better but it will take you longer to get to the city (about twenty minutes by bus – there is no railway station).

Glebe Village Backpacker's (9660 8878) 256 Glebe Point Rd. This is a great, big, busy place, set back from the street in a couple of dark, somewhat gloomy old houses. A great place for meeting people, planning, relaxing, talking; and the proximity to some of Sydney's most interesting neighbourhoods and restaurants makes it a real winner for about $16.

YHA Sydney Summer Hostel (9557 1133). Located in St Andrew's College, University of Sydney. This is a weird one, open only between December and February, when the college dwellers are elsewhere. A useful location, though, and the facilities are excellent.

Glebe Point YHA (9692 8418) 262 Glebe Point Rd. Busy, excellent facilities and services, without too much of the YHA strong-arm approach. Highly recommended, at about $17.

Wattle House (9552 4997) 44 Hereford St, Glebe. Smaller than most, but friendly and very quiet. A very nice change from the Party Zone atmosphere which prevails at most Sydney city 'packer places. About $17.

Darlinghurst and Surry Hills

Fashionable and interesting suburbs just south of the city heart. And yes, we do spell Surry like that, although no one seems to know why. Taylor Square and Oxford St have been officially declared the Gay and Lesbian Zone, or Pink Precinct, of Sydney – but they won't make an issue out of it if you don't. This is another area with great food, often at quite reasonable prices. Lots of clubs and night life around here, too.

Nomads Captain Cook Hotel (9331 6487) 162 Flinders St, Darlinghurst. Part of a well-regarded national chain of backpacker's, with a very high standard of service and accommodation. Comes highly recommended at $16. Pickups and transport assistance readily available.

City Road Working Holiday Hostel (9310 7627) 94 City Rd, Chippendale. Big and slightly untidy, oriented more towards long-term and working visa visitors. Not especially party-prone, it operates a no-smoking policy.

Kangaroo Backpack (9319 5915) 665 Sth Dowling St, Surry Hills. Very friendly sort of place, well located. Costs under $15 per night at the base rate. Very well regarded.

Bondi Beach

It's a fair way from the city centre, but that doesn't mean Bondi is dull or suburban. Plenty of cafés and nightlife and there are some very decent beaches nearby. Mind you, if you've come to Australia for the beaches, you should get out of Sydney! Go North, young man. Or woman.

Bondi Beach Guesthouse (9389 8309) 11 Consett Ave, Bondi Beach. A good place, not too jammed with people. Starts at $15 per night, with a maximum of four guests per room. And yes, it is indeed very close to Bondi Beach.

Lamrock Hostel (9365 0221) 7 Lamrock Avenue, Bondi Beach. Friendly, popular, long-established and their rates don't tend to vary as much as most other places. The Lamrock is very good value at $15.

Coogee

Another beach region, a little south of Bondi. This is another nice, bright area with cafés and nightspots as well as beaches, although it's all on a much smaller scale than Bondi. Public transport to the city is easy, with the bus taking about twenty minutes, but as the accommodation is so far from the 'action' (except for the large Coogee Bay Hotel), you may be able to find it a little cheaper.

Bondi Cigars

No, these are not an Australian version of the Havana. A Bondi Cigar is, in fact, a long, brown, cylindrical object occasionally found floating in the surf at Bondi. Due to an unfortunate juxtaposition of a sewage outflow, some tricky currents and Australia's best known beach, 'Bondi Cigars' (sometimes known as 'Brown Trout') were an occasional feature of Sydney's surf for many years. Of course, that's all been fixed now. Really.

Surfside Backpacker's (9315 7888) 186 Arden St, Coogee. Clean and excellent, with balconies, beach views, friendly, laid-back atmosphere and fine facilities. Starts at about $13. There is a gym almost next door if you're into that sort of thing.

Coogee Beach Back-packer's (9315 8000) 94 Beach St, Coogee. Groovy and inexpensive, very popular and quite close to the beach.

Manly

Manly is a nice, relaxed place on a neck of land which faces the ocean but backs onto the harbour. It's about twenty minutes by fast ferry (the Harbour Cat) to Circular Quay and forty minutes by a big, real ferry. There's a big beach. The two reasons to stay there are because it's quieter than the other places listed in this book and because of the chance to cross the harbour twice a day.

Manly Beach Resort (9977 4188) 6 Carlton St, Manly. A hip and friendly place, does pickups and deliveries to the airport for $5. Very well regarded, with good facilities and atmosphere. Starts at about $16.

Manly Backpacker's Beachside (9977 3411) 28 Raglan St, Manly. Another highly regarded, very popular spot, quite close to a very decent beach.

Harbourside Hotel (9953 7977) 41 Cremorne Rd, Cremorne Point. This is on the northside but closer to the city than Manly, in a quiet residential area. Excellent location right on the harbour, a short trip by public transport to the city centre, the Opera House and all that good stuff. Starts at about $15. Excellent, slightly manic atmosphere which may get a little too noisy and party-ish for some, but a very worthwhile place anyway.

Food

This is where I draw the line. There are probably as many restaurants in Sydney as there are in the rest of New South

Wales. You can get food in the style of almost anywhere in the world; I even saw a Nepalese restaurant, called the **Yak and Yeti**, in Glebe. What do the Nepalese eat, for God's sake? I wish I'd had time to find out. You need a separate book just to begin to find out what's going in Sydney restaurants and fortunately such a book exists. It's called *Cheap Eats In Sydney* and will cost you about $8; it lists literally hundreds of places where you can stuff yourself stupid for $20 or so. The best places for lots of good restaurants are **Glebe Point Rd, Glebe, Oxford St, Darlinghurst** and **King St, Newtown**. Hit these streets before it's too late (say by 7 p.m. on Friday or Saturday nights) and you'll have no trouble finding something good. The general rule, of course, is to avoid anywhere that's empty on the grounds that the locals probably have a reason for avoiding it.

Below is a list of bargain eateries. But if I had a full wallet (at least $50 per person) and one night left to live, I would head off to the **Darley Street Thai** for its amazing, Thai-influenced seafood and other delights. 28 Bayswater Rd, Kings Cross, shoes and booking essential (9358 6530).

Some of the following nosheries are BYO (bring your own alcohol) although some are licensed. You can tip the staff 10 percent if you like, but many people don't.

Johnnie's Fish Café: 57a Fitzroy St, Surry Hills. Bulk cheap seafood, very tasty.

Mekong: 711 George St, Central. Savagely cheap, specialising in Thai, Cambodian, Vietnamese food. Good stuff.

The Astoria: 9 Darlinghurst Rd, Kings Cross. Yes, the same place as the backpacker's accommodation. Good, filling fare at miserly prices. Plus atmosphere to burn, oh yes.

Betty's Soup Kitchen: 269 Crown St, Darlinghurst. Soup, bread and damper (a slightly scone-like Australian bread).

Chinatown Centre: 25 Dixon St, Chinatown. Chinese food. No booze. If it were any cheaper here, they'd be paying you to come inside.

Hare Krishna Food Centre: 329b King St, Newtown. Vegetarian food, Indian in style, very good. Price is whatever you can afford to donate, usually. You may have to put up with a dose of strange, saffron-hued religion, depending on when you're there. Still, it's entertaining as well as tasty.

Iku: 25a Glebe Pt Rd, Glebe. Heavy on the 'Ick'. No sugar, no meat, no dairy products, all organic, rainforest-approved, dolphin-free, Happy Banana food. It's cheap, though, and if you're inclined towards this sort of thing, I suppose it's good to know it's there.

Mother Chu's: 735 George St. While we're at it, these people claim to be entirely free of MSG.

Laksa House: 182 Oxford St, Paddington. God, I love a good laksa. Supercheap excellent Malay food lives here.

Napoleon's Hotel: Kent/Margaret Sts, City Centre. Cuts out the middleman, lets you grill your own damn steak at lunch. Cheaper that way and you've got nobody to blame but yourself.

Pizza the Hutt: Everywhere. Lunch specials $5 eat until you can't breathe any more. Unfortunately, it's not really food, is it?

Tandoori Centre: 149 Oxford St, Darlinghurst. Curry Lives Here!

That's all you get from me. So long as you are in Sydney, you are rarely any great distance away from somewhere cheap and reasonably tasty …

Miscellaneous

Nightlife

Well, this is just a little subjective, isn't it? The best, if obvious, advice is to talk to other travellers about your needs. In general I find most 'packers are happy to allow their social lives to be determined by the hostel where they're staying. Two suggestions for a good range of restaurants and bars are **Campbell Parade**, **Bondi** and Oxford St from the city to Paddington. (For the latter, when you reach the Verona Cinema complex in Paddington you've reached the end of most of the action.) Oxford St also has plenty of nightclubs, both straight and gay.

Shops

David Jones has two big and very good department stores in the city. The men's store on the corner of **Market** and **Castlereagh Sts** has an excellent food hall in the basement, which also sells a reliable range of Australian wine. (In most liquor stores you have to be an expert to pick the good ones from the indifferent; price is rarely an indication of quality). David Jones' women's store is diagonally across the road, on the corner of **Market** and **Elizabeth Streets**. There are several good camping stores clustered around **Mountain Designs** at 499 Kent St in the city (9267 3822). Good general bookstores are listed in the introduction to this book and the **Travel Bookshop** is at 20 Bridge St in the city (9241 3554). The **Mambo** design company store is at 17 Oxford St, Paddington while Australian surf-influenced fashion can be had at **Hot Tuna** at 180 Oxford St.

Buying a Car

In New South Wales, buying a legal car means that firstly, the car should have a valid 'pink slip', which shows that it is roadworthy. Cost of a 'pink slip' should you wish to sell a car is about $25 and can be obtained from most mechanics. Most petrol stations have a mechanic. Next, you should be certain that the car is unencumbered – ie, that it's not stolen and nobody owes big money on it already. You can ascertain this by telephoning the **Registry of Encumbered Vehicles** (9600 0022) seven days a week from 9.00 a.m. to 5.00 p.m. Remember that you also inherit any outstanding parking fines and the like, so be certain to call and ask.

Ideally, the car you buy should have current registration as well, which includes mandatory third party injury insurance (though it doesn't cover collateral damage at all). Should you decide you want more complete insurance coverage, you may find difficulties getting a local insurance company to handle transients. Try **Kings Cross Car Park** for insurance, on 1800 808 188 (free call).

If the car's registration has lapsed when you buy it (check the sticker on the windscreen and the registration certificate the seller must give you), or will lapse shortly thereafter, you can expect to pay another $300 to $500 to the government for renewal of registration, depending on the size and age of the vehicle. Check with the **Roads and Traffic Authority**

(9662 5000) if you want to ensure that the vehicle's registration is current.

Selling a car outside the state in which you buy it is tricky. To sell it, you will need to transfer the registration to the state where you are selling it, which will involve further inspections and paperwork. It can be done, however and cars from Down South can be expected to have slightly better resale value in the Deep North, because the climate and road conditions of the Deep North are absolute hell on vehicles. In Sydney, the easiest way to buy a car is from the **Kings Cross Car Markets**, in the Kings Cross Parking Station on the corner of Ward Avenue and Elizabeth Bay Rd. Selling of vehicles is limited to travellers, which is nice, but kind of limits the range of vehicles. If you want to expand your choices a little, go and look at the Sunday **Flemington** car markets, near Flemington Railway Station twenty minutes train ride from **Central Station**. There are also many hundreds of vehicles sold privately every day through advertisements in the *Trading Post* magazine and the classified advertisements sections of the *Sydney Morning Herald* (Wednesday and Saturday) and the *Telegraph* (Saturday and Sunday).

One method of getting a vehicle is to arrange a buy-back with a dealership. Ask at your hostel for any dealers who work this way – then ask at another place, and another. On the good side, this can be a very effective means of purchasing a reliable car, with a reasonable guarantee of getting some money for it at the end of your trek. In effect, you lay down a lump-sum deposit to the value of the vehicle and when you return, you get your deposit back less a fee for the use of the vehicle. Of course, if you're planning to sell the car in Cairns this gets a bit tricky – you'll need a contract that states the arrangement can be taken over by another person, and you'll have to convinve that other person (the buyer in Cairns) that the deal is safe. Read the contract very carefully, to be certain you're not going to be stiffed for a lot of unreasonable expenses when you bring back the vehicle. It is reasonable for the dealers to expect you will return them a clean, roadworthy vehicle. It is not reasonable for them to demand that you cover the cost of all kinds of minor repairs, rustproofing, re-upholstering, etc.

If you get a car you must join the NRMA. This is NSW's motorists' association and by joining it you are automatically also covered by the Queensland association. They'll come and fix your car when it breaks down and they also provide free maps and accommodation guides and a good travel service. Branches are everywhere, but the main one is at **151 Clarence St**, Sydney (13 2132).

Staying On

If you plan to stay in Sydney for at least a few months, look up the **Shared Accommodation** sections of the Wednesday and Saturday *Sydney Morning Herald*. Most people want to share their house with people who will be around for longer than a few months, but some won't mind.

Work

Assuming you have a work visa, which you should have arranged before you left home, you can apply to the government's **Commonwealth Employment Service** (CES) for help in finding work. They have branches everywhere, but their head office number is 9379 8000. Otherwise try the newspapers.

Sport

Cricket is played in summer, rugby league, rugby union and soccer in winter. The main sports grounds are located at **Moore Park**, a fifteen minute bus ride from the city. If you want to sail a boat, look up **Boat Hire** in the **Yellow Pages** phone book. Look up **Surfing Equipment** for boards and lessons if you want to surf. (The best beaches for the experienced are **North Narrabeen** and **Long Reef**, but check with the surf shop by phone to make sure it's good on the day.)

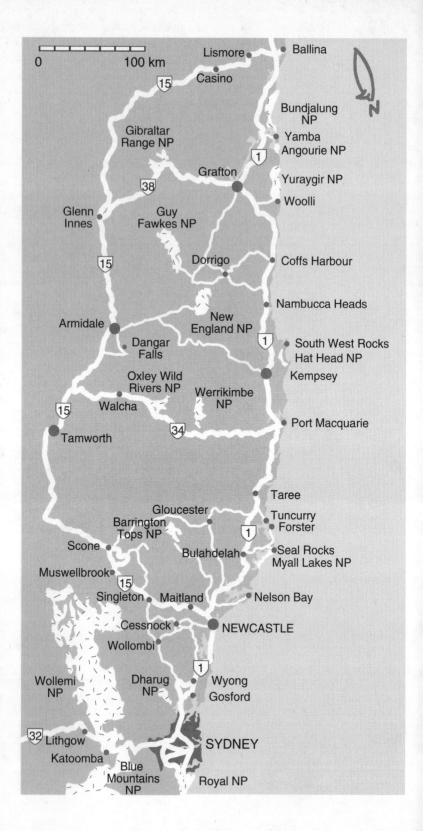

Sydney to Ballina

There's a whole string of remarkable places along the coastline, here, plus the wineries of the Hunter Valley. The trick is to avoid, or at least not linger in, any of the large towns along the coast, such as Newcastle, Port Macquarie and Coffs Harbour. What you're here for is the mind-bogglingly beautiful, isolated beaches, the exquisite national parks, the inland rivers and stands of rainforest and the tiny little towns tucked away in jewel-like bays up and down the shore. The beaches and the surfing here are about as good as they get along the east coast of Australia.

Dirk's Dozen

1. **Ride the wild surf:** Crescent Head, Hat Head, South-West Rocks and a dozen other nameless, beautiful, broad, desolate beaches in the area. If you don't know how to surf, go to Coffs Harbour and learn. Then come back and do it.

2. **The Hunter Valley Winery tours.** Don't miss one of the best winemaking regions of one of the world's best wine-making countries.

3. **Barrington Tops National Park:** Wild, secluded, exquisite. Those World Heritage people knew their business, didn't they?

4. **Port Stephens:** Gorgeous. Best bet is to walk into the magnificent Myall Lakes National Park just to the north, take the 21 km Mungo Track hike to Hawks Nest and then get a boat across the mouth of Port Stephens to Nelson Bay.

5. **Drive the Waterfall Way** up past Dorrigo and check out the **Dorrigo Rainforest Centre** with its skywalk slung high in the rainforest treetops.

6. **Go whitewater rafting** down the Nymboida River. Top stuff.

7. **Hide out** in the utterly isolated coastal villages in Yuraygir National Park.

Dirk Dumps On

1. **Newcastle.** A nice enough place, but if you want city, Sydney is right there. And if you want wild and magnificent coast, well, just half an hour or so north, the coast is even more splendid and far less busy and crowded than at Newcastle. Still, Newcastle is a good base from which to go raiding the Hunter Valley.

2. **Port Macquarie:** Same arguments as Newcastle. It's not much of a

city and there's a lot of fantastic coastline in the vicinity. Stop in, have lunch, resupply and move on.

3. Taree and the World's Biggest Fibreglass Bull.

4. Coffs Harbour – ooh, shit, there's a lot of tacky tourist stuff here. Great surf school, though and it's central to a lot of good stuff both inland and on the coast. Okay, I may not like Coffs, but I suppose that it is at least necessary.

5. Weekends in the Hunter Valley. You might find half of Sydney there. There's even a rumour they increase the prices on Saturday and Sunday.

The Hunter Valley

Once you get away from Newcastle at the bottom of the valley, this is a magic land of little coal-mining towns, rolling pastures, green mountains and wine, wine, wine. Ooh, yes, I love the Hunter Valley. The wineries start in the lower valley area around **Cessnock** and finish up in the **Upper Hunter**, near Scone. The heart of the valley is the **Hunter River** itself, which winds its way down to the sea at Port Hunter, next to Newcastle. The **New England Highway** runs up the guts of the Hunter Valley, from Newcastle through Maitland and Muswellbrook to Scone. What you'll need is the free guide to the wineries and map called *Hunter Valley Wine Country*, which you get from the **NSW Travel Centre** in Sydney or the **Cessnock Visitor's Centre** on Abedare Rd in Cessnock (049) 90 4477.

Aside from the excellent wine to be had from the Hunter, there are a number of other things which should be visited, including the nearby **Goulburn River National Park** and the remarkable **Barrington Tops National Park** to the north. Using Newcastle or the inland town of **Maitland** as base of operations and foraging out on a one-or-two day basis, I'd say that the Hunter Valley can easily occupy a good week of your time.

Wine-making got started in the Hunter Valley back in the 1820s, but it was James Busby – who later went on to establish the famous Treaty of Waitangi as Government Resident in New Zealand – who really got the ball rolling. When Busby took off for New Zealand in 1833, he handed on the job of getting wine out of the Hunter to Dr Henry Lindeman and in fact Lindemans are still a force to be reckoned with in Australian wine today. In 1843, Lindeman was granted Cawarra and he turfed medicine (which was a shitty job in the 1840s anyway) for full-time wine-making. He was doing quite well, by all accounts, when Cawarra burnt to the ground. Thus, it was back to medicine for Dr Lindeman. He went off to the goldfields in Victoria, near the Murray river and earned himself a useful stake in grape money before he returned to the Hunter and got back into the wine scene. Probably the highest point of this early phase of Hunter River wine-making was the presentation of a Hunter champagne made by James King to Napoleon III in 1855. Remarkably, the French judges of the Paris Exhibition of that year admitted that the champagne in question didn't suck – probably the first and last time the French have ever had anything good to say about Australian wine.

In the first half of this century, the dominance of South Australian wines made the Hunter wine industry fade and a lot of vineyards were converted into grazing pasture. By 1960, there were really only three varieties of grape (Semillon, Hermitage and White Shiraz) being grown in commercial quantities in the Hunter. The goal was not so much quality as quantity and alcohol content. At that time, Australians preferred their wine heavily fortified and the Hunter Valley wasn't really a good place to produce such wines.

These days, more than twenty varieties of grape grow in the Hunter Valley, including Semillon, Cabernet Sauvignon, Traminer, Rhine Riesling and Chardonnay. The Hunter Valley is particularly noted for its very good white wines, especially the Semillons, which are the equal of almost any in the world.

If you go to the Hunter Valley from Sydney, the scenic route is to take **Victoria Rd** out of the city to the west, follow the signs towards **Windsor** and **Richmond** and, at either of these places, take the turn-off to **Cessnock** or **Singleton**. This takes you along modest and scenic back roads right up to the edge of the Hunter Valley and means you can avoid Newcastle. It takes longer to reach the Hunter, but it gets you into the middle of the bush a lot quicker than taking the freeway up north.

Stuff To Do

The Wineries: If you don't like wine and wineries, then you should just cruise through the Hunter without stopping on your way to Barrington Tops. Otherwise, it's going to be wine, isn't it? The real problem with visiting wineries is that invariably, you're going to want to taste the stuff. Now even if you spit it back out (horror!) after a dozen wineries or so, you're not going to be fit to drive. And remember: even riding a bicycle with a blood alcohol content in excess of .05 percent is illegal, so you're not going to get around it that way, either.

There's only two possible solutions. One is to appoint a member of the party as designated driver, whereupon they act as sober chauffeur to the rest of the drunken louts in the crew. This is fine if you happen to have a non-drinker in your group … but otherwise, one member of the party is going to spend one of the longest, saddest, driest days of their life. Of course, to be fair, you'll have to come back again the next day with someone else in the driver's seat.

Another possibility is to hook in with one of the various half-day wine tasting tours which leave from Newcastle. This will cost you about $40, so it's a sight more expensive than taking your own vehicle. Also, you'll only get to visit a limited number of wineries and it won't be you that chooses which ones. On the other hand, your driver won't spend all day complaining, either. It's a tough call. For tours you can try **Hunter Vineyard Tours** (049) 91 1659.

Now, other than wine, there are still a few funky things to see around the Hunter. About twenty kilometres above Scone, near Wingen on the New England Highway, is a place called the **Burning Mountain**. Back in the 1820s when the first Europeans got here, they thought the place was an active volcano. The reality is considerably stranger. It appears that underground seams of coal are burning here and may have been doing so for some 6,000 years, based on their rate of consumption. There's not a whole lot to see, obviously, as this is an underground fire, but there is a nice walk of about 2.5 km up to some of the vents where smoke pours out of the ground. The concept of the earth burning underfoot alarms me and I think the Burning Mountain is pretty nifty.

Barrington Tops: The other absolute must-see in the area is the World Heritage-listed **Barrington Tops National Park**. This is another big one, at nearly 39,000 hectares. It's not easy to get into. If you've been to Scone, you can continue on to **Gloucester**. There're also roads in from Maitland and **Dungog** which can be reached from the Pacific Highway near Raymond Terrace. Barrington Tops National Park is a fantastic area, studded with dramatic cliffs, hills and plateaus. The whole thing is based around two high plateaus. There are pockets of rainforest, plentiful clear creeks and waterfalls and a number of very fine walking trails. The only problem is that in winter, being so high up, it can get damned cold. Occasionally it even snows, which isn't really what you expect from Australia I suppose. A good and cheap accommodation base is **Barrington House**, a guest house (049) 95 3212, or you can camp at **Gloucester River**. Maps are available at tourist information centres around the area.

Shelter

The Hunter Valley is quite a popular and well-patronised area, but it's largely agricultural and there's a fair bit of money around. As a result, backpacker's accommodation isn't exactly springing up like mushrooms. Probably your best option is the **Newcastle Backpacker's** (049) 693 436 at 42 Denison St. It's a friendly, clean place with beds under $15 – and the owners can tell you a few things about the Hunter Valley and its wineries.

Accommodation in the Hunter isn't all that easy. There are no hostels as yet and nor are there likely to be in the near future. You can try for cheap rooms in the pubs at some of the really small towns like **Denman**, **Merriwa** or **Castle Rock**, but this is a hit-or-miss proposition, especially in the summer months, as they're often full.

There's a couple of caravan parks in Cessnock, if you want to set up a tent – **Valley View** (049) 902 573 on Mount View Rd is probably the best value. There's also the **Maitland Caravan Park** (049) 332 950 in Maitland, but on the whole, even camping in the Hunter Valley region is difficult. There is a reasonable sort of campsite way up at **Glenbawn Dam** near Scone (head to Dangarfield and turn left at the signpost) which you might want to try. From there, you can access the Upper Hunter wineries, then take a trip around to Barrington Tops National Park.

Food

Who cares? Stop for lunch at one of the pubs in Maitland, or up in Muswellbrook, which is pretty. Try out some of the local bakeries, if you must. Other than that, see what you can manage to nibble at the wineries.

Many wineries put out bread or cheese to help cleanse the palate between swilling down the wine. If you visit enough wineries in the space of a day, you can feed yourself as well as get satisfactorily tipsy.

Port Stephens

Port Stephens is not a town, but a beautiful bay about 50km north of Newcastle, off the Pacific Highway. The highway actually crosses one of the upper reaches of Port Stephens bay at the town of Karuah. It is easily accessible from both Sydney and Newcastle by bus and aside from being utterly charming, offers a variety of possibilities to the traveller.

Most of the facilities and development have occured on the southern shore of the entrance to Port Stephens, at **Nelson Bay** and **Shoal Bay**, at the end of Nelson Bay Rd, which goes back to the Pacific Highway. In terms of accommodation, there's a couple of good hostels in the area. **Samurai Beach Bungalows** (049) 821 921 on Frost Rd and Connell Close is a new and pretty place in a nice setting, with friendly management and cheap beds, usually well under $15. It has another advantage, depending on your inclinations: Samurai Beach is a nude beach. Of course, just south of Samurai Beach is **One-Mile Beach**, which has totally bodacious surf, so take your pick: tanning or tubes.

The **Shoal Bay YHA** (049) 842 315 at 59-61 Shoal Bay Beachfront Rd is part of a converted motel complex. It is very well regarded by travellers, but prices vary depending on the time of year.

Stuff To Do

In Port Stephens, the best options are as usual, surf and watersports. At the western end of Shoal Bay proper is a somewhat historic lighthouse

Flinthart's Journal

At last I've made it to Port Stephens. I've been wondering about this place ever since Sydney, where a seriously stoned packer named Kelvin burbled on and on about the place for what seemed like hours, but may have been days.

I think he was right about the place. He waffled a lot about clear blue waters, sunrise out of the ocean, brilliant surf, forest walks, koalas and crap like that. He also babbled about dolphins. I checked in and took a walk down the beach. Kelvin wasn't wrong - there were dolphins playing in the surf. Very cute.

I kept walking up the beach, off to look for white pointers.

which has been restored to its quondam glory. It's a pretty place with splendid views out across the bay and it has a bit of information on local history.

Renting boats to sail on the sparkling waters of the bay is a pleasant thing to do, especially as the local dolphins pretty much consider all boats to be their big fibreglass buddies to chase. If you like that sort of thing, you can also book yourself on a cruise around the bay, which lasts about two hours.

Port Stephens, while it may not be laden with heavy history and sophisticated entertainment, is an extremely pleasant and pretty area. I'd rate it a really good place to come and recover from Sydney (or the Hunter Valley) before you set off the rest of the way up the coast. It's also relatively undeveloped, which is nice compared with places like Port Macquarie and Coffs Harbour, which are still ahead of you …

Food

Food locally is a bit limited. You might try the RSL, or the pubs, for the usual pasta-steak-seafood-salad arrangements. A little more upmarket is **Scales Restaurant** (049) 842 699 at 106 Magnus St, who do a kind of surf & turf arrangement. Alternatively, consider going down to the **Fishing Co-op** wharf and actually buying some hands-on fresh uncooked-type seafood all your own. That's if you can cook, of course.

Bulahdelah and the Myall Lakes

A little over two hours north of Sydney on the Pacific Highway is the mountain town of **Bulahdelah**. Once a major source of alum, it's now a forgotten little place. It's main claim to fame is that Australia's best living poet, Les Murray, lives nearby. His ancestors were timber cutters and it's from around here that the sleepers for the Trans-Siberian Railway were cut. (This is just one of those essential facts the other guide books will not tell you.) Not far north of Bulahdelah is the turnoff to New South Wales' tallest tree, known as **The Grandis**. Follow the signs from the turnoff to the pocket of rainforest which holds the tree. You won't regret it. The enormous tree – Eucalyptus grandis – and its brethren are a truly awe-inspiring sight, well worth the diversion.

Stuff To Do

Down Lakes Rd from Bulahdelah is the village of **Bombah Point**, in the **Myall Lakes National Park**. This is a wonderful place, easily accessible from Sydney by hopping on a **Great Lakes Coach** 008 043 263 from the **Sydney Coach Terminal**. It's about 31,000 hectares in area all up, much of which is occupied by a fantastic series of freshwater lakes. The coast consists of about 40km of most excellent white, sandy beaches and there's even a couple of offshore islands with spectacular fishing.

The Myall Lakes park is just crammed with wildlife. Inland you can reasonably expect to see kangaroos and wallabies, koalas and dingoes, while offshore, dolphins regularly do their thing in the surf. At the north end of the long beach strip is the tiny village of **Seal Rocks** and from time to time, it is even possible to see the Humpback Whales as they pass on their migration.

Myall Lakes is a fairly popular park and it abounds in campsites. One of the easiest to reach is across the very entertaining vehicle ferry from **Bombah**, down near Mungo Brush on the **Bombah Broadwater**. **Mungo Brush** (not Basil's long-lost cousin, but a very small town) also has a caravan park where you can stay.

There's bugger-all development in and around Myall Lakes, which is very comforting given its proximity to Sydney and Newcastle. This is an excellent place to spend a few days walking, swimming and taking photographs. If you're feeling the need for a certain amount of adventure, you might want to take the 21 km **Mungo Track** walk, which links Mungo Brush with the little village of **Hawks Nest** to the south, at the entrance to **Port Stephens Bay**. (Then you can get a boat across to the south side and explore Port Stephens Bay for a while. This is a really cool option). Even if you haven't got a vehicle of your own, there's nothing to stop you tripping out from Sydney for a few days camping between the lakes and the sea.

Forster-Tuncurry

North of Bulahdelah, off the highway proper, Forster-Tuncurry is the name of twin towns on either side of the sea mouth of Wallis Lake. Neither is particularly large, but the place is relatively popular, especially in the summer, although still not yet heavily developed. Forster is the larger of the two towns, on the south shore of the lake mouth. The beaches and the clear, winding blue waterways of the lake entrance, as well as the splendid lake itself which is one and a half times the total size of Sydney Harbour, make Forster-Tuncurry a pleasant enough place. But at this point, especially if you've lingered since leaving Sydney, you might want to push on to the superior beaches further up the coast.

Stuff To Do

We're not exactly in the wilderness here, but it's still a pretty neat place. Check out Seven Mile Beach south of Forster for surf, or Nine Mile Beach north of Tuncurry for more of the same. The area is rife with dolphins and even the occasional small whale. Look out for them around dawn; you may find yourself sharing a wave with some finned companions.

The still waters of Lake Wallis are a marvellous place for boating,

Jim Makes A Discovery: So there I was in a pub in Brisbane. This guy I'd never met before just walks up and starts talking to me and I'm thinking - gee, these locals are friendly.

He seems like a nice guy and we talk for a while. Then, out of the blue, he offers me a goddamn condom. I stop dead and look around. Have I come to a gay bar or something? No, it doesn't look like that.

I turn back, smile sort of weakly and tell him no thanks, I brought my own.

He looks puzzled and says something about me looking dry.

I figure the guy is queer for sure. I don't want to say that I'm wet, because it sounds kinky. What do I do? I nod and agree that I'm dry. So he goes to the bar and comes back with a beer. A goddam Fourex beer.

Just like the brand of condom is named, back home in the States. Some things take a bit of getting used to. I'm still laughing at that beer commercial where they sing, 'I can feel a Fourex coming on'. I want to take a video of that one home for my parents.

---

canoeing and learning to sailboard without all those nasty waves. Contact the Great Lakes Aquatic Centre (065) 555 633 for further information on rental of watersports equipment.

If you do get hold of a boat, you owe it to yourself to go up the Coolongolook and Wallingat rivers. It's a fair trip back to the Wallingat State Forest; close to 15 kilometres by water, so unless you're a fit sort of paddler, a round trip of 30km might be something you want to dodge. Rent a boat with a motor. Note that as the Wallingat State Forest is exactly that – state forest – you can camp back in there free of charge, so long as you take care and observe the rules of good camping. This is a wonderful chance to get away from your vehicle and the hostels for a while. The Wallingat Forest is a particularly pretty region, more than worth overnighting in – and you might even be able to hook a fish or two out of the river.

Shelter

The only hostel in the area is the YHA-affiliated **Dolphin Lodge** (065) 558 155 at 43 Head St. This is a new, clean, delightful place with beds under $15, which is good for the only hostel in such a popular, pretty area. The beach is only spitting distance away from the hostel and it's a real charge to get up and watch the sun come up out of the Pacific. Despite the lack of hostels, there's no shortage of caravan parks. Camp sites go for between $10 to $13 and the range of facilities is usually good. These places can get very busy during the school holidays, so it may be advisable to phone ahead if you're travelling at that time of the year.

Smuggler's Holiday Village (065) 546 666 45 The Lakes Way, Forster

Great Lakes Caravan Park (065) 546 827 1 Baird St, Tuncurry

Forster Beach Caravan Park (065) 546 269

Tuncurry Beach Caravan Park (065) 546 440 Beach St, Tuncurry

Food

Local seafood is the word. Check out **The Little Mermaid** (065) 555 144 in Tuncurry – it's Danish oriented and the Danes have long known a thing or two about dealing with fish. Mind you, eating fish in a place named The Little Mermaid seems a bit tasteless. **Andy's Waterfront Restaurant** (065) 545 019 on Wharf and Ray St in Tuncurry also has a way with seafood, especially their excellent fresh seafood platter.

Cheaper food is as usual available from the local pubs and clubs, including the **Lakes & Ocean Hotel** in Little St and the **F-T Memorial Services Club** (065) 549 506 in Strand St, Forster. If you're feeling lazy, call for pizza or ribs from the **Southside Pizza House** (065) 555 400 at 4 South St in Tuncurry. They deliver and the hostel is within their range.

Taree and the Manning Valley

About 30km north of Forster-Tuncurry and back on the Pacific Highway, **Taree** is a place best ignored by the traveller, especially the architecturally crippled Big Oyster. Unfortunately, you can't miss the place – the entire fraggin' building is shaped like a gigantic oyster. I suppose it makes a change from Big Fibreglass Things. Anyway, if you drive on from Taree, though the highway runs inland from the coast, there are a number of access roads leading to little villages with what is by now the usual brilliant beaches and surf. Worth noting is **Crowdy Head**, at the south end of **Crowdy Bay National Park**. It has splendid cliff-top scenery and an excellent walk along the base of the cliffs, with yet another incomparable beach. There is camping permitted at a couple of spots in the area, but they are unimproved and you may need to carry your own water. Still, I'd rather overnight here than at Port Mac, further along.

Inland, up the **Manning River** from Taree, there are a range of parks, forests, waterfalls and picturesque little towns. The area is worth a drive through, perhaps even a full day trip, although leaving the glorious coastline around here is a wrench.

Port Macquarie

With about 30,000 people, this resort town marks the beginning of the long run up the seriously gorgeous subtropical coast. The town itself is fairly placid, with a high proportion of retirees and family holidaymakers and there's a bit of a 'ho-hum, so what'? feeling about it after the dramatic scenery of places like **Hat Head** to the north, or **Crowdy Bay** to the south. It's a nice little town, but nothing special. It still warrants a stop, though personally, I'd push on and overnight somewhere else. It was the third settlement established on the continent, set up as a place of secondary punishment by Macquarie for the really tough convicts. Oh, how the face of punishment has changed!

You might hear this place referred to simply as *Port* by the locals. The early settlers were so worn down by the harsh environment inland that Australians adopted the habit of abbreviating a lot of place names and words. Wagga Wagga, for instance, is usually called just *Wagga*. Journalists are often called *journos*. For other reasons, which escape me at the moment, people in the Bush would refer to Sydney as *the Big Smoke*, or simply the *Smoke*.

Stuff To Do

You can surf, waterski, snorkel, dive, parasail, fish, take scenic flights, etc, etc. It's not quite as full-on as places like Byron Bay and the Gold Coast yet, of course, but give it time. Sailboarding on the quiet but breezy river waters is a fine option and it's nice to rent a small boat and pootle round the river as well.

Worth doing is the boardwalk at the **Sea Acres Rainforest Centre** (065) 823 355 which runs through more than a kilometre of seaside rainforest. Although the entry fee is a bit steep at about $8, it is well set up and educational, worth doing before you plunge into the wild and woolly rainforests further north.

I also quite liked the little observatory at **Town Beach**, on Lord St. Port Mac doesn't have too much light pollution and in the evenings, you can go down there and take a look through a really big telescope at the skies above. Costs about $2 and it's a pleasant walk anyway.

Stuff Not To Do

Unless you're drunk or stoned, you won't really enjoy **Fantasy Glades**, which is this tacky children's fairytale park. And looming as a threat of things to come in Port Mac's future, you can give a big miss to **Peppermint Park** with its waterslides and its mini-golf and video games … mind you, playing miniature golf when you're seriously chemically imbalanced with a group of like-minded companions can be quite entertaining.

In And Out

The train line doesn't run here, so you can forget that. All the long-distance buses stop in Port Mac, in Short St. Sydney is about five hours away; Brisbane more like seven. It costs about $35 to get to Sydney and $45 to Brisbane. **Lindsays Bus Line** (065) 531 277 have an office here in Port Mac, where their buses stop. Most others stop in **Short St**.

Shelter

Lindel Traveller's Hostel (065) 831 791, 2 Hastings River Drive: a fair way from the action, but it is a well-appointed, well-run place with friendly management, good facilities and a lively atmosphere. Has a good reputation amongst travellers. Beds are under $15.

Port Macquarie YHA (065) 835 512, 40 Church St: much closer to the town centre. Another nice, clean, friendly place. Value at less than $15.

Backpacker's Headquarters 015 200 692, 135 Horton St: Cheapest hostel in town, but you get what you pay for, don't you?

Food

Have a look in town along Clarence St, William St and in the arcades off Horton St and William St. There's nothing really outstanding here in Port Mac, but there is a nice, wide selection of cheap and pleasant cafés and eateries. Local seafood is quite good if you can get it, notably at **Cray's**, on the river at Fishermans Wharf. It's not cheap, but it's good. Cheaper seafood (read 'fish and chips') can be had from **Macquarie Seafoods** on Short St and from the **Tickled Trout** in Clarence St.

Port Macquarie to Nambucca Heads

The highway runs slightly inland for a way. Ignoring (advisedly) the town of **Kempsey**, there's a string of great little places on the coast proper, including **Crescent Head**, **Hat Head** (interesting name) and **South West Rocks**. Crescent Head is a Mondo Surf Mecca; the beach shelves very, very gently, the waves form well offshore and you can cruise in for a very long ride indeed. All three of these sites are damnably pretty, particularly Hat Head, which is surrounded by national park and South West Rocks. South West Rocks also boasts the excruciatingly picturesque **Trial Bay Gaol**, a beautiful sandstone building set on a stark, rocky head. It was built last century and housed the odd POW in WWI. I wonder how much you'd have to pay to be imprisoned there now. As it stands, you have to pay about $3 just to get in, which is pretty ironic when you think about it.

There's no hostel accommodation hereabouts, but there are plenty of caravan parks and campsites. Although access to the area is pretty much limited to private vehicle, if you do have your own car, please, don't miss this wonderful little stretch of coastline. I urge you.

Nambucca Heads

On the mouth of the Nambucca River, this is a really top spot. It's a pretty little town, slightly off the highway proper, with a lot of local activities. Surprise, surprise, there's a brilliant string of beaches nearby, with some excellent surf. The local 'packer's place is the **Nambucca Backpacker's**

Hostel (065) 686 360 at 3 Newman St. Beds are under $15, the facilities are spotless and more than ample and the whole place has a relaxed and friendly atmosphere. There are also several local caravan parks, including the **Headland Caravan Park** (065) 686 547 near the main surf beach. Nambucca has fine local bushwalking and canoeing on the Nambucca river, which is broad and calm in the sheltered waters near the mouth. Whitewater rafting, scenic flights and local fishing are also highly commendable.

North of Nambucca Heads there are two little hamlets called **Urunga** and **Mylestom**. Neither of these is anything special – but as usual, they lie upon indescribably beautiful beaches. They are well off the beaten track and both of them have convenient and comfortable caravan parks. Mylestom even boasts a hostel: **Caipera Riverside Lodge** (066) 445 245 on the main street. Beds are less than $15 and this is such a pleasant place you may want to stay for a few days.

Coffs Harbour

Named for a bloke called John Korff who took shelter here in 1847, this is a not-particularly-special town on the coast, about two hours south of Byron Bay. True to the name, it's got a nice little harbour and the local scenery is pleasant, so Coffs is undergoing a serious tourism and development boom.

The town itself is actually a bit sprawled out these days. The Pacific Highway goes through the centre incognito, under the name of Grafton St – but if you're driving through, all you have to do is avoid making any sudden turns.

The place got started back in the 1860s as an outlet for the gorgeous Red Cedar and rainforest hardwoods which were coming out of the near north and west. If things had been left at that, Coffs would probably have died a natural death when the timber industry started winding down, but no! Some fool had to go and introduce bananas and now they're all over the place. Which leads directly to something too hideous for words – the **Big Banana**.

Now it's true that Queensland is reputed to be the Big Thing homeland of Australia, what with its Big Cows, Big Fish, Big Pineapple, pathetic Big Crab and a zillion other oversized objects. Nonetheless, Coffs Harbour boasts what may be the biggest and baddest of them all: the almighty Big Banana, on the coast road running north out of the town – a place to be avoided like herpes, syphilis, gonorrhea and crabs all in one venereal region. Consider it a warning: when the Big Things start to spring up, somebody has obviously taken a major cash interest in the area.

The end result of all this investment is an area which is growing faster than the local infrastructure can handle. Coffs is a nice place to visit, but I'm buggered if I'd want to live there. Best bet is to use the place as a base to visit the gorgeous hinterland surrounding. On that basis, the place is worth about a week.

Special Note on Coffs Harbour: Seeing that it's a big resort place, it's very popular with the families. Prices tend to go up sharply during the

The Car From Hell: Simon from Wellington spoke to me in a Sydney pub. 'Yeah, I been up to the North already. Me and a mate, we bought this car in Sydney. Thought it was an old Ford Escort. It looked okay and we had a buy-back deal and everything, so we thought it would be alright. I didn't know anything about cars and neither did me mate.

'Things started falling off before we even got to Coffs Harbour. The driver's side mirror was stuck on with glue, we found out. And the muffler was mostly made of that bog stuff. About then, we realised we'd been done, but we thought we'd just go for it anyway.

'Between Brisbane and Bundaberg, I learned a lot about motors. Especially about head gaskets and rings. And about radiators too. Remember what I said about it looking like an old Escort? Well, somehow, they'd managed to get a fucking Toyota engine into the thing. At least, that's what the mechanic said when we took it to him. He wouldn't work on it, but he was a nice bloke – lent us tools and garage space and even gave us a few pointers.

Being stuck in Bundaberg, we got work picking for a while and made enough that we decided not to bother taking the car back to Sydney to sell. That was a good decision. Halfway between Rockhampton and Mackay, there was this incredible noise and the car just went crazy. Smoke went everywhere and sparks and we just jumped out as fast as we could and ran away. Thought it was going to blow up.

'It didn't, though. Turned out that the bastards who'd bodgied the Toyota engine into the car had done some shitty welding to make up for the wrong-shape engine mounts and the engine had just basically fallen out half onto the road. I've never seen anything like it.

'Me and my mate got our packs out of the thing and just walked away. I've been hitchhiking ever since.'

school holidays, the longest of which occur in the December-January period. Ring in advance if you're going to Coffs. The last thing you want is a horde of sweaty, screaming children polluting the visual and auditory landscape.

Stuff To Do

This is another tourist mecca, which means you can do practically anything. Jetski, surfing, abseiling, rock-climbing, bushwalking, parachuting, indoor rock-climbing, waterski-ing, bungy jumping, scuba-diving, balloon rides, scenic flights, horse-riding etc. There's also a local zoo. Nothing particularly special, but it does have the inevitable koala-fondling sessions, so if you've managed to miss that part of the Australiana Experience, now's your chance to make amends. Anyway, if you want to try any of these things, just ask at either of the hostels.

One of the best things about the string of beaches running up the north coast of New South Wales is the truly splendid surfing conditions to be found there. Really, if you can't surf, you're missing a major experience in this region. Many hostels have boards which guests can use

How Australia

Long ago, Australia was peopled by geeks and grommits, who did not worship The Wave, nor followed they The Board. Then, in 1915, while much of the world was lost within a minor war in the Northern Hemisphere, a great and enlightened man came to Australia. And the name of this man was 'Duke' Kahanamoku and he came from the wise and perfect island of Hawaii.

And Duke did look upon the nation that was Australia and he saw that many were the miles of perfect beach and countless were the splendid tubes that did crash upon those beaches. Then did Duke say to himself, 'Wherefore is it that there are no Australians in the surf?'

But when Duke asked of the Australians, 'Wherefore is it that thou dost not partake of the surf?' Then did the Australians laugh at him and call him 'silly person,' and cry out with derision.

Yet wise was Duke Kahanamoku. Seeing that Australia knew not of The Wave, nor of The Board, wise Duke took unto himself a plank of sugar pine and with great skill did he work it and carve it until it was a thing of beauty. And then did Duke Kahanamoku raise the plank above his head crying, for free. The problem is that surfers are a bit of an in-group, an elite clique of blonde, tanned swine who seem to have been born with fins, gills and torsos which could frighten Arnold Schwarzenegger. There are few things more embarrassing than taking your deadly-pale flabby flesh to a beach like Byron Bay and trying out a surfboard for the first time while surrounded by high-speed predators who make balancing on the face of a three-metre wave look as easy as scarfing up a Big Mac. Bastards.

Fortunately, there's a way to avoid this ego-destroying experience. When you hit Coffs Harbour, you need to contact the **East Coast Surf School** (066) 515515. They run a 6-hour Beginner's Course for $68, all equipment provided. The good thing about this is that not only do they teach the basics of surfing and bodyboarding, but they'll teach you about all kinds of stuff like rips, tides, currents, swells and first aid as well. That way, when you wimp out in terror at the sight of your first fifteen-footer, you can always tell everybody else that there was some technicality which prevented you catching the beast. At least you'll sound like you know what you're talking about.

Seriously, though, this is a very good value investment. Surfing is

Got The Surf

'Behold! I bring you The Board!'
   Still did the foolish people of Australia laugh and cry out in their numbers, saying, 'Go home, ya prawn."
   But wise Duke was nothing loth and went he to Freshwater Beach. There did he point to the ocean and cry out, 'Behold! I bring you The Wave!'
   And still the people of Australia did ignore wise Duke, except for those who threw the empty bottle of the beer at his head.
   And so did Duke descend into the holy surf, with his Board beneath his arm. And the waves did rise up before him and behind him and yet with his Board, Duke was master of all. Back and forth cut he and many the tube he shot.
   Then did the people of Australia gather, crying 'Behold, a miracle! This man walketh upon the water and lo, the wave itself doth bear him up.'
   And thus did the way of The Wave and The Board come to the Land of Promise and still to this day doth the sugar-pine plank of mighty Duke Kahanamoku hang much revered upon the wall of the Freshwater Surf Club.
   Here endeth the lesson.

big-time fun and the majority of players have little time for geeks who don't know basic wave etiquette and right of way. (On the other hand, surfers themselves often have deeply Nazi tendencies, especially where body-boarders and mere swimmers are concerned. Many's the time I've been forced to give pushy surfers a lesson in Advanced Drowning off the beaches around Tweed Heads.) Take the time to learn how to do it right and you'll have the chance to practice for yourself at some of the world's premier surf-beaches. East Coast Surf also have an hourly rate, if you figure you don't need the full course.

Got a few bucks? Consider a heli-rafting trip. The **Whitewater Rafting Professionals** (066) 544 066 are prepared to take you and your gear by helicopter to stretches of the river you can't get to otherwise. And the only way out is downstream, by raft. While it's still reasonably safe, a helicopter ride over the local rainforest terrain is a big bonus and the rafting qualifies as reasonably serious adventure stuff.

Local scuba-diving is reasonable. Water clarity is good and a full PADI course is about $350: **DiveQuest Centre**, (066) 541 930. This usually includes a dive on the **Solitary Islands**, which are probably the finest diving in Australia outside the Barrier Reef. On the other hand, the water is a fair bit colder down here than it is up north. If you're on your way north, you should probably stick to surfing and save the time and expense of a scuba course until you hit the Barrier Reef. Definitely dodge the local snorkelling. It's cheap, true – you can hire everything you need down at the jetty for under $20 for the day – but without a local, inshore reef, it's not exactly a rivetting pastime.

If your timing is good, the **Bellingen Markets** are held every third Saturday of the month in **Bellingen Park**. This is one of the better markets around. At last count, they had something over 250 stallholders, with all kinds of stuff to buy, eat and watch.

Weird Shit

About 45km south of Coffs, west down Valla Road, is the Big Fat Worm Farm. (065) 695 297. They farm worms there. Earthworms. Big, ugly, squirmy ones. You can buy them for bait. You can buy them for your garden. You can pick them. Pack them. Race them. Or you can just watch them writhe ...

You can get a bit of food at the Worm Farm, if your appetite holds out. Being of a deeply twisted nature, I found it a fascinating place to stop for lunch and it only cost $5 to get in. Say – did you know that Australia has the world's biggest fucking earthworms? It's a Gippsland species, which gets to be up to three metres long ...

All the surf beaches are actually north of the town proper, but they're easy to get to and you can rent boards from **Coopers Surfshop** (066) 521 782 on High St, near the jetty. (This is not too far from the **Aussitel Hostel.**) **Diggers Beach** to the north is an excellent surfing beach, but is not patrolled. Beginners beware.

Coffs is also the place from which to organise white-water rafting on the **Nymboida** River. While it's not as warm and comfortable as Tully and the Barron river in the Deep North, the rafting is quite good in summer and the scenery is well worth the effort. Also, since things are a little more developed down here than they are up north, at least one company offers four-day rafting trips, all-inclusive of food, transport, camping and gear. Of course, the price is about $440, but being all-inclusive, that's practically economical – and the local rivers and rainforests are outrageously beautiful. If you decide to do rafting here, poke around a little. There's about half a dozen different companies in the area and if you ask around, you may be able to latch onto a special seasonal offer.

Shelter

The town has only two hostels. **Albany Lodge** (066) 526 462 is the local YHA, at 110 Albany St. It's only a block from the main road to the harbour proper, but it's about a klick from the town centre. It's a nice sort of a place, with beds for under $15 and a line on most of the activities in the region. They've also got a few bicycles and surfboards to be had and it keeps much more liberal hours than your usual YHA.

Further out from the town centre, but closer to the old harbour, is the **Aussitel Backpacker's Hostel** (066) 511 871. Again, beds are less than $15, but this place is a little more busy and crowded. Not that the standard of accommodation suffers for it, never! It's just that this is a very lively hostel, with a heavily used barbecue area and a swimming pool. (Above the pool is an odd sign: 'Topless Bathing Permitted'. Permitted? Who's going to stop them? Shouldn't that sign read: 'Topless Bathing Strongly Encouraged'?) Once again, the management are very clued-in and can help you organise just about any kind of local tour or activity which exists. They also organise pickups, beach trips and social excursions. Very groovy.

Food

Food here is pretty much what you'd expect from a big tourist area. It ranges from not outstanding and fiendishly expensive, down to dirt-cheap and still not outstanding. Most of the pubs have reasonably priced counter meals and the local seafood is fresh and tasty.

Down by the harbour and the Jetty, at the end of High Street, there's a cluster of ethnic restaurants, most of which do seafood. They're not especially cheap, but the food's decent enough. Try the deplorably spelled **Fisherman's Katch** (066) 524 372 for reasonably priced seafood. They like you to make reservations in advance, though. The **Chinese Fountain** (066) 511 978 produces a fair semblance of Chinese/Vietnamese food at backpacker-friendly prices, while the **River Kwai** in the Jetty Village specialises in Thai food. It's not bad.

Flinthart's

Coffs Harbour - Some Places To Avoid. First on the list is the Elvis Bar at the Moonee Tavern. This was the place which led me and a Manchester lass named Annabel to the Great Clog Barn disaster. Expensive drinks, crappy decor and a necrophilic homage to a man who wasn't that fucking great while he was still breathing.

Next on the list, of course, is the Big Banana. If you actually need to be warned to avoid a place with a twenty-metre fibreglass banana out front, I don't figure this book will do you much good anyway.

Not far below the Big Banana is Storyland Gardens, whose major claim to fame is a building shaped vaguely like a gigantic pink boot. Something to do with the old woman who lived in a shoe, I think.

Then there's the Plaster Fun House, where you can go to - well, make things out of plaster and paint them. Hmm. We ducked out the side way and wound up hiding out at the Elvis Bar, where we hit the red wine and met some Americans who had a whole load of shitty Nimbin hashish that they had to get rid of before they flew out of the country.

And that, of course, led to Annabel's crippling hangover, which in turn led to her being

Inland From Coffs

Along the Pacific Highway south of Coffs Harbour by about 25km, you will see a turnoff to the West. This is a fantastic detour to take, if you have the time. The road in question is known as the **Waterfall Way**, and it winds its way through rainforests up the mountains to the beautiful little town of **Bellingen** and thence to **Dorrigo**, finishing up in **Armidale**. Now, while neither of the two towns is any world-beater, the local countryside is more than delightful enough to justify a couple of days.

Bellingen proper has a backpacker's (066) 551 116, plus local pub accommodation. Dorrigo, on the other hand, is pretty much without budget accommodation. Fortunately, there are campsites and caravan parks all over the area, if you have a tent.

This is a very beautiful area, best seen by simply taking a leisurely drive over whatever roads take your fancy. The entire tableland is mazed with little roads, ranging from two-wheel dirt tracks to well-

Diary

sick in The Clog Barn. I don't blame her for that, though. This place says proudly 'Visit Holland Without Ever Leaving Coffs Harbour'! Well, if I wanted to visit Holland, I'd go to fucking Holland, wouldn't I? Not some horrible little mock-Tudor bastardisation called 'The Clog Barn'.

It was an unhappy moment. Perhaps if Annabel could have just sucked on some fresh air in the open for a while, she would have returned to a more normal colour. Sadly, the Clog Barn featured not only a giant model Dutch Village, but Coffs Harbour's Largest Range of Collectable Spoons. I mean, even if you were perfectly okay, you'd be a little queasy at that concept, right?

Well, Annabel took one brief look around and engaged in a major repaint of most of the model Dutch Village - including one or two bystanders - in a nasty shade of Gastric Yellow. Ten points for aesthetic sense, I figured - but absolutely zero for tact. By the time this book is written, the name of Flinthart will be reviled across most of Australia.

Mind you, with a range of places like that in it, I was never planning to go back to Coffs Harbour anyway.

kept shady laneways. Even if you do no more than follow the Waterfall Way itself, there are a myriad of excellent places to stop.

The **Dorrigo Rainforest Centre** (066) 572 309, about 3km short of Dorrigo in the **Dorrigo National Park**, boasts a really excellent set of raised walkways, allowing you to enter the dense canopy of the rainforest itself. This is a real treat, as it is up in the canopy where most of the rainforest action actually occurs. Look for the famous orchids while you're taking the walk.

Aside from the Rainforest Centre, the number of walks and waterfalls in this region is phenomenal. Listing them all would be impossible – but a few of the more attractive and interesting places are:

Dangar Falls, just outside Dorrigo on the abandoned Cedar Rd.

Chandler Falls, in Wollomombi Gorge, between Dorrigo and Armidale. Camping permitted, with amenities provided – and the falls themselves are reputedly the highest in Australia, at 220m from top to bottom.

The Tallow-wood Grove, deep in the abandoned Cedar Rd out of Dorrigo. This grove of trees estimated to be at least 600 years old has been left as a memorial to the plundered forests of the region.

Guy Fawkes River National Park. North-west of Dorrigo, it requires determination to get in, but there is a beautiful campground and most of the pools along the Guy Fawkes River still have platypus living in them.

Even if you can't find time or transport to explore deeply in this area, just passing through it makes a lovely diversion. If you do have transport and a tent, I'd say this region is worth at least a week. You can easily intersperse wilderness camping with short stints in the little villages and if the beautiful forests and mountains get stale, you can always nip down to the coast for a beach break.

North of Coffs

Between Coffs Harbour and Grafton, the highway doesn't actually get to the coast much. However, there's a whole string of wonderfully isolated beach villages along here, mixed in with the excellent **Yuraygir National Park**. First of these is **Red Rock**, about halfway to Grafton. If you go down the well-marked turnoff from the Pacific Highway, you will find the **Yarrawarra Aboriginal Cultural Centre** (066) 492 355. The centre itself isn't anything great, but it does have a pleasant campground and an interesting array of art from the local Gumbaingirr tribe. Also, for $6 you can take part in a two-hour guided walking tour which takes in local Gumbaingirr sites, including camps, ochre (basis of traditional paints) quarries, middens, stone/tool workings and ceremonial sites. This is a very worthwhile excursion, if you have the time. Unfortunately, it's a ways north of Coffs and not easy to get to without your own transport. If you do take this option, you might consider staying overnight in **Red Rock**, by the coast at the end of the road. It's a terribly pretty little area, with the usual fantastic, isolated beaches. The only useful accommodation is the caravan park (066) 492 730 which is quite near the river inlet. This is very good value, with tent sites at under $10.

Just across the river is the southernmost reach of the **Yuraygir National Park**. You can hire canoes locally to go paddling up the peaceful river, which is a lovely option and quite cheap at about $25 per day.

Next turnoff to the coast along the highway leads to **Wooli** ('wool-eye') and **Minnie Waters**. These two are both very ordinary little holiday villages – but once again, the beaches are absolutely extraordinary. It's hard to explain just how fine these little places are, with their nowhere-at-all atmosphere and their deserted million-dollar beaches with perfect surf. After a while, one runs out of appropriate words: they all start to sound alike. And of course, they are – because each has its perfect beach, its little national park forest and its placid river inlet teeming with birdlife – but on the other hand, there's a world of difference between them all.

What can I say? If you have your own transport, you shouldn't miss this opportunity. Even if you're on the bus, or following your thumb, you may still be able to get to one of these beaches. The **Wooli Bushland Holiday Park** (066) 497 519 is prepared to collect people who phone from Grafton, for example. Like as not some of the others would do the same.

Grafton

A nice country town on the Clarence River. It's worth a lunch stop and a bit of a wander round, but doesn't really rate an extended stay. Hire a canoe; paddle over the river to **Susan Island** and walk through the rainforest which shelters a truly colossal colony of fruit bats. Fruit bats, or Flying Foxes, as they are known, are a common, but very large, species of fruit-eating bat. Fully extended, their wings span more than a metre.

Fruit bats are harmless, relatively friendly animals, although they have a powerful musky odour. They are the bane of orchardists throughout the tropics and although they are protected as are all native species, fruit growers often take potshots at them anyway. During your stay on the East Coast, you will no doubt hear them at least once, screeching and squabbling in nearby fruit trees at night. Similarly, the vast beating of leathery wings close above your head on a dark roadway by night can be quite alarming, the first time it happens to you.

Past Grafton, the coastline presents more of the same and quickly returns to the sort of thing found in Yuraygir – little, isolated towns, national park and desolate, wonderful beaches. On the south side of the mouth of the Maclean River is the little town of **Angourie**, which has some of the most excellent and challenging surf on the coast. Definitely for experienced surfers only, however, as local conditions are hazardous.

On the north side of the mouth of the Maclean River, the tiny town of **Iluka** marks the southern entrance to **Bundjalung National Park**. About 6km north of Iluka is the large privately-operated Woody Head camping ground. The local wildlife is friendly to the point of being a little alarming and the national park itself is magnificent, including a fantastic stand of rainforest. The beaches are, of course, uniformly magnificent and the dune environment is wonderfully unspoiled. There are also some unimproved campsites within the park boundaries. At the north end of the park, in a typically Australian environmental paradox, a large stretch of the land is sealed off, set aside for use as a military bombing and target practice range.

Between Bundjalung National Park and **Broadwater National Park** is the little fishing town of **Evans Head**, at the mouth of the Evans River. Camping is not permitted in the Broadwater National Park, but Evans Head has the fine Silver Sands Caravan Park (066) 824 212 in Park St, with frontage to both the beach and the river.

Broadwater Park is worth a walk through, especially early in the morning if you happen to have overnighted at Evans Head. Birdlife and wildflowers are the most significant aspects of the place. There are also numerous Aboriginal shell-middens, marking the site of long-ago oyster-feasts. The park protects an area of wetlands and heath just behind the dune, with a large salt lagoon. The local Bundjalung Aborigines believe that the lagoon has a spirit-woman guardian. Named Gaungun, she appears as a light in the swamps by night and during the day she is the black rock on the beach where the Salty Creek channel runs down to the sea.

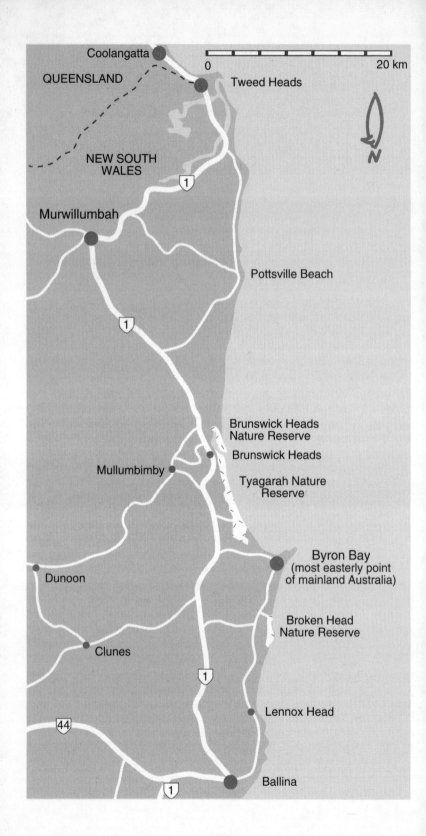

Coolangatta

QUEENSLAND

Tweed Heads

0   20 km

NEW SOUTH
WALES

① 1

Murwillumbah

Pottsville Beach

N

① 1

Brunswick Heads
Nature Reserve

Brunswick Heads

Mullumbimby

Tyagarah Nature
Reserve

Dunoon

Byron Bay
(most easterly point
of mainland Australia)

Broken Head
Nature Reserve

Clunes

① 1

Lennox Head

① 44

Ballina

① 1

Ballina to Tweed Heads

Oooh, this is pretty country. The whole of the coast is lined with magnificent surf beaches, almost entirely deserted once you get away from the main centres of population. There's not many of those centres, either: Ballina is just north of the Broadwater National Park and only has about 15,000 people. Then there's Byron Bay itself: something of a Big Tourist Mecca these days, but locals are continuing to fight a ferocious battle to ensure that it retains something of its own character. In fact, they've just had a very big win against Bastard Club Med, who wanted to put up their usual tasteful sort of multi-story megaresort next to one of the wonderful local beaches. Last of the three is Tweed Heads – but it's so far north, you might as well consider it part of the Queensland Gold Coast.

This is one of the three high spots of your trip (the others being Sydney and the Cairns/Barrier Reef Thing) and you should spend some serious time here. Inland, a swag of old volcanic mountains ensures that the area gets plenty of rain and the soils must be some of the most rampantly fertile in Australia.

Dirk's Dozen

1. **Surf**, surf and more surf. The beaches are this area's best feature.

2. **Byron Bay** – a buzzy little town where the New Agers, the Ferals and the tourist operators have combined with magic surf to produce a very cool destination.

3. **Hang gliding** at Byron Bay. Costs about $70 for a tandem flight. Best spot in Australia, if not the world, for hang gliding.

4. Slow drive the **coastal route** between Byron Bay and Tweed Heads. Unbeatable scenery.

Dirk Dumps On

1. **The Big Prawn** at Ballina – enormous fibreglass seafood is always a bad thing.

2. **Byron Bay** at Easter, Christmas or New Year. Crowded, tense and pushy.

Ballina

Fishing and holidaying seem to be the things which hold together this little town, set on the north shore of the mouth of the Richmond River. It's small, reasonably pretty and quiet. There's not a great deal of heavy tourist push here yet, so it's still a nice place just to drift through.

The buses run through Ballina, following the Pacific Highway. Mostly, they stop on the highway proper, near **The Big Prawn**. (Yes, it's a Big Thing. No, it isn't in Queensland. Technically, anyway.) **Kirklands** (066) 865 254 has a depot in Cherry St in the town proper and does a lot of local stuff, so if you were going to go inland to Lismore from here, (about $8 and a bit over an hour's drive) they're the folks you should talk to.

If you decide to stay in Ballina, there's not exactly a big range of cheap options. The **Ballina Traveller's Lodge** (066) 866 737 is a nice, clean, well-run YHA affiliate which will give you a bed for under $15. They've got a pool and things like bikes and watersports gear, and all in all, it's a pretty decent place to spend a couple of days.

If you've come for the surf, though, you might want to try **Flat Rock Camping Park**. It's about 5km north on the Pacific Highway from Ballina, with all the appropriate amenities, but it's a tent-only place. This is nice, if you're tired of dirty great caravans full of bickering children. (Mind you, there's any number of caravan parks proper in Ballina, if that's what you want.) It's only $10 to put up your tent and the Flat Rock grounds have the advantage of being right there, next to the beach – and what a beach it is!

There's a nice little café in Ballina, if you get hungry, called **Shelley's On The Beach** (066) 869 844 on Shelley Beach Rd near the junior surf club. Prices are good, the food isn't bad, but the view just can't be beat. There aren't many restaurants that advertise 'whale-watching breakfasts', after all. Mostly it's just dolphins – but any morning where you get up and watch the sun come up out of the clear blue Pacific with the day's first cup of hot coffee in your hand, well, that's a good morning, I think.

Other than surfing and having breakfast in Shelley's, Ballina doesn't offer a whole lot of excitement. There's good sailing in the area, of course. If you're interested, you can contact the people at the hostel, or go to the **Tourist Information Centre** (066) 863 484 just off River St (which is what the Pacific Highway happens to be named at that point).

Lennox Head

About a third of the way from Ballina to Byron there's a little town called **Lennox Head**. It's situated on yet another excruciatingly pretty piece of shoreline with magical surf. There's also a small freshwater lake there, near the beach, if you want a break from the saltwater. Lennox Head is another place ideal for surfers, but with limited facilities for anyone else. Nonetheless, it's a terribly pretty little place. If you want to stay there, try the **Lennox Beach House Hostel** (066) 877 636. Beds under $15 and the place practically redefines the idea of relaxed. This is a great place to chill out for a few days, take it easy, catch some sun and plan your assault on the north. (PS: Try the excellent bread at **Café Fino**.)

Byron Bay

Ask any Australian who lives within 1,000km of the place about **Byron Bay**. The answer you get will always be the same: 'Oh – it used to be such a nice place. Now, though – well, it's all gone commercial, hasn't it?

This, as they say in the trade, is bullshit.

It is true that Byron Bay, with only about 5,000 people in it, boasts more accommodation and more small businesses than practically anywhere on the coast. And it is true that the main street is no longer a camel-track. However, that's where the 'commercialisation' comes to an end.

Byron Bay is a very pretty little town. The Pacific Highway enters from the south as Bangalow Road, does a dogleg across the railway line and exits as Ewingsdale Rd, with a couple of other name changes in between. It has a beautiful, rocky headland – **Cape Byron**, the most easterly point in Australia – with a real monster of a lighthouse and a couple of the most fantastic beaches around.

The local community recognised long ago that Byron wasn't going to be a sleepy little village forever. However, some of those locals have quite a bit of clout (Paul Hogan is one of them), and they decided that if development was going to occur, then it was going to happen on their terms. No high-rise buildings. No Bastard Club Meds. No enormous shopping malls. And get this: somehow, as yet, no MacDonalds, Pizza the Hutt, Burger Bastard, or in fact, any of those suckers. You've got to love a place which has managed to achieve that!

As a result, even though the businesses have gone upmarket and prices aren't what they used to be, Byron Bay still retains the flavour of a

Captain's Log, James Cook 1770 World Surf Safari: 'Truly, this land must be the Ultimate Tubemeister's Paradise. This day we rounded a rocky headland and discovered a glorious beach with the most exceedingly bitchin' curl. I ordered the immediate waxing of my finest stick and proceeded at once for the action while that fool Banks took sightings and samples.

'At the end of the day, I have decide to name the headland Cape Byron. Banks applauded my choice, saying that he felt the poet would be honoured by such a gesture. Banks thinks he's so hip, just because he's a member of the Royal Society. Ha. Show's how much he knows. Little did he realise that I have not named this headland for that big-shirted hippie poet at all, but for his very cool grandfather, who was a major waxhead. His own World Surf Safari back in the '60s was way legendary, dude, and inspired my own efforts towards this journey.'

busy little village. Full marks to the people who've kept it that way and bollocks to the whingers who complain about how commercial it all is now!

Stuff To Do

Relax! If ever there was a place purpose-made for relaxing, it was Byron Bay. Of course, if you wanted to do something active, there's no shortage. Swimming is brilliant, as is the local surf and you can get surfboards and boogie boards from most of the hostels. The trip to the lighthouse is very pleasant – there's some good walking trails and a wonderful view to be had. There's something really enchanting about watching dolphins in the surf. It sounds like New-Age wanksterism, but it's just that they seem to be having so much fun …

There's a good dive site about 3km offshore, at **Julian Rocks**. It's not really up to the standards of the Great Barrier Reef, but the waters are usually pretty clear and there's an abundance of life. You can do a dive course locally, if you want.

Since Byron Bay is a Big Backpacker Mecca, you can do quite a lot of the usual adventure bullshit, but some of the more irritating options – like cable water ski-ing and nude bungy jumping – seem to be absent. Not to worry. There's plenty of other places to catch up.

Hang gliding off the platform up near the lighthouse on **Cape Byron** is a real buzz. You can learn to glide, locally, although of course it's a touch on the expensive side. You can also take a flight in an ultralight aircraft from only $50, which is a lot of fun. Naturally, you can go skydiving as well.

If you have the time and interest, take a look at **Colin Heaney's glass-blowing studio** (066) 857 044 at 6 Acacia St in the industrial estate north of Byron proper. Colin's gorgeous, brilliantly coloured works can be found in stores up and down the coast, but this is an opportunity to watch a genuine artist at work in an ancient and fascinating craft. Costs nothing to go and take a look and the glassware ranges from somewhat garish to utterly spellbinding in beauty.

Byron Bay also has a pretty significant night-life. Nothing quite so crass as a proper night-club, but there are quite a few bars and eateries which encourage live music – **The Piggery**, for example, or the well-known **Railway Bar** near the station proper. The music varies, but is frequently of a much higher standard than might be expected and once a year at Easter time, Byron Bay goes a little ape-shit holding a **Blues Festival**.

And this brings me to Byron Bay's one solitary note of warning: During the big holidays, it can get very bloody crowded. The Blues Festival got itself quite a reputation for a while there and drew crowds of bikers amongst others. End result of that was a massive increase in police presence for the Easter period in Byron and a rather tense atmosphere. Things also get hairy around New Year. Personally, I'd avoid the place during these two times.

Any other time, though, Byron Bay is excellent.

In And Out

Happily, Byron is on the **Murwillumbah-Sydney** train line and you can catch a swift, comfortable XPT to or from Sydney for under $85. This is a good option, if you weren't wanting to check out everything in between – cheap, comfortable and relatively fast. The railway station in Byron is just off **Jonson St**, quite near the information centre and the main bus stop.

Bookings for the buses can usually be made at the **Information Centre** (066) 858 050 in Jonson St, opposite the instantly recognisable **Community Centre**, with its garish murals. Byron Bay is well serviced by buses. Brisbane will cost you about $25, Sydney roughly $60, Coffs Harbour about $30 and you can also head across to Melbourne (about $120) and even Adelaide ($150) if the fancy takes you.

Shelter

Arts Factory Lodge (066) 857 709 Skinner Shoot Rd. Roomy, friendly sort of place which has cheap beds and permits camping. Costs about $10 for a bed. Atmospheric, very entertaining clean and comfortable place to stay, but a little further from the all-important beach than most.

Cape Byron YHA Hostel (066) 856 445 Byron & Middleton Sts. It's a bit over the top, all clean and spiffy and new with a little shopping centre and a pool and everything. Costs about $15 per night. Fine, but lacking a certain laidback atmosphere which Byron Bay cultivates.

Backpacker's Inn (066) 858 231 29 Shirley St. Closest hostel to the beach. Big, well appointed, well-laid out, comfortable place with all mod cons and accessories. Costs about $15 for a bed.

Backpacker's Holiday Village (066) 858 888 116 Jonson St. Relatively near the bus stop, though it's out from the town centre and the beach. Smaller place, but quite popular and as usual for Byron, well-supplied and maintained. You can usually get a bed here for under $15.

Belongil Beachouse (066) 857 868 Childe St. Totally groovy place, across the road from the beach, comes with its own rather good little café. This is a good thing, because it's a fair way from the town centre. Mind you, that makes it even nicer to stay in if you ask me. Expect to pay about $15 for a bed.

There's also a few caravan parks, if you want to put up a tent. Once again, it's not a lot cheaper than staying at the rather good hostels and, in school holiday periods, finding a place in any of the caravan parks can be a major trial.

Snapshots

Carl Has To Change His Shorts: From the first day I told my folks back in San José that I was going to Australia for the summer break, everyone started telling me what a dangerous place it was. I mean, they'd all seen Crocodile Dundee like a hundred times and everybody talked about the crocodiles and the snakes and all that kind of stuff. I just laughed at them. It was kind of fun, you know – going to this place where there's all these weird animals and everybody thinks its going to be some kind of big adventure.

Anyway, I came into the country at Sydney, but I went straight to Melbourne to meet with some Aussie friends who'd come to California the year before. They were really good to me. I met everyone, went to all the places, had a really good time.

But they told me all these fuckin' stories, right? About snakes and jellyfish and crocodiles and especially about sharks. 'Cause they've got all those Great Whites down at the south of Australia, don't they? Boy, they really loaded me up.

After Melbourne, I caught a bus for Byron Bay because I'd heard how good the surf was and how it was supposed to be this really pretty, laid-back place. It was a long bus trip. We went right up through the middle of nowhere and got in pretty late at night. I just went to my hostel and crashed.

Clarks Beach Caravan Park (066) 856 496 Lighthouse Rd.

Suffolk Park Caravan Park (066) 853 353 Tallow Beach. (about 5km south of town).

First Sun Caravan Park (066) 856 544 Main Beach. Very little shade.

Food

Wow! No international junkfood tyrants with their pinstriped slaves asking you if you want coffee with those fries. I love it! Personal favourite: check out **Earth & Sea Pizza**, on Jonson St near the roundabout. First time I had a pizza there, the quality surprised me so much that I went back and ate pizza the next two nights running. They also do pasta. Gets

Snapshots

Woke up early in the morning, grabbed a board and went to the beach. It was everything they'd told me it would be. Those waves were fuckin' beautiful. Six feet tall, clear as glass and the water felt great. I paddled right out and just lay on the board for a while, feeling the morning sun.

Next thing I know, this big dark shape shoots through the water under my board. I just about shit. I'm pulling my hands and feet out of the water, trying to make sure everything's still there and then right beside me, this big dorsal fin comes up.

I did shit, I swear. I started screaming about sharks and paddling like crazy for the shore. All the way in, I thought for sure I was gonna be bitten in half by some monster fuckin' great white.

I got about three quarters the way in to the beach when the adrenaline burst faded and I just had to stop paddling and breathe. Then I noticed that there were a couple of other guys in the surf and they were just killing themselves laughing at me. That didn't seem right, so I took a look around.

Yeah. You guessed it. It was just a couple of fucking dolphins. I was totally pissed. I felt like a complete jerk.

You're not gonna put my real name down or anything, are you?

quite crowded, so you're better off ordering take-away and eating in the park overlooking the beach.

Popular and interesting, not to mention cheap, is the **Old Piggery** restaurant, which now serves up excellent vegetarian food as well as providing one of Byron Bay's most hallowed live music venues. A visit to The Piggery is probably a quintessential part of The Byron Experience.

For slightly meatier fare, check the beach end of Jonson St, where you will find the **South Indian Curry House**. More fine curry with **Oh! Delhi**, in the Feros Arcade. Another good Asian place is **Kips**, in the Plaza shopping centre, which cooks up cheap Thai/Malay food.

For breakfast in superb surroundings, try the **Beach Café** on Clarks Beach. It isn't exactly cheap, but they do a fine stack of buttermilk pancakes and it's a wonderful place to sit and kickstart the day.

At the top of the hill overlooking the beach on Jonson St is the **Beach Hotel**. Aside from providing the usual range of reasonable pub food, this is a marvellous place to sit and drink and watch the ocean. Big and spacious, with heaps of atmosphere. I've spent many a long drunken afternoon in there when its been too wet to hit the beach – there's nothing so nice as sitting in a warm pub, nursing a whisky, watching the rain fall on the beach in the afternoon.

Most of the food places are clustered around the central roundabout and up Lawson and Jonson St. A simple walk through this area will offer you more choices than you know what to do with and if it's just a snack you're after, the place is crawling with coffee shops and little cafés.

Tweed Coast

North of Byron Bay, the Pacific Highway turns inland. However, there is a coastal route to follow as well and just for the drive alone, it's well worth the effort. However, there's not a lot of development anywhere on the coast between Byron Bay and Tweed Heads (which is really part of the Gold Coast, by now). This isn't actually a bad thing. The end result is thirty kilometres or more of stunningly beautiful beach coastline, which is practically deserted along its whole length. There's a couple of villages

here and there – the largest is **Brunswick Heads**, with about 1700 people – but for the most part, it's empty.

There are campsites scattered here and there along this coastal route, mostly completely unimproved. There are also caravan parks in most of the little towns and at **Cabarita Beach** (locally famous for surf that just won't quit), there's even a little hostel – **Emu Park** (066) 761 190.This is a wonderful, out-of-the-way spot and with a nearby freshwater lake, it's got a bit of something for anyone.

Flinthart's Journal

Mindy wanted to ride a camel. She saw the sign just before Brunswick Heads – 'Camel Safari', it said. I wondered out loud why it didn't say 'Danger! Camel Safari'. Mindy pouted and opined that I had lost my sense of humour. I despise women who pout. In fact, I despise men who pout as well.

I stuck around long enough to see Mindy mounted on the back of a huge, evil-smelling, foul-tempered, shaggy spit-factory. I smiled, waved until she was out of sight, then left her pack with the operators of the Camel Brothel and headed south.

Paying money to ride on a camel is stupid. Riding camels is not fun. Camels are not fun. Camels are angry, ugly, mutinous monsters who really would spit in your eye as soon as look at you. Anyone who says different is probably trying to sell a bunch of surplus camels.

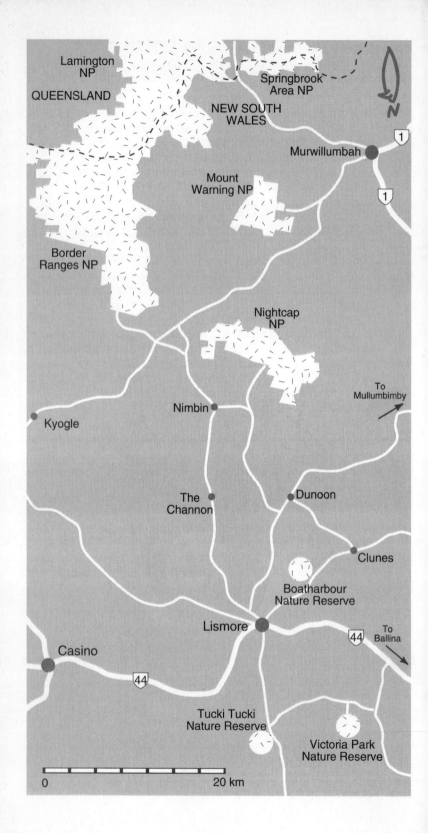

The Big Scrub

Only the Australians could ever label such an impossibly beautiful region with a name like 'The Big Scrub'. The term refers to a basin of once-rainforested country from about Lismore up to the Queensland border. Many millenia ago, there was a truly fucking enormous volcano here. I mean very large indeed. The old volcanic core is still visible as the dramatic upthrust of Mt Warning, just south of Murwillumbah. The result of all this volcanic upheaval was a series of raised plateaus surrounding a hilly basin of the most astonishingly fertile and well-watered soils. While much of this lower region has been plundered for timber, including the famous Western Red Cedar, during the last two hundred years, there are three areas of World Heritage-listed rainforest remaining as national park. Due to the volcanic upthrust, these regions remained cool and moist throughout the last umpteen billion years and the forests there are reckoned to be as close to the original forests of Gondwanaland as anywhere on the planet.

Dirk's Dozen

1. **Just drive:** Drive through the maze of little roads which connect the multitude of tiny towns with hamlets and villages that barely rate a spot on the map. Drive through rolling green fields, through dense, dark rainforest, along crystalline creeks and rivers. Buy a map, then ignore it. Get lost. Get found. Get lost again. This is a wonderful place to be. Look especially for the Tweed Range Scenic Drive, out of Kyogle into the mountains.

2. **Check out Nimbin**, where the Hippie still thrives: This village is officially the sister city to Woodstock – the famous Woodstock of the festival in the USA. Reason being, apparently, that Nimbin once had its own Aquarian festival, back in 1973. Only the place was so green, so inviting and beautiful, that most of the groove dudes and hipsters never left and the place is like some kind of weird karmic time warp back to the glory days of the early seventies.

3. **The Channon Markets:** Just the drive to get there is lovely. Stay for half a day or so, eat, drink, buy weird things, then go for a swim at one of the waterfalls in the area. Wonderful stuff. The Channon is a little town off the road between Nimbin and Lismore. The markets occur at the showgrounds just outside town on the second Sunday of every month and they are just wonderful. There's food, bands, all kinds of bizarre clothes, jewellery and oddments for sale and just walking around the show ring a couple of times is easily worth the effort of getting there.

4. **World Heritage Rainforests:** Get into at least one of those Heritage-listed national parks. If there is magic left in the world, this is a

good place to start looking for it. Try at least for the Border Ranges Park, on that Tweed Ranges Scenic Drive – and do the Pinnacle walk.

5. **Climb Mount Warning** so you arrive at sunrise, when you will see the sun breaking over the Pacific Ocean. You see, the peak of Mt Warning is the very first place in Australia to see the morning sun, being so far East and so high. There's a New Age rumour that Mount Warning is one of the four corners of the world, or something. But climb it anyway. You'll need to be fit. Allow four hours return and take a jumper and some water. And a camera.

Dirk Dumps On

1. **Pathetic Nimbin dope deals:** Don't bother buying marijuana in Nimbin unless you're really hanging out. The locals have quite a trade going and its a very tourist sort of thing. They'll spot you coming about six miles off and you'll find yourself paying $100 for a couple of foils of shitty leaf.

Getting Around

Notable towns in the Scrub are **Lismore** (the largest, in the south), **Murwillumbah** (up north in the Tweed River Valley) **Kyogle** (inland to the west) **Mullumbimby** (just in from the coast near Brunswick Heads) and **Nimbin**, somewhere near the centre of it all. There's a very decent highway which runs from **Ballina** to **Casino** and inland which passes straight through Lismore. From Casino, another reasonable (read 'sealed, at least') road runs north to Kyogle and naturally, there's a road from Kyogle to Murwillumbah, but that one's not fully sealed and tends to be a bit rough. Still, it's no more than an hour from any of the towns to any other, unless bad weather intervenes.

Actually, there's a maze of interconnecting roads up in that area. They follow old trails, wander over ridgelines and peter out into mysterious camel-tracks that disappear into the depths of the rainforest. Driving and navigating through the Big Scrub is invariably a hilarious comedy of errors – unless you're really trying to get somewhere, in which case it can be alarming.

The **XPT train** out of Sydney runs through Lismore, Mullumbimby, Kyogle and Murwillumbah, which is damned convenient. Lismore itself is

a kind of nexus and mysterious buses are always coming and going. Best bet is to deal with **Kirklands** (066) 221 499 which is actually based in Lismore.

Definitely your best option is to drive. If you haven't got your own vehicle, con somebody else into taking you for the trip. Failing that, try renting a car out of Byron Bay or Ballina. There's a couple of companies which will get down as low as $35 per day plus about 15c per kilometre. A private vehicle is the only way you will get the chance to really enjoy losing yourself in this delightful part of the world.

Hitch-hiking is possible in the area and is often more successful than it is elsewhere in Australia, because of the very high proportion of Ferals and New-Agers who live in the area. It's a pretty laid-back region without a lot of serious crime, but the usual rules on hitch-hiking most definitely apply.

Lismore

The unofficial capital of the area with a population approaching 30,000. Lots of good productive rural land around, but there is a certain amount of life and interest to the town generated by the Ferals and Alternatives and by the students from the local university campus. Lismore has a nice hostel, the **Currendina Traveller's Lodge** (066) 216 581 on Ewing St, with beds for under $15. It's a bit rule-bound, though, so it's not as much fun as it ought to be. There's also a couple of caravan parks if you simply want to put up a tent. Talk to the people at the **Information Centre** (066) 220 122 if you're interested in joining any of the local bush tours or camping treks, or if you would just like to organise your own tour of the region.

Lismore is a friendly, pretty town, but there's not a whole lot of interest there. Possibly the best thing to do is to take a river cruise to Ballina by way of the **MV Bennelong** (066) 217 729 for about $45. This is a very relaxing journey with marvellous scenery.

Kyogle

About 3,000 people in a fairly ordinary little country town. The only real budget accommodation here comes from the caravan park. **Kirklands** buses run there and the **Sydney/Brisbane XPT** can be caught into or out of Kyogle for about $75. The northern road out of Kyogle leads to the **Border Ranges National Park**, which includes some of that World Heritage-listed rainforest. Kyogle makes a nice lunch stop on a leisurely driving tour of the Scrub.

Murwillumbah

A sizeable little place on the **Tweed River** about fifteen to twenty minutes drive out of the Gold Coast. From **Murwillumbah**, there's a lovely inland drive north through the **Numinbah Valley** to **Nerang**, which lets you cut off quite a stretch of the harrowing Gold Coast drive, if you're going on to Brisbane. Actually, the Numinbah Valley is worth a visit in its own right – see the mention in the Gold Coast Hinterland.

Murwillumbah is propped up by bananas, sugar-cane and tourism. It's a nice but unspectacular sort of town, which provides shopping and support for the whole of the Tweed Valley and the northern half of the Big Scrub. If you visit, you can stay at the **Mt Warning Backpacker's YHA** (066) 723 761 at 1 Tumbulgum Rd. Beds are under $15 and the place is pretty fantastic. The managers know the area quite well and can help you organise even the most unlikely of itineraries.

Most of the buses stop at the railway station, near the highway. Buses run out of Murwillumbah for Brisbane, Sydney and Lismore, as well as to the coast. The Brisbane/Sydney XPT train stops in Murwillumbah.

Best things to do in and around Murwillumbah are canoeing on the Tweed River – which is broad and placid at this point – and walking up the **Mt Warning track**. This is a well-marked trail which leads all the way to the top through yet more of that magic rainforest. It's quite a long, steep walk and you'd do well to carry water with you.

While you're in the area, you might want to ignore **Avocado Adventureland**. Avocadoes are a delicious tropical fruit with smooth, yellow-green flesh. They are not an adventure. Any sentence or idea which links 'Avocado' and 'Adventure' without the words 'Smeared all over the body of your favourite super-model' is blatantly lying.

Mullumbimby

Nice little town of about 2,500 people, best known for the legendary *Cannabis cultivar* dubbed Mullumbimby Madness. The Madness was a sticky reddish smoke which did the rounds in the late seventies through early eighties and can still be obtained if you know the right people. Be sure that your head is firmly attached to your body before you do anything rash.

Mullumbimby is the town where Nimbin Ferals go when they burn out and have to return to civilisation. It's full of semi-reformed hippie sorts making a living in arts and crafts and as a result, the local Arts Gallery is well worth the effort to visit. There's no really cheap accommodation in Mullumbimby, though, and at best, the place warrants a day-trip. Myself, I'd give it a nice extended lunch-break visit at the local pub.

Nimbin

Uh-oh. Careful – you may be treading on somebody's legend. This is a small, difficult-to-reach village about 30km north of Lismore in the mountains. **Nimbin** is the Feral Person Capital of Australia. Back in the seventies, there was something of a rock festival here and ever since then, there's been a slow trickle of people coming in to drop out and lead an alternative lifestyle. Nimbin is – well, it's Nimbin. The name itself carries a wealth of meaning in Australia.

It's a bizarre little place, with a raffish, ramshackle sort of air. Half the people there are the most mind-bendingly sincere, eco-guerilla, tree-hugging commune-dwellers you will ever meet on the face of the earth. The other half are just plain strange. The place is run on marijuana and the Unemployment Benefit. Buying dope in Nimbin is as simple as walking into the Rainbow Café on the main street. Unfortunately, it's also pretty pointless. Unless you actually know somebody locally, you'll prob-

Snapshots

Mark & Jenny Do The Time Warp: We're from Philadelphia. Like the movie. Except it's a really straight-down-the-line kind of city, so visiting Australia was a real adventure for both of us.

We had bus passes that we'd bought back in the States, but trying to use them around Nimbin was impossible. We met these really friendly people in Murwillumbah, though, who said that it was easy to hitch-hike, so we thought we'd give it a try.

Getting into Nimbin was easy. The first guy who picked us up outside Murwillumbah took us all the way there in his beat-up old pickup truck. He even took us into the Rainbow Café and introduced us to some friends of his.

They were just the friendliest people. We talked and talked for hours and then they gave us a lift down the road to Granny's. Not only that, but they gave us a couple of reefers of their own stuff. We took a walk that evening and tried it out. Shit, was it strong.

That was the real problem. We'd only budgeted an overnight stay for Nimbin, but we got so stoned that we couldn't wake up early enough in the morning to hitch-hike out, so we decided we'd take a walk and a swim and leave early the next morning.

That's what we did. Only that evening, there was a local dance, which was lots of fun - and somebody else went and got us stoned. Again.

The next day we met these Feral People at a local swimming hole. They showed us around a bit and we got hideously stoned all over again.

And the next day.

Actually, in the end, we were there for five days before we could get our heads straight enough to get up in the morning and just plain leave. Some trip!

ably wind up paying an inflated price for a pretty inferior product. On the other hand, if you do know who to talk to, the locals take quite a lot of pride in their home-cultivated strains. A Nimbin *cultivar* recently took out a major award at the Amsterdam Marijuana Show.

Accommodation in Nimbin usually means **Granny's Farm** (066) 891 333, a YHA affiliate on the local creek. Costs less than $15 for a bed. It's only a few minutes by foot from the centre of town. It's not as big and flash as a lot of places, but it's plenty friendly and the setting is very nice.

Food means anything on the main street. You can get decent counter meals quite cheaply from the **Freemasons Hotel** and there's half-a-dozen other places around selling any of a variety of cheap and healthy food. Check out the **Rainbow Café** for seriously weird atmosphere as well as cheap food. Also, the **Nimbin Bakery** in Cullen St is a source of truly remarkable breads and pastries. Interestingly, though they state the bread is baked without animal fats, they also offer baked pigs and meats for special occasions.

The countryside around Nimbin is fantastic. This is a good place to base yourself for a couple of days if you want to do some rainforest walking and swimming. There are two or three waterfalls in walking distance – although it can be quite a walk – and the people at Granny's can help you with navigation. For atmosphere, scenery and simple bizarre fun, Nimbin is definitely one of the must-see places of the Scrub.

National Parks of the Big Scrub

Nightcap National Park. About 30km due north of Lismore, accessible through **The Channon** and through Nimbin. Camping is permitted in the **Whian Whian State Forest** which adjoins. Camping is also permitted in the **Terania Creek** area, reached by travelling through The Channon, which has excellent walking and swimming. Beware heavy rains which may maroon you at Terania Creek if you're not careful.

More very fine walking trails around **Mt Nardi**, reached through Nimbin. Look for the giant Brush Box trees in the area, some up to 1,500 years old. There are some wonderful views to be had in this area. If you're feeling energetic, you might consider making the 8km or so walk along the historic **Nightcap Track** between Rummery Road in the Whian Whian forest and Mt Nardi. This track was once a packhorse trail, the first overland link between the Richmond and Tweed valleys. It was primarily a mail route and when it was in use, it took the mail three days to go from Lismore to Murwillumbah. Walking it will give you some idea of the troubles that beset the timbergetters who once plagued the area.

Mt Warning National Park. Impossible to miss, Mt Warning looms over Murwillumbah and **Uki** like a giant green Quasimodo. The mountain got its name from Captain Cook, who was having a bad day; it was named as a nice, visible landmark to help avoid **Point Danger**, which he also named. Local Aborigines, however, called it **Wollumbin**, meaning 'cloud-catcher' – which is a much groovier name. Access to the park is from a side-road off of the road from Murwillumbah to Uki, about 10km south from Murwillumbah.

At the base of the mountain, about a kilometre up the approach road, is the **Wollumbin Wildlife Refuge and Caravan Park** (066) 795120, where you can put up a tent for about $10. It's a nice quiet little place, next to a lovely creek. An excellent thing to do is to put up here for the night, then take off and make the walk up the mountain to catch the dawn.

Border Ranges National Park. So called because it sits along the Qld-NSW border, this is a very big park. About 32,000 hectares, in fact, chockablock with ancient rainforest, inaccessible mountain peaks, sheer cliffs, mighty waterfalls and practically anything else you could want. Except McDonalds, of course.

Easiest part to access is the **Tweed Range Scenic Drive**, which loops off the road between Uki and Kyogle. It isn't all that easy to find, but make the effort. It's about 60km long altogether, a winding gravel road through the mountain tops with fantastic views and gorgeous, isolated walking tracks through the rainforest. If you can find it, the very best site is the **Pinnacle Lookout**. This is nothing short of breathtaking. About 8km past the signposted **Blackbutts Picnic Area**, the lookout itself is only a five minute walk from the road. If you've got a head for heights, though, you can actually walk out along the knife-edge ridge to the sheer, isolated rock of The Pinnacle itself. Do it. This Is Really Funky.

One important note: a large stretch of this road is one-way traffic only. It's designed so that you can loop around and come back without coming nose-to-nose with other vehicles on a road sometimes barely wide enough for a decent fart. The problem is, the 'one-way' signs aren't always overly visible, being set in rainforest as they are. Look carefully; people get unreasonably cranky if they come upon you going the wrong direction. (Wankers. No sense of fun.)

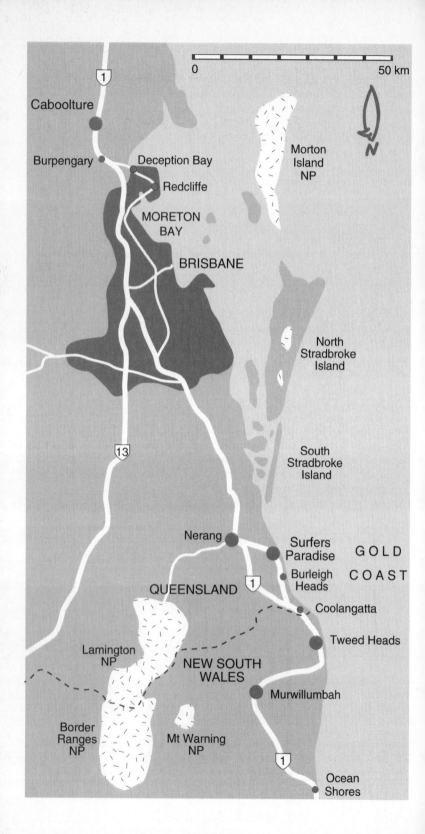

South-east Queensland

This is the most densely populated area of Queensland, as it includes the capital, Brisbane. Fine beaches and a beautiful hinterland in the Gold Coast just over the border from NSW have led to viciously intense development, producing a foreshore at Surfers Paradise which could grace Kowloon Harbour. Brisbane itself is a big, fairly quiet city, with absolutely no beaches or surf at all. Local museums aren't too bad – the Queensland Art Gallery has a notable collection of Australian moderns, especially Ian Fairweather. Also, Moreton and North Stradbroke Islands offer very useful quiet getaways, with more magic surf. These sand islands are a small but viable alternative to Fraser Island if you can't get that far.

The Sunshine Coast has been extensively developed for tourism as well, mostly in terms of its excellent beaches. However, the Glasshouse Mountains and the pretty villages of the D'Aguilar Ranges north of Brisbane are worth visiting as well. But on the whole, this is an area I would suggest you don't waste too much time on.

Dirk's Dozen

1. **Moreton** and **Stradbroke Islands.**

2. **Surf**, especially at Noosa.

3. **Cooloola National Park**. Rent a canoe and go paddling.

4. **David Fleay's Wildlife Sanctuary** at the Gold Coast – possibly Australia's best.

5. **Lamington National Park** inland from the Gold Coast. An extension of the Barrier Ranges World Heritage Area with a brilliant three to five day trek.

Dirk Dumps On

1. **Gold Coast** during any of the school holidays or the infamous **Schoolies Week**.

2. **Gold Coast** during the March **Indy 500** race festival.

3. Crowded American-style **theme parks** at the **Gold Coast**.

4. Nauseating and stupid '**tourist attractions**' springing up on the **Sunshine Coast**.

> The perfect Queensland day goes like this: a surf beach, a sunny day, a cold beer, a mud crab, a big spliff, a really good sweaty bonk and a great big cold juicy mango to round it off. If you can manage even one single day with that kind of itinerary, you might as well turn around and go home. No, in fact, you might as well just kill yourself; you've had the very best out of life that you'll ever get.

The Gold Coast

This is not my kind of thing.

The **Gold Coast/Surfers Paradise** area consists of a solid strip of heavy development and urbanisation, stretching from the border of NSW practically all the way up to the southern end of Moreton Bay. It's been a holiday spot for over a century, beloved for its marvellous beaches and for the green, mountainous, well-watered hinterland. And to be fair, the beaches and the surf are genuinely shit-hot.

Sadly, there's fuck-all else left of the area. The hinterlands have been heavily cleared and logged, except for designated national parks. And the foreshore! You might as well be in Florida or Hong Kong. The place is just one long, crawling strip of traffic and neon.

Still, if you want a few days of high-energy holidaying, with the best aspects of both a busy city and a top set of surf beaches, the Gold Coast has its attractions. Personally, I cringe every time I have to drive through the place. It gives me the shits in a big way.

Dirk's Dozen

1. **Fleay's Wildlife Park** – probably the best-managed and most comprehensive Australian wildlife park in the state, if not the entire country.

2. **Currumbin Bird Gardens** – amazing displays as the thousands upon thousands of vibrantly colourful lorikeets come storming in to be hand fed, morning and evening. Wear a hat.

3. **Surfing.** Especially at Burleigh Heads, if you know what you're doing.

4. **Lamington National Park:** for the fit and adventuresome, the **Caldera Rim Walk** which takes upwards of three to four days is utterly unforgettable. Otherwise, even day-tripping is worth doing.

Okay. Take a deep breath. One thing you don't do is laze around and relax, oh no – not with the pressure on to spend the bucks, party up. Let's deal with the everyday stuff first. Seeing that the Gold Coast is Big Tourist Mecca, you can do the usual range of stuff. Skydiving, biplane rides, parasailing, rock-climbing (indoors and outdoors) bungy jumping and all the variations thereof, waterski-ing (boat or cable), scuba diving (not particularly good around here), motorcycle/bicycle/rollerblade rentals and tours, bla bla bla bla … if you want it, you can do one of two things. You can ask your hostel to help you out, or you can contact the **Gold Coast Regional Information Centres**. There's one in the **Cavill Ave Mall** in Surfers (07) 5538 4419 and one in **Beach House Plaza**, Marine Parade, Coolangatta (07) 5536 7765). The whole purpose of these places is to help you spend your money. That service, at least, comes free of charge.

Now, however grudgingly, I must admit there are a few useful things to do on the Gold Coast. Number one, of course, is surfing. The surf at **Burleigh Heads** is world-class and internationally famed. It's not for the faint of heart, as the waves roll in to a shore of jagged rock, but the rides are out of this world. Of course, all the local blonde surf gods know that too and they have a kind of private-property, proprietorial attitude to the place. Don't try it unless you know what you're doing and for pity's sake don't let on if you're from another country

Another useful thing about the Gold Coast is the sheltered water-way behind **The Bar**, at the northern end of the strip. This is a really good place to learn a few basic watersports skills. You can learn to sail small boats here, or try waterski-ing, or any one of a number of things and all in complete safety. Except for the occasional shark. Again, talk to your hostel or the Tourist Authorities, or just check the Yellow Pages for watersports schools.

If you've got some kind of a deep, dark, kinky thing for theme parks, this is the place for you. **Dreamworld**, on the highway to Brisbane, is a poor man's Aussie Disney-clone. I think it's about as exciting as picking my nose, but it does have the usual selection of rides and people in over-sized animal suits. It's perpetually in financial difficulties however, and last I heard they were about to flog it to yet another Japanese corporation.

Warner Brothers Movie World, in the same area, is cloned from the famous Universal Studios in Los Angeles. Lots of annoying stunt shows, a few rides, souvenir stands and quasi-informative, fully-scripted tours of dysfunctional movie-making facilities which don't even begin to answer anything like an intelligent question. And still more people in oversized animal suits. Ho-hum. Oddly enough, though, this is a very popular place. And I freely admit, some of the rides are pretty cool, especially the **Lethal Weapon**, if you like being flung around at high speeds in a chair dangling from a demented railway track. (Which I do.) Nobody dies, though.

Sea World, on the Broadwater just north of Main Beach, is probably the best of the lot. Performing sea creatures, more fucking rides and souvenirs, waterski shows … I like dolphins, though. And whales. And sharks. I really like sharks. All of the theme parks cost between $30 and $40 to enter and most of the rides are free once you're in.

If you've got the time, **Fleay's Wildlife Park** on West Burleigh Rd at Burleigh Hds is a cut above the usual koala brothel. The place was established by a chap called David Fleay, who actually did some important and valuable work in the field of naturalism. Among other things, he was the first to successfully breed platypus in captivity and the park maintains a very high standard to this day. There is a very wide range of native birds and animals, well-treated and well-presented and the park itself is quite an attractive place. It's more than worth the $9 it costs to get in.

Not far from there, on the Gold Coast Highway at Currumbin is the **Currumbin Bird Sanctuary** (07) 5534 1266. Back in 1946, a bloke called Alex Griffiths started feeding the local lorikeets, apparently to stop them shredding his gladioli. This was a big mistake. Lorikeets are a highly gregarious group of brightly coloured, noisy parrots and they hunt in packs. Soon, Mr Griffiths was widely known as 'the guy with the birdshit all over him' and his neighbours were moving away in droves. Didn't stop him or his lorikeets though, by God.

Personally, I suspect poor old Griffiths had bitten off more than he could chew. I mean, he was feeding and entertaining literally thousands of the savage, noisy bastards. How could he stop? How do you explain to a giant flock of ravenous lorikeets that the birdy num-nums are no longer going to occur and would you all please go back wherever you came from?

In 1976, Alex Griffiths finally worked out the solution to his problem. He gave the property and the sanctuary to the government, which runs it to this day.

Actually, the Bird Sanctuary is pretty neat. It's attractive, well run, stocked with quite a wide range of both bird life and the odd animal and it only costs $14. Try to be there between 8am and 9.30am, or 4pm and 5pm. That's when the lorikeet feeding sessions are held. You've got to see it to believe it. These are definitely not shy, timid birds.

An excellent day-trip by bicycle (if you're prepared for a strenuous ride) is the **Mt Cougal National Park**. Essentially, you turn off the Gold Coast Highway at Currumbin Creek and follow Currumbin Ck Rd inland as far as it goes. It's a long, winding, very pretty ride through a green valley, terminating at a small rainforest park, with some really good rockpool swimming. Take a picnic lunch.

Also at Currumbin, in Tomewin St between the highway and the sea, is the **Chocolate Expo**. It's actually a factory which makes quality chocolates. The stuff is all hand-made right there in front of you and very pleasant it is, too. Okay, it may not be the excitement high point of your trek, but it will taste a whole lot nicer than, say, your mouth the morning after hitting the Surfer's Paradise nightclubs.

Oh yeah. The nightclubs. Okay, prepare to party down at:

The Globe (07) 5538 7444. 5 Beach Rd, Surfers Paradise.

Cocktails & Dreams (07) 5592 1955. The Mark, Orchid Ave, Surfers Paradise. Big 'packers place, with meal and drink voucher deals with most of the hostels, lots of wanky party activities, hard drinking and dancing. 'Packer's meat market, basically.

The Tunnel (07) 5536 8400. Orchid Ave, Surfers. Popular, runs a variety of different kinds of music.

Actually, if you just cruise up and down Orchid Avenue when you're in the nightclub frame of mind, you'll find something sooner or later.

Getting out of the Gold Coast proper and into the hinterland is a good idea. Although rampant development has thoroughly arse-holed most of the area near the Gold Coast proper, there are still a few very groovy spots to be found in the general vicinity. Mostly, you'll need your own transport to reach them, but it's possible to rent a small car from various places on the Gold Coast for quite reasonable rates, down at $30 per day or below. (Of course, that's for a week or so. It's a bit more to rent just for the day.)

Following the highway back around through **Nerang**, you can get into the **Numbinbah Valley**. This is very green and beautiful, with lots of impressive granite and rainforest. Check out the **Natural Arch National Park** on the east side of the valley – it's a little over-used, especially on weekends, but the glow-worm cavern with the waterfall that crashes through the rock ceiling is still quite impressive. It makes a rewarding walk, especially because you can swim in the rock pool when you get there.

If horse-riding appeals, this is magnificent country for it. Contact **Yowgurrabah** (075) 5334 4137 in the Numinbah Valley about doing a half-day ride through some of the best scenery around. Costs about $40; they supply all the gear, the guide and they match the horses to your level of skill and experience, which is comforting.

Lamington National Park is beautiful subtropical mountain rain-forest, with brilliant walking and swimming. Actually, the **Lamington Plateau** rates very highly with me – rugged wilderness area that you can really enjoy getting lost in. They lost a whole aeroplane in there once, years ago: the 'Stinson', it was called. The survivors were stuck on the mountainside for days until a local named Bernard O'Reilly organised a

rescue. (Apparently, the first thing they wanted to know when they were officially found was Bradman's score in the cricket test against England.) The O'Reillys still operate a very fine guest house in the Lamington area. If you've got time, a walking trek into the park is great. You can camp in there, so long as you get permission from the National Parks people at **Green Mountains**.

Another option for the Lamington Plateau is to take part in an organised bushwalking/mountain bike camping expedition. A weekend will cost you around $200, which ain't cheap, but since they feed you, provide all the equipment and get you in and out, it's not unreasonable. Contact **Borderline Bike Adventures** (07) 5545 3412 if you're interested.

If you've brought a halfway decent camera with you, consider joining up with a **Photo Geographic Day Safari** (07) 5534 8662. This is really only for people who actually want to take a few interesting photographs. If you're happy with the usual selection of out-of-focus, overexposed snaps of people whose names you can't quite remember, lurching drunkenly around hostel swimming pools, then forget it.

Personally, I think these photo safaris are a brilliant idea. You cough up $100 and bring your own camera. They provide lunch, transportation, tripods, permits from National Parks and Wildlife and a roll of film. (Bring more of your own. Definitely.) You get instruction from a pro photographer on how to do the nature shot thing and then they send you into one of the wildlife parks so you get to try out your skills on all kinds of creatures. After that, you do a rainforest run, through one of the World Heritage listed parks in the area.

This is a really brilliant arrangement. I mean, there's nothing so embarrassing as coming home from a great trip overseas with a bunch of shitty photographs. How can you make people properly jealous of your holiday with shots of the back of somebody else's head? At last, you'll be able to go home with crisp, clear photographs of things like crocodiles and cassowaries, kangaroos and koalas and you'll be able to nonchalantly explain to everyone that you took the snaps yourself.

Things To Avoid At The Gold Coast

Where to start? There's so much gross shit here. The first thing to consider would have to be **Schoolies Week**. This is a grotesque 'coming-of-age' ritual which occurs at the end of every academic year in late November. Thousands upon thousands of graduating schoolkids from Brisbane and all around come to the Gold Coast for a week of utter drunken frenzied brain-death.

It's a total mess. All the accommodation is snapped up and everywhere you go, herds of drunken seventeen-year-olds are making total dicks of themselves. Every year, the papers go apeshit with reports of underage drinking. The cops come out and arrest everyone in sight. The landlords complain about kids trashing their flats. The kids whinge about the ripoff prices charged by the landlords … yet still, they come.

Now if you're thinking this sounds like an opportunity to score some cute little schoolgirl/schoolboy tail – well, you're not the first to think of it. The only thing during Schoolies Week more nauseating than watching the Schoolies themselves, is watching the wet-lipped, slack-mouthed, sweaty-palmed drooling hordes of pathetic panty-sniffers who come out of the cracks in the sidewalk to ply the kids with booze and dope.

Next on the list of Things To Avoid would have to be the school holiday periods. The Gold Coast has been a sort of family penance to be done three times a year, every year, by Australians since time immemorial. Come those fateful days in January, May and August, the place just fills up with anxious, hypertensive parents and brutal, greedstricken cartoonfreak rugrats. This is not a sight for the faint of heart. I would be happy to pay very, very good money indeed just to be a long way away from the Gold Coast during the school holidays.

Flinthart's Journal

What is it about the Gold Coast? Something about it always grabs my attention, right down at the level of my gonads. Maybe it's the smell of money – big money, coming loose in freely spent gobs of ill-gotten illicit cash. Huge hi-rises built on foundations of sand and flogged off for three times their value before they're even half-complete ... hordes of Japanese tourists with baseball caps and golf habits that can only be assuaged on the $120 courses attached to every resort in sight ... fat councillors with numbered, anonymous accounts getting fatter every time a bleach-blonde hooker turns a trick.

Bucks. That's what it's all about. Good, honest greed. Sure, they've made a total fucking eyesore of a beautiful piece of coastline. Sure, fat pigs keep turning over megabucks by converting swampland into ultra-chic addresses with sad names like Fortress Harbour or Safety Bay. Sure, you can't walk three metres down Orchid Avenue after dark without some weasel-face in cheap Asian knockoffs of expensive European labels trying to hustle you into some dubious bar full of peroxide blondes with tits from Silicon Valley ... but hey! It's *caveat emptor*, right?

Let the Buyer Beware.

There's only two kinds of people on the Gold Coast. Sharks and itty-bitty super-tasty pilchards for the sharks to eat. Yum yum!

Then there's **Indy Season**. A few years ago, some silly bastards got the idea that what the Gold Coast really needed was to host one of the Indianapolis 500 formula races. Thus, every year in March, they start to fuck up the already chronic traffic problems by turning half the most important roads in Surfers into a racetrack. Hundreds of thousands of people turn up. No accommodation is available. No peace or privacy can occur. Americans arrive in droves.

I guess those are the three biggies. There's plenty of other stuff to avoid, though. Any tour or cruise through **Sanctuary Cove**, for example. Sanctuary Cove is one of these highly dubious swampland developments rammed through by good buddies of the old National Regime in Queensland. It's this ultra-chic walled suburb full of people with more money than sense – the kind of social maggot who's not secure enough with themselves to live anonymously, but have to gather in groups to reassure themselves that they're important. Paying money to go on a tour through their home territory would interest me only if shotguns and ammunition were thrown in for free.

Then there are the various canal cruises. Listen up: the waters behind **The Bar** are very, very placid. Climbing into a large power cruiser with forty or fifty other people and putt-putting through expensive canal developments, looking at high-rise skylines, eating shitty smorgasbord luncheons is just fucking boring. Don't do it.

Then there's golf. I'm sure that ordinarily, you're quite good at avoiding golf. I am. Trouble is, with so much Yakuza money being laundered here in the Gold Coast, it seems there's a golf course behind every goddamn public toilet.

And **Twin Towns Services Club**! Jesus fucking Christ on a hellbound Harley Davidson! Enter that place and you risk being instantly forced into a coma from which there is no awakening. Twin Towns is a special kind of hell where they send old people to watch all of those crappy entertainers you see who put out albums pushed by K-Tel at 2 am during the Creature Feature on Channel Ten. I mean, game show hosts get to sing at Twin Towns. And long-forgotten one-hit disco wonders, still in their original suit of glittery flares. Put a torch to the place!

Then there's **Jupiters Casino**. There are better ways of losing money than hanging around in a mega-tasteless Las Vegas-style clip joint. What's the point? You want the thrill of gaming, go to the track. At least you can watch the dogs and the horses. Look, if you've got a bunch of bucks you don't want, you can always send them on to me. I promise to find good homes for them all.

And theatre restaurants. I hope there's a special place in hell for the bastard who invented theatre restaurants. Unless you genuinely think that Benny Hill was a comic genius; unless you enjoy paying shitloads of money for crappy food served by irritating waiters in cheap costumes; unless you actively enjoy being bored stupid by the drunken antics of your fellow diners, you would be well advised to regard theatre restaurants in the same kind of light as a good dose of syphilis. Except that it's more fun catching syphilis than it is going to a theatre restaurant.

In And Out

Naturally, the Gold Coast has its very own airport, at **Coolangatta**. Fly to/from Sydney for about $270, Melbourne $400, Adelaide $440, Perth $650. Aside from the very recently arrived commuter train to Brisbane, there is no rail service to the Gold Coast. You can catch that train to Brisbane for about $10, though, and from there, if train travel is your little heart's desire, you can clickety-clack north, south, or west as you will. Alternatively, you could catch a bus to Murwillumbah and board a Sydney-bound train from there.

Many regular buses come down from Brisbane, if you're coming in from the north – not least being that nifty Jupiters Casino bus. (By the way, don't try to take a backpack on the Casino bus – they only want to move people who look like they're going to the coast to spend some bucks at the casino.)

There are two full-on **Transit Centres** on the Gold Coast. In Surfers Paradise, it's on the corner of Cambridge Rd and Beach Rd. Down in Coolangatta, the transit centre is on the corner of Warner and Griffith St.

Bus fares out vary between the three main carriers – **McCafferty's** and **Greyhound Pioneer** are roughly the same, but **Kirklands** undercuts them significantly on the more local runs. Brisbane will cost you about $12; Byron Bay is about $20 ($15 from Kirklands) and Sydney is anywhere from $65 to $75.

One very important note: hitch-hiking into or out of the Gold Coast is most definitely a bad idea. For starters, the local traffic conditions are absolutely shitty and anybody who pulls over for you is likely to cause a major accident. On top of that, the rapacious nature of the area seems to breed violence and weirdness. As long as you stick to doing pretty much standard tourist things, you'll be fine – but stepping outside the dotted lines can very easily bring you a lot of trouble. Even if you've been hitching on every other stage of your journey, I strongly recommend that you pony up the bucks for a bus fare through this area.

From south to north, the main regions of the Gold Coast – now all thoroughly blended into one another, are – **Coolangatta**, **Currumbin/ Palm Beach**, **Burleigh Heads/Miami**, **Mermaid Beach/Broadbeach** and **Surfers Paradise**, which includes **Main Beach** and **Southport**. The Gold Coast Highway snakes right through the lot, usually as the main street. If you're just trying to get around or through the Gold Coast, DON'T STICK TO THE GOLD COAST HIGHWAY. The Pacific Highway parts company with the Gold Coast Highway just short of Currumbin and heads inland to Brisbane at a much more effective pace. Following the Gold Coast Highway is just a good way to give yourself hypertension.

Shelter

Coolangatta YHA Hostel: (07) 5536 7644. 230 Coolangatta Rd, Bilinga. Costs under $15 for a bed. Reasonably good place, close to the beach (aren't they all?) and the airport, but not much else.

Big Backpacker's: (07) 5538 4633. 2623 Gold Coast Hwy, Broadbeach. Big. Very, very big. A converted nursing home, in fact. A bed costs about $15. The place is big, clean and practical, but not a lot of fun in itself.

Couple O' Days: (07) 5592 4200. 18 Whelan St, Surfers Paradise. It's cheap, coming in at $12 or less for a bed, but slightly tatty these days.

Surfers Paradise Backpacker's Resort: (07) 5592 4677. 2835 Gold Coast Hwy, Surfers Paradise. Costs about $15 for a bed. True to the name, the place comes with everything – pool, parking, gym, etc. Backpacking ain't what it used to be, is it?

Surf & Sun Backpacker's: (075) 538 7305. 3323 Gold Coast Hwy, Surfers Paradise. A converted hotel, very close to the beach, with a full-on, rage-til-ya-puke party atmosphere. Good facilities, but who's going to sleep?

Cheers Backpacker's: (07) 5531 6539. 8 Pine Avenue, Surfers Paradise. Big, new, clean and glossy. All the right stuff, including pool and barbecue facilities. Costs under $15 for a bed and once again, you'll get all the partying you can stand.

Trekkers: (07) 5591 5616. 22 White St, Southport. Probably the least irritating of the Gold Coast hostels. An old house, renovated up for the task of holding 'packers. The job has been done well and the place has a nice feel to it. They don't overstuff their dorms, either. Good value at about $15.

Gold Coast Backpacker's Resort: (07) 5531 2004. 44 Queen St Southport. Big, modern and cheap at about $12 for a bed.

There are also quite a few caravan parks scattered along the Gold Coast. They're no cheaper than the hostels and frankly, if you've come all this way to go camping, I'm fucked if I know why you'd want to camp in a caravan park on the Gold Coast. If you feel you must, though, try these:

Main Beach Caravan Park: (07) 5581 7722. Main Beach Pde, Main Beach. Tent sites under $15.

Miami Caravan Park: (07) 5572 7533. 2200 Gold Coast Hwy. Tent sites under $15.

Burleigh Beach Tourist Park: (07) 5581 7755. Goodwin Tce, Burleigh Heads. Tent sites under $15.

By the way: you'll be wasting your time if you try to find a spot in the caravan parks during the school holiday periods. The camping grounds are invariably filled to the brim and families actually keep coming back to the same reserved site on a yearly basis for bloody generations. You practically have to inherit a tent-site on the Gold Coast for school holidays.

Food

Seeing that most of the Gold Coast is dedicated to separating tourists from their bucks, you might well expect that there would be a very large range of places for eating out. You wouldn't be wrong. Eating cheaply,

Snapshots

Vicki from Dover: I am absolutely never ever going to go home. I mean, what's the point? You can hardly ever get mangoes in England and even when you do, they're never in very good condition.

Did I mention that I've become a mango addict? Oh God, I should have said that first. Mangoes. Oh my God, how have I spent twenty-one years without mangoes? I love them. I love the way they taste, the way they smell - that wonderful, sort of musky perfume. And the texture. I mean, not so much the wild mangoes. They're a bit stringy, although they'll do if there's nothing else available - but what about a big, perfectly ripened, juicy Bowen Mango? And some of the other varieties too. Strawberry mangoes and peach mangoes. They're really beautiful. I swear, when I take the first bite out of a big, fresh mango, the flavour just jolts right through me. All the way down to my crotch. Like sex, but it tastes better and lasts longer.

Do you know what I really want to do? No, truly. I mean, it's really kinky, but I think it sounds like heaven on earth. Oh God - what am I saying? You must promise me that if you publish this, you won't use my real name. Promise? Do you promise? Good. All right then.

What I really, really want to do, more than anything else in the whole world, is to be naked with Brad Pitt. In a jacuzzi. Full of ripe mangoes! There - I said it! Brad! Brad? Wait for me! I'll bring the mangoes!

though and enjoying it – that can be tricky.

Pub food is ever reliable and even on the Gold Coast, can be affordable. Try some of the surf-lifesaving clubs for similar fare.

If you've a yen for Japanese food, there are (perhaps unsurprisingly) a number of rather good Japanese restaurants in the area. Don't expect any bargains, but the quality and authenticity of the food is necessarily quite high. Try **Donto Sapporo** (07) 5539 9933 at 2763 Gold Coast Hwy in Broadbeach; you may not be able to afford much more than sushi, but it will be good sushi. At the cheaper end of the Japanese scale is **Cha Cha**, at the intersection of Surf and Victoria Avenues in Broadbeach. Cheaper than chips and very nice.

For an unusual food experience, try out **Medina's Stone Grill Café**

(07) 5538 1833 in Victoria Square on the Broadbeach mall. Basically, they cook your food on very hot rocks. Nice rocks, though − smooth, pretty pieces of granite and basalt. It's supposed to be very healthy, because there's no oil involved and it does impart an interesting sort of taste.

Actually, the Broadbeach mall is a good place to go looking for almost any kind of food. Thai, Indian, Mediterranean and of course, the ubiquitous burgers. A more reasonable sort of place for the budget is **Woody's Surf Restaurant** (07) 5538 0883 on the corner of the Gold Coast Hwy and Rosewood Avenue. The fare is pretty average, though fresh, well prepared and presented. They're clearly cashing in on the budget surf crowd, but with nothing costing more than $10, who cares?

Down in Burleigh Heads, the **Old Burleigh Theatre Arcade** on Goodwin Tce packs in a number of cheap and useful eateries, including a good Malay place and the popular **Montezuma's**, which naturally specialises in Mexican food. There's another **Montezuma's** in the Aloha Building at 8 Trickett St in Surfers Paradise. They're bright, cheerful places with a good line on food for about $10-$12 and a wicked way with the tequila.

If you're too drunk or too tired to go out, you can always try ordering in. **Lai's Chinese** (07) 5572 0122 will supply a range of standard Chinese dishes for about $10-$12. Delivery will cost $3 unless your order comes to more than $16. It's not a bad deal and there's some tasty options on the menu.

Down in Coolangatta, if you can bring yourself to enter the dire precincts of the **Twin Towns Services Club**, they have a snack bar with very decent meals at under $10. Also, the **Coolangatta Pie Shop** at 50 Griffith St is well known for its pies, pastries and bread. On weekends, it's open 24 hours, which can be very handy.

And in Surfers Paradise, just go to the **Cavill Avenue Mall**. The place is positively crawling with cheap food from all over the world.

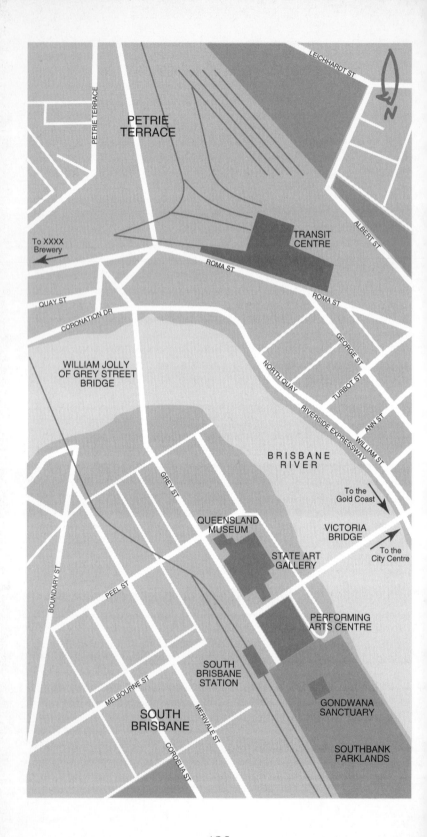

Brisbane

It is very popular to dump on Brisbane as a travel destination these days, so I'll jump right on the bandwagon and agree. So far as backpackers go, Brisbane's a bust. It hasn't got the night-life of Sydney, the culture of Melbourne, or the accessibility of Adelaide. The local transport is erratic and expensive and accommodation is at a premium. It is, however, a pleasant, friendly, easy-paced city with most of the facilities and amenities you'd expect from a place this size.

Best possible use for Brisbane, if you're on the road, is as a stopping place, where you catch your breath. Take a couple of days and chill out. Poke around. Sleep late. Eat modestly and well. After all, from Brisbane, you make the long run up to the Deep North, or you plunge into the strange decay of the South. Brisbane is not a place to see of its own.

Of course, it does have a few things to recommend it. I mean, I lived there for years – there must have been something, right? Let's see. There's the Gateway Bridge: sure, it's just another single-span concrete bridge over a muddy estuary, but hey, for a while there it was averaging more suicides than the Golden Gate. That's gotta be interesting, right?

That's Brisbane for you.

Brisbane is an easy place in which to orient yourself. The Brisbane River squirms muddily through the heart of it, with the city centre proper tucked into a bend about halfway between the Bay and the reservoir. There's only one city-heart section and the rest of the city sort of radiates out from there. Surrounding the centre and the godawful Queen St Mall, the older suburbs such as West End, Paddington, Fortitude Valley, Kelvin Grove and Highgate Hill still retain a little of the sort of lazy, small-town, big-verandah 'character' for which the city was once known. This 'inner ring' pretty much marks out the area that's actually worth walking about in. Most of the rest, with the exception of Queensland University and its immediate surrounds, has this monotonous sort of 'post-war' flavourlessness to it which rapidly jades even the most inquisitive traveller. Brisbane is an oasis of proper city surrounded by a groaning ocean of evil suburbiana.

Another reason for sticking mostly to the city centre is Brisbane's utterly appalling public transport system. In comparison with any other city of similar size anywhere else in the world, Brisbane's public transport is practically crippled. It's expensive, unreliable, poorly co-ordinated, doesn't go to most of the places you'd like it to go and stops functioning at an unconscionably early hour. If you stick to the city centre, at least you won't be forced to stand in the infamous cab queues along with hundreds of others at three in the morning …

Dirk's Dozen

1. **XXXX Brewery Tour** (07) 3361 7597: Okay, I like beer. Nonetheless, it's a cheap and interesting sort of tour anyway. And they give out free samples. Comes highly recommended from several veteran pissheads I talked to from a whole range of nations.

2. If you like drinking, head next for the **Story Bridge pub** at Kangaroo Point. It's an ex-bomb shelter and a fine place to hide from the summer heat. What another guide book might call 'a Brisbane institution', that is if it was in the habit of recommending places where bikies drink. But it's cool, very cool.

3. If you like painting, check the **Art Gallery**, if only for a walk out of the heat. There's a reasonably good collection, including Australia's best range of work from that Ian Fairweather chap.

4. A day trip to **North Stradbroke Island**, the poor man's Fraser Island – a 35km long island of fine white sand, hung on an extinct volcanic core, studded with lakes and strange wetland forests.

5. Visit **Moreton Island**, another enormous, mostly deserted sand island with fantastic, desolate surf beaches, clear lakes, huge sand dunes, forests, swamps, shipwrecks, lighthouse …

Stuff To Do

Fortitude Valley fancies itself a little rough after dark, but if you travel in pairs, you won't have any problems. Leave the pack at the hostel, though, right? The Valley carries what little overt sex trade prudish Brisbane boasts and frankly, it's not worth the effort. There's a couple of clubs that cater to the stressed and rabid businessman, but there's nothing like even the limited colour and life of the Cross down in Sydney. Also in The Valley, **Chinatown Mall** is a waste of time, unless you're looking for a cheap feed. It's small, fairly ugly and blatantly commercial without being particularly exotic.

If you're into nightclubs, there's a few of those in the Valley as well. Nothing particularly swish or challenging; try **The Zoo** in Ann St for laidback atmosphere, a bit of food and pool tables. Dodge the clubs and bars in the city centre; with the notable exception of **The Treasury**, they tend to be expensive and full of bad-mannered, drunken wannabe yuppy types.

The **Valley Mall** is awash in places to buy expensive coffee these days. Big privilege; sit out on the cobbles under an umbrella and watch the drunks stagger past. The coffee places are all pretty much the same; there's not much sense in choosing one above any other. **MacWhirters** on the corner of Wickham and Brunswick is a neat piece of work. Somebody redeveloped a building from the twenties and instead of just knocking it down and pouring plastic over it, they actually used the building to house a whole bunch of small businesses. Again, there's nothing particularly outstanding here, but it's nice to see a development which doesn't use the same evil architecture as every other plague-rotted mall on the planet.

The city centre proper is a place which has had most of the character and taste developed out of it during the eighties. **Queen St Mall** is a clone of hundreds of thousands of malls all over the world. The corruption-crazed National Party government of that era also encouraged the obliteration of most of the older, more interesting buildings in the city centre, replacing them with glass and steel needles. The exception is the old **Treasury Building**, which now houses a casino and wouldn't look out of place in downtown London. Also, **City Hall** on Albert Square is a nifty old building, with a museum tucked away inside. Take a ride up into the clock tower for the view and the adrenalin rush of The Bells at Twelve. On the whole, though, the centre of Brisbane is a commercial wasteland, devoid of taste or interest.

Across the **Victoria Bridge**, at South Bank, an attempt has been made to give the city some life. It could have been worse. There's a large, free-entry lagoon-style swimming pool which is extremely popular, a pleasant river-front boardwalk, some carefully-landscaped parkland and a couple of 'attractions'. Skip the **Gondwana Rainforest**, unless you don't intend to ever set foot in the real thing.

The South Bank complex also includes a couple of pleasant pubs, a few (generally overpriced and not particularly good) restaurants, a rather good night market which operates Friday evenings and the **Performing Arts Centre**. Across the street from the Arts Centre is the **Art Gallery** and the **Museum**. Both are worth a look in, entry being free except for special exhibits. The Art Gallery has a useful collection of Australian artists, including Queensland's greatest son (well, he was born in England – but he died here) Ian Fairweather.

Lone Pine Koala Sanctuary (07) 337801366, while not as big or impressive as Alma Park Zoo, is still worth a look-in if you haven't yet done the mandatory koala-cuddly thing. Best bet is to take a river cruise from North Quay in the city centre down to **Fig Tree Pocket**. They make it easy for you: you can cough up an all-inclusive $15 return for the river cruise and Lone Pine all in one.

Weekends mostly shut the whole city down. This is the cue for the **Riverside Market** to open up, on Eagle St, near the ferry stop. Riverside Markets are fairly swish and while you won't find any really amazing bargains, there's a lot of really good stuff there. In particular, take a look at **Pendragon Boots** – they make a wild buskin.

And that's about it. Frankly, if you don't know anyone in Brisbane, Sunday afternoons could easily start to look like the eighth circle of Hell. Rest and recuperate; consider taking a few day-trips to the surrounding areas. Then, when you're good and ready, hit the road again.

Day Trips

North Stradbroke Island. Take a Stradbroke Island bus out of Roma St at the Transit centre. It will take you out to Cleveland, where you'll catch a water taxi across to 'Straddie'. Costs about $25 return. Straddie is a poor man's Fraser Island – a 35km long island of fine white sand, hung on an extinct volcanic core, studded with lakes and strange wetland forests. It has a couple of things Fraser doesn't: small towns, for example, where supplies, including the all-important Beer, can be purchased at prices which aren't too ruinous. **Dunwich**, on the western side, is the largest town and even has an ANZ bank, which is about the only place to deal with money, with the exception of a couple of EFTPOS locations. Unfortunately, as the western shore faces Moreton Bay, the swimming sucks and the surf is non-existent.

The eastern shore, while less convenient, is essentially one long, glorious stretch of deserted sand, pounded by massive Pacific surf. You can hang around **Point Lookout** village, if you like – rent surfboards, eat at the local pubs and clubs – but I think the best thing to do is grab some supplies and take off down the beach for a few days. There are a bunch of official campsites on the island, but at this point, nobody seems too concerned if you want to do a spot of camping just off the deserted beach a few kilometres from anywhere. That is, nobody minds so long as you don't light fires, abandon your rubbish, or do anything else stupid or antisocial.

There's a particularly good hostel on Straddie, conveniently sited at Point Lookout, near the beach. It's the **Stradbroke Island Guesthouse** (07) 3409 8888 which will bed you down for about $15. Best thing about it is the pickup bus it runs from Brisbane, opposite the Roma St Transit Centre three days a week for about $5. It helps if you book and they will also pick up from some of the Brisbane hostels.

Actually, it's quite remarkable that Straddie has remained so beautiful and largely deserted when you realise that it's only spitting distance from the two largest cities in the state. It's a popular daytrip destination for locals and can get a little crowded during Christmas and Easter, but on the whole, the place has been well looked after and you can have a really great time trekking around it for a pittance.

Moreton Island. Still another enormous, mostly deserted sand island with fantastic, desolate surf beaches, clear lakes, huge sand dunes, forests, swamps, shipwrecks, lighthouse … Moreton is less developed even than Fraser and isn't easy to get around on. You can take your own 4WD vehicle across from **Whyte Island**, near the mouth of the Brisbane River, for $85 return (including passengers), or just tough it out on foot, for $18. Most of the island is national park and there are designated campsites with water, where you can put up a tent for the piffling sum of $3 per night. Camping on Moreton is a really lovely option. It's not nearly so heavily used as Fraser or Straddie and has almost all the best features of both. There's a couple of small villages on the island, but supplies are relatively expensive, so if you're thinking of a prolonged camping trip, be prepared to carry a lot of your own food.

It's not difficult to navigate on Moreton Island – there are quite a few old tracks left behind from the sand-mining days and seeing that it's only about 35km long and 10km across at the widest, walking is a much more reasonable option here than on Fraser. There's a popular and expensive tourist resort on the western side of the island at Tangalooma and they operate a ferry which can be used to daytrip as well, for about $25. It's a lot faster than the vehicle ferry.

If you want to see something of the famous sand islands of southern Queensland and can't bear the idea of slogging around Fraser in the company of a horde of other backpackers, Moreton Island is a very good compromise. Contact the **National Parks and Wildlife** office in Brisbane, 160 Ann St, (07) 3227 8185 about maps and camping permits before you go.

Snapshots

Jim from Oregon: I don't know why the Europeans don't like Aussie beer. It tastes pretty good to me. First time I ever left the States - except for Canada and that don't count - I came to Australia. Landed in Brisbane. I stayed at a place in New Farm, near a pub on … what was it … Brunswick St. They had a lot of backpackers there. It was a good place, with a lot of atmosphere.

Only thing I couldn't work out was why I kept getting filthy drunk. First night, I had six beers and they had to practically carry me back. All these British guys kept laughing at me. I thought it was the jet-lag though, so on the second night, I set out to show them what I could do.

This time, I got through eight beers in two hours and they really did have to carry me back. I threw up all over the place. Next morning, I had a bit of a thought and looked at the label on the beer.

Well, shit! It said 5 percent alcohol! In America, the label on the beer usually won't tell you how much is in it, but I know that most of the American brews are about 2.5 percent - what you guys call a Light Beer. Only for us, a Light Beer means lo-cal. Anyway, in America, if it's over about 4 per cent alcohol, you're not supposed to call it beer at all. You're supposed to call it Malt Liquor - and only hard-core drunks buy malt liquor. Now I know why all the Aussies I met in the States used to laugh at Budweiser!

The Sunshine Coast and the Gold Coast. These day trips are easy to do and relatively cheap by commuter train, from the **Roma St Transit Centre**. In fact, for my money the best possible way to see the Gold Coast – if you insist on seeing it at all – is by way of a daytrip out of Brisbane. Check out the **Jupiter's Casino** bus from the Transit Centre at 9am daily – costs $10 return, (which is cheaper than the usual bus-fare anyway) and they give you a meal voucher and a $5 casino voucher as well – so in essence, the ride comes free of charge.

Reaching the pretty villages and scenic drives of the **D'Aguilar Ranges** and the **Glasshouse Mountains** north of Brisbane requires a vehicle of your own. Overnight car rental will cost you a little over $50, with a security deposit against accidents or theft, of $500. This deposit is usually taken as a debit slip against your credit card and returned to you once the car is returned intact. The trip is well worth the effort, however. This region abounds in scenic winding roads, little out-of-the-way parks and waterfalls, country pubs just laden with atmosphere and bizarre little craft shops in peculiar mountain villages.

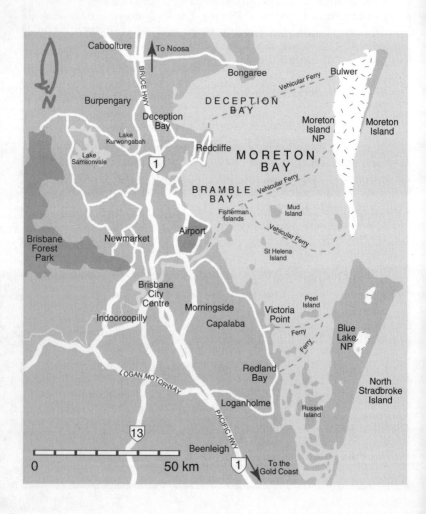

The **Gold Coast Hinterlands**, including **Lamington National Park**, **Numinbah Valley**, **Mt Tamborine** and the **Springbrook Plateau** are also easily accessible as a daytrip from Brisbane. It is even possible to find daytrip bus tours to this region, which features beautiful rainforests, precipitous waterfalls and excellent walking tracks. Costs vary between about $40 and $55, depending on whether or not lunch, etc is included in the return trip. Contact **Far Horizons** (3284 5475) or **Allstate Scenic Tours** (3285 1777) if this sounds like a good idea to you.

In And Out

Brizz isn't nearly so confusing as Sydney. There's one big highway south, one big highway north and a westward one which leads to Ipswich and Certain Doom. Don't go that way. They all play banjo with their toes. Rail and bus routes both converge on the **Roma St Transit Centre**, a humungous complex about three blocks northwest of the city centre. This spot handles everything, including the only bus to the airport. (Remember what I said about Brisbane and public transport? Can you believe a capital city with no train and only one hourly bus to the airport? Weird!)

If you need road maps or advice on roads, call the **Royal Queensland Automobile Club** on 3361 2444.

Trains are an excellent way of day-tripping out of Brisbane, as regular commuter trains go to both the Sunshine Coast and the Gold Coast. Phone 13 2232 for information and bookings, or just go straight to the **Railway Travel Centre** at Central Station, Ann and Edward Sts in the city heart. Train to the Sunshine Coast is about $20 return and the trip one way takes a bit over an hour. Train to the Gold Coast is about the same. Train any further in Queensland is a hideous and painful waste of time and money.

Buses, as usual, are the mainstay of the budget traveller. In Queensland, the two companies you're likely to deal with are **Greyhound Pioneer** (13 2030) and **McCafferty's** (3236 3033), both of which operate out of the Roma St Transit Centre. Going northwards, the fare scheme is roughly this: Noosa – 3 hours, $15; Hervey Bay – 5 hours, $35; Rockhampton – 10 hours, $60; Mackay – 15 hours, $87; Townsville – 21 hours, $120; and Cairns – 24-28hrs, $135.

Hitching is entirely plausible, but the best way to do it is to catch the electric commuter train to the end of the line and then look for an appropriate bit of highway. Hitching the highways close to or actually within Brisbane is a serious losing proposition.

Air travel is another option. Brisbane's airport is well outside the city centre and is very poorly serviced indeed by public transport. The domestic and international terminals are actually quite widely separated, but there is a shuttle bus that runs between the two, fortunately. There are frequent flights to Sydney and Melbourne, Rockhampton, Mackay, Townsville and Cairns and international destinations in Europe, America, New Zealand, the South Pacific, Asia and Papua New Guinea.

Again, if you are planning any air travel within Australia, it is far, far cheaper to book from overseas. Domestic air travel in Australia is prohibitively expensive. If you suddenly decide there's something you absolutely must see that's not on your itinerary, see if you can get there by bus, train, or car before you resort to making last-minute air bookings.

Presuming that you must do so, however, fares one-way from Brisbane are approximately as follows: Sydney – $250; Melbourne – $380; Darwin – $600; Perth – $650; Cairns – $400; and Rockhampton – $220. This is a rough indication only. Fares fluctuate wildly depending on the season, the financial climate, the whims of the Government and what the pilots had for dinner last night. Ask around if you decide to travel by air and remember that hostel noticeboards are often a good source of information regarding unwanted air tickets.

Shelter

Not being such a major destination as Sydney, Brisbane is rather less well-catered for in terms of budget accommodations. Also, since there isn't the same degree of competition as, say, Cairns or Airlie Beach, there's not a lot of incentive on hostel-operators to really chase after business and service and facilities are (to be charitable) somewhat variable. This is one place where it would definitely repay your efforts to read the guidebook and to spend a few dollars on the public phones in the Roma Street Transit Centre before deciding where you were going to spend the night.

New Brisbane YHA: 392 Upper Roma St (07) 3236 1004. Very handy to the Roma St Transit Centre, situated between the somewhat yuppiefied suburb of Paddington and the city centre proper. Good facilities, cost about $16 for non YHA sorts; suffers from lack of parking and that peculiar brand of YHA Nazism which is the bane of travellers the world over.

City Backpacker's: 380 Upper Roma St (07) 3211 3221. Again, the location is very handy. A relatively new, well-cared for facility. Non-smoking, about $13. A bit soulless.

Somewhere To Stay: Brighton/Franklin Sts, Highgate Hill (07) 3846 2858. Big, bold and brassy. Probably comes closest to the kind of all-in service you might expect from a decent inner-city hostel. Lots of accommodation options, down as low as $12. Pool, great facilities, plus lots of information and assistance available. A little large, though – has some of that 'hotel' feeling, rather than the comfortable anarchy of a proper hostel.

Sly Fox Hotel: 73 Melbourne St, South Brisbane (07) 3844 0022. Great location, in an old hotel right next to the State Museum and Performing Arts Centre. Easy walk to the South Bank complex, the city centre and eclectic West End. Lively and energetic, which is a plus in Brisbane. It's a little noisy, though – the pub often has live music. Also, being an older building, it's somewhat worn and the kitchen facilities aren't really up to speed. Lots of atmosphere, though. Good place to come if you're looking to party down and cheap enough at under $15.

Balmoral House: 33 Amelia St, Fortitude Valley (07) 3252 1397. Recently refurbished, clean, very well appointed and somewhat chillingly quiet. This YHA affiliate is definitely not a party zone. Under $15, but really, only for the up-at-5am calisthenics and muesli mob.

Courtney Place: 50 Geelong St, East Bris (07) 3891 5166. Nice place, quiet and comfortable, with a good setup. Reputedly, the house was purpose-built as a family home by a chap with a disquietingly high sperm count and far too many offspring. Slightly out-of-the-way, but buses and ferries to the city are available. About $12.

Banana Benders: 118 Petrie Tce, Petrie Terrace (07) 3367 1157. Petrie Terrace is a major arterial road in Brisbane's choked inner-city traffic flow. The hostel is quite decent and the location is convenient, but don't try to hear yourself think during the rush hour. About $13.

Aussie Way: 34 Cricket St, Petrie Terrace (07) 3268 2823. Down a side street from Petrie Terrace proper, this is a quiet and unassuming little place. Good value at about $13.

Pete's Palace: 515 Brunswick St New Farm (07) 3254 1984. A somewhat ramshackle three-storey job with loads of atmosphere. Looks as though it may have been a brothel at some time in the past and the decor is somewhat unusual, but it's got all the appropriate fixtures and fittings. About $12 and worth the price if only to get a feel of what Brisbane can be like when it's in the mood. (Eccentric as all hell.)

Atoa House: 95 Annie St, New Farm (07) 3358 4507. A complex of three adjacent houses. Relaxed, friendly, off the beaten track and blessed with plenty of yard space. Beds start at about $15, but they may let you put up a tent in the back yard for under $10.

Food

The City of Brizz is relatively new to the concept of cheap, enjoyable food. Mostly, eating out in the past has been either a dreary family ritual of glutinous grey Chinese noodles and chips, or a monumentally expensive exercise in Eurofood-snobbery. Fortunately, things have begun to open up a little and it is now possible to eat moderately well on a budget without leaving the state.

The cheap munchies scene in Brisbane is very much a locality thing. Look in the Valley for good Chinese food in the **Chinatown Mall**. The **Valley Mall** is also home to a never-ending stream of al fresco cafés and coffee shops, which serve pleasant food at a price which for Brisbane, is okay.

Special recommendation goes to **Lucky's Trattoria** (07) 3252 2353 in 683 Anne St, near the Red Garter, down in the Valley. Excellent Italian food, with enormous servings at very affordable prices. Most importantly, though, it's a relaxed and friendly place, with bulk atmosphere and sassy waitresses. Also, the proprietor – Lucky – is something of a fixture in Brisbane. He's had the place for more than a quarter of a century and if you can get him talking, he'll tell you more about the place than any guidebook could ever hope to.

Over in West End, amidst the plethora of coffee shops (amongst which **Café Babylon** on Boundary St and **The Three Monkeys** at the West End Roundabout must be rated the absolute standouts) **Qan Heng's** serves up extremely good Vietnamese food at ludicrously low prices. West End in general is a good place for wandering around and fossicking for food: if you like Lebanese nosh, try **King Ahiram's**, at the intersection of Vulture and Boundary streets. Not far away is the **Greek Club**. Brisbane has a fairly sizeable Greek community, sited mostly in West End and if you like Greek food, the Greek Club next to Mowbray Park is the place to look.

The city centre itself is a bit sterile and most of the fooderies are of the 'shopping-mall foodcourt' variety. Notable exceptions are **A Kabab** at 227 Albert St, which makes a cheap and very mean kebab with all the trimmings and the **Irish Club** at 175 Elizabeth St. This last is an amazing place. Looks perfectly ordinary from the street, but once you get inside, it's positively huge. It's open to visitors and serves good solid Irish fare at very reasonable rates. An excellent place to stop for a bite and a pint of reasonably decent Guinness.

Paddington is another area replete with interesting eateries. Unfortunately, due to the 1980s Invasion of the Killer Yuppies, Paddington prices tend to be hurtful. Still, if you want a truly memorable seafood feed, try **Gambaro's**, near the intersection of Caxton St and Petrie Tce. Your budget will hate you, but you will never forget the experience. Ask for the Thai Chilli Mud Crab.

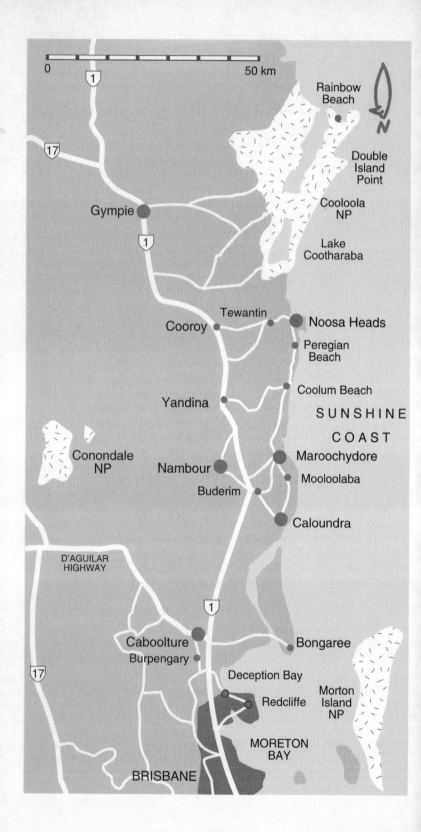

Noosa and the Sunshine Coast

There's a whole stretch of really lovely terrain that starts about 70km north of Brisbane, at Caloundra and continues through Maroochydore and Noosa all the way up to Rainbow Beach. The shores are fine, broad, gorgeous sandy beaches with magnificent surf and just inland, the dramatic Glasshouse Mountains rise all grey and jagged out of an ocean of green. There's pretty little villages, winding roads, waterfalls, patches of rainforest – all in all, a near-paradisical sort of location.

Unfortunately, everybody knows about it. As a result, most of the rainforest is gone, the pretty little villages have got their hooks out for the tourist dollar and the beach regions have undergone extensive development. Of course, it's still possible to have a great time and thoroughly enjoy the Sunshine Coast; you're just going to have to bear with the fact that you're not the first person to think of it … You might want to drop in on Noosa and then head on to less developed areas further north.

Stuff To Do

Rule One – On The Sunshine Coast, We Surf. Grab a board and hit the tubes, dudes. Doesn't matter whether you're a rank amateur or a rated pro; the surf along this stretch of coast is absolutely brilliant. There's room enough for everyone, even the oft-despised Boogie Board riders.

Of course, when you're done surfing, there's quite a lot more to be seen and done around here. Top of the list would have to be hiring yourself a canoe and disappearing up the **Noosa River** into **Cooloola National Park**. This is an exquisite, brilliant excursion. The waters are tranquil and extensive, lined with undisturbed native vegetation. There are also quite a number of campsites set up along the Noosa River well into Cooloola and being a national park, permits cost only $3 per night. Personally, I rate a two or three day canoe-camping excursion into **Cooloola** as the standout, must-not-be-missed piece of action on the Sunshine Coast. Expect to pay $30-$50 per day for rental of a big Canadian-style canoe – but if you're careful, you'll fit two people, minimal camping gear, plus supplies into the one canoe. Excellent value.

A pleasantly off-beat way to spend an evening is to make your way to tiny **Pomona**, about 20km northwest of Noosa. There's bugger-all to be seen or done here, with the notable exception of the most excellent **Majestic Cinema** (074) 852 330, built in 1921 and still going strong. The Majestic screens old silent and classic films and the owner accompanies on his pipe-organ in the manner of the original silent cinemas. Catch the weekly showing of Valentino's 'Son Of The Sheik' for a really entertaining evening.

Saturday mornings, in the nearby village of **Eumundi**, the famous **Eumundi Markets** come to life. Shouldn't miss this, if you have any flea-market genes anywhere in your body. There's over 200 stalls and the place is expanding at a frightening rate. They've got practically everything for sale there, including the delicious local fruits and vegetables. And naturally, the town is positively infested with craft shops, galleries, potteries, antique shops and all sorts of Ye Olde Goode Stuffe like that. Worth a look-in.

At **Yandina**, not far away, you can find out anything and everything you ever wanted to know about ginger at **The Ginger Factory**. It's a bit tourist-oriented, but personally, I like ginger. Ginger wine, ginger beer, preserved ginger, gingerbread … yeah, ok – it's a personal taste. Mind you, it's free to get in and they've got a whole bunch of other stuff there as well, like a wildlife park and train rides, so it's not a complete waste of time. Helps if you like ginger, though.

If you have access to any sort of vehicle at all, a day spent driving around the **Glasshouse Mountains** is worth the effort. The mountains, jagged, cragged old things, are volcanic cores which jut inexplicably up from the surrounding plains like petrified giants. There's no camping-grounds around here, which is a pity, but there are any number of picnic grounds, walking tracks, lookouts and rock-climbing areas. A number of companies in both Brisbane and the Sunshine Coast organise rock-climbing expeditions to these precipitous peaks; check with your hostel for details of cost and the amount of experience required.

It would be a good idea, if you were in the area, to check out the Glasshouse Mountains while you still can. Although a small part of the area is now designated national park, large parts are quietly under threat from quarrying, with the support of the area council. Local residents and visitors alike are horrified by the prospect of the magnificent peaks being turned into gravel, but big bucks are what count in Queensland, as usual – and gravel means money.

On the way to Maroochydore, just south of Caloundra, the **Queensland Reptile Fauna Park** (074) 941 134 has a very good range of creatures, well-kept and displayed. Demonstrations include snake-milking and occasional crocodile feeding. This is an excellent opportunity to familiarise yourself with the slithery bastards before you have to run the risk of confronting them in their home territory, further north.

If you've managed to avoid the giant aquariums at Sydney and Townsville, then you might consider a visit to **Underwater World** at Mooloolaba. It's supposed to be the biggest in the southern hemisphere – though the one in Sydney makes similar claims – and has the inevitable walk-through perspex tunnel so the fish can look at you properly. Costs a bit, at about $15, but to be fair, it's a hell of an oceanarium and if you can't catch up with the others, you might want to try this one. Of course, diving on the reef is a much more interesting option.

If your stay on the Sunshine Coast occurs around New Years Day, you should certainly consider visiting the **Maleny-Woodford Folk Festival.** This is a massive event and getting bigger. It lasts five days and attracts thousands and thousands of people from all over the place. Every aspect of folk culture, music and craft is represented in some form and there is quite a strong Aboriginal presence, which is refreshing, to say the least.

Actually, the Maleny/Woodford region is another really pretty area. **Maleny** itself is a nice little village, set high in the mountains. Drive around; you'll find parks, waterfalls, walking tracks, old pubs with lots of ambience, amazing views of the coast and a hundred other diversions. It's especially nice because it's cool, breezy, green and not too heavily touristed as yet.

In And Out

Dead easy, from Brisbane. The **Bruce Highway**, (the main route north) parallels the coast, with turnoffs at regular intervals for the various settlements on either side. It's about an hour's drive in a private vehicle.

Another way to do it is to take advantage of the fast and comfortable electric commuter train service which these days runs about as far north as Nambour. Catch the train from the **Roma St Transit Centre**, or from **Central Station** in the city heart. It'll cost you under $12 to get out there. This is a lot easier than hitch-hiking and if you haven't got your own vehicle, is definitely the preferred option. Unfortunately, getting from the train line to the coast can be quite difficult. Buses run to the coast from **Nambour** station and **Cooroy** station, but for the rest, it's hitch-hiking, walking, or an expensive cabfare. If you're planning on staying on the Sunshine Coast for a while, it's a good idea to call one of the hostels in advance and see if you can get a pick-up from the nearest railway station. Most of them will be happy to co-operate.

Naturally, since the highway runs through the region, you can get on any of the long-distance bus services, although only **Greyhound Pioneer** will actually leave the Bruce Highway and detour down to the coast. **Suncoast Pacific** (074) 431 011 are really the people you want to talk to about bus services to and from Brisbane and along the coastal strip: they run about ten buses a day and of these, quite a few actually swing past the airport on their way out of town! These leave from the Roma St Transit centre at all hours and the fare to Noosa will set you back about $15. It'll take nearly three hours, though.

Going north from the Sunshine Coast is a little more twisty. Regular long-distance train stops at **Yandina** and the **Nambour** rail-point, and from here you can catch the **Sunlander**, the **Queenslander** and every other one of the boring trains on offer. **Greyhound Pioneer** runs a daily service in and out of Noosa, from the bus terminal at the corner of Noosa Dve and Noosa Pde. **McCafferty's** don't bother with Noosa at all. **Greyhound** also do a daily service in and out of Maroochydore, to the **Suncoast Pacific Bus Terminal** on First Avenue.

Shelter

Most of the backpacker action is concentrated at Noosa, on the northern end of the Sunshine Coast strip. Noosa has become a bit of a mecca lately and despite locals growling about overdevelopment and strict rules on what and where you can build, the place is starting to look a bit too much like a suburb composed of Club Meds for my taste. Nonetheless, the local terrain is pretty amazing and what with the strong social scene as well, there's quite a few very good places to stay. Competition has ensured that the degree of service and the facilities available are up there with the best of backpackerdom anywhere.

Koala Beach Resort: 44 Noosa Dr (074) 473 355. This is a very popular spot, linked to the other Koala Resort in Hervey Bay. It's a kind of self-contained 'packers resort, all in one. A converted motel, you can get a bed for under $15, or you can get an entire room to yourself for substantially more. The place has watersports gear and bicycles, information on sights and tours, cheap meals, a pool, good facilities, a bar, a savage social and party scene and I suppose, if you wanted to, you'd never have to leave at all.

Noosa Backpacker's Resort: 9-13 William St, Noosa (074) 498 151. Excellent facilities, very popular. Boasts a small Thai restaurant! Very helpful in arranging tours and trips. A bed is less than $15.

Melaluka Units: 7 Selene St, Noosa (074) 473 663. I wonder why they continue to mis-spell Melaleuca? (Ti-tree, source of the medicinal oil.) Doesn't matter. Top facilities for about $15, in any one of a bunch of units in the area. Check the sauna and the laundry facilities.

Backpacker's On The Beach: 26 Stevens St, Sunshine Beach (074) 474 739. The usual for Noosa. Beds under $15, all kinds of beach gear and bicycles available, excellent accommodation and facilities.

Camping at Noosa

What with the fine climate and the delightful local scenery, camping in the Noosa region is more a pleasure than a way of stretching the budget. For the most part, though, local camping is actually no cheaper than the hostels, since it's pretty much limited to caravan parks. Try the **Munna Point Caravan Area** at Russell St in Noosaville (074) 497 050. Nice locality and you can get a tent site for only about $11.

Slightly south of Noosa, the splendid beaches at **Coolum** and **Peregian** have been considerably less developed. The surf is still quite good, though, and accommodation for the budget traveller is available. **Coolum Beach Backpacker's**: 285 David Low Way, Coolum Beach. (074) 716 666 if you're prepared to go camping. The Peregian Beach Caravan Park (074) 481 223 on the David Low Way has sites for about $12 in a pleasant setting. On the foreshore of Coolum proper is the Coolseas Caravan Park (074) 461 474, operated by the local council which has sites for under $12.

Further south still, the Maroochydore/Mooloolaba area has three hostels.

Cotton Tree Backpacker's: 15 The Esplanade, Maroochydore (074) 437 544. Lovely old place looking out on the river. A bed costs about $12.

Sunshine Coast – Places To Avoid: Wherever the natural beauty of an area brings in the tourists, sooner or later some prawn starts thinking in terms of Giant Fruit. I don't know why this is. Anyway, the sight of the 15m tall Big Pineapple looming over the skyline at Nambour nearly frightened poor Benko into barfing up his breakfast kelp. Or whatever the green stuff was he'd eaten. He pointed at this awful monstrosity and jabbered away in furious Japanese, of which I understood not a word. Didn't matter. Some ideas are universal. I nodded a lot, shouted 'Banzai' occasionally and when he paused for breath, passed him the bottle of Ouzo. We managed to get by without anyone having to commit seppuku.

He managed to accept the weirdly-bent Ettamogah Pub with the ageing Model-T on top, probably because he didn't know it was a franchise based on a cartoon strip, but down at Bli Bli, poor Benko's eyes bugged out of his head again. This time he was staring at the bloody awful Bli Bli castle. I don't blame him. I have friends who are big on the medieval re-enactment thing; every year, they spend days standing around Caloundra's Abbey Museum sweating in meticulously crafted metal armour under the staggering Queensland sun. The sight of a Ye Olde Concrete Blocke Medieval Castle complete with Ye Red Fibro Turrets sends them into rabid paroxysms every time they pass it.

Just for kicks, I surreptitiously guided the Red Terror off the highway, back around near the airport to Nostalgia Town. Like many Japanese, Benko was a big golf fan. Nostalgia Town was the final straw for him ... he must have simply had too much of a sense of good taste to bear it. Last time I saw him, he was standing in the middle of the Graveyard Mini-Golf, holding a putter like it was a katana, threatening this enormous American woman in a livid purple muu-muu and screaming in hi-speed samurai.

He was too uptight to be a good navigator anyway, I figured.

Maroochydore YHA Backpacker's: 24 Schirrman Dve (074) 433 151. Neat, tidy and well-kept, with a real line on local events and entertainment. Very laid-back so far as YHA places are concerned. Costs about $12 a bed, a little more for non-YHA members.

Suncoast Backpacker's Lodge: 50 Parker St, Maroochydore (074) 437 544. Not bad. Has all the usual facilities and the bed price is $12, or thereabouts.

If you go as far south as Caloundra on the Sunshine Coast, you reach the limit of the decent surf beaches. After this, it's all Moreton Bay until you hit the Gold Coast. Caloundra has been a family outing site for Brisbane since it was a penal colony, so as a result, the place is kind of built-up. There's no hostel action there at the moment, so if you decide that Caloundra is the place for you, it's going to be either a caravan park, or start shelling out the bucks.

Hibiscus Holiday Park: Bowman/Landsborough Park Rd (074) 913 342. Tent sites about $10, on-site vans available.

Food

Noosa is the big noise in food hereabouts. In fact, Noosa is a big noise in food no matter how you slice it. Check Hastings St for a plethora of very fine dining – though the prices are a little on the brutal side. Style plays a big part too – Noosa is very trendy and stylish. See **Saltwater** at 8 Hastings St (074) 472 234 for open-air rooftop dining, for example – although their fine take-away section downstairs is more likely to suit a traveller's pinched budget.

More affordably, the **Bay Village Food Court** has a whole range of the usual food purveyors. Open for lunch, they also do dinner in the money season. In Noosa Junction, on Sunshine Beach Rd, **Roma Pizza** is locally famous for its all-you-can-eat pizza/pasta nights. $6 or so and you supply your own wheelchair to roll your groaning, overstuffed self away afterwards.

Down in Noosaville (these names get a bit monotonous, don't they)? there's a couple of good value venues. The **Villa Noosa Hotel** has cheap drinks and decent pub fare for a pittance and on Gympie Terrace, near the river, the **Noosa Yacht & Rowing Club** does the same kind of thing. Never knock a good pub meal; it may not be haute cuisine, but frequently, pub food is just about the best value around.

In Coolum and Peregian, with the lower level of development, it's pretty much catch-what-you-can. There's a sufficiency of little eateries to be found, but nothing that really stands out as value for money.

Maroochydore boasts **Leftys BYO** (074) 437 891 at 24 The Esplanade. Mexican-Mediterranean Food; it's not exactly super-cheap, but there's plenty of it and it's rather good.

Down in Mooloolaba, try the **Wharf** complex on the river. There's a whole bunch of Food places in there, some of which are quite cheap – especially in the Food court in the middle of the place.

Gympie

A pretty little town about 200km north of Brisbane, it bills itself as the Town That Saved Queensland. In the 1860s, the colony of Queensland was up shit creek financially. A banking crisis brought the situation to a head and in desperation, the government put up a truckload of cash for anybody who could find payable gold in Queensland. Enter a chap named James Nash, who found gold in the Mary River. He collected the cash and precipitated the first of the Queensland gold rushes – some 15,000-odd diggers who went utterly berserk all over the area. The Gympie fields produced some good finds, including the famous Curtis Nugget, which was a lot bigger than a lump of gold has a right to be. However, the gold rush pretty much marked the high-water point for Gympie. Nothing much of note ever happened there again and aside from rich local agriculture, the place is still living off its fame as a gold-mining town. The place is on the main highway, but it isn't really worth a stop, except perhaps for lunch. Turn east for the coast from here, if you want to see something decent.

Cooloola National Park

Bordered to the south by Noosa and ending at Rainbow Beach to the north, Cooloola National Park is a remarkable and beautiful stretch of terrain. The undeveloped wilderness terrain includes mangrove estuaries, heathlands, forests of several kinds, lakes and of course many kilometres of isolated, beautiful sandy beaches.

It's a huge place – over 54,000 hectares of land. It is possible to drive through it from north to south in a conventional vehicle, despite the fact that it's mostly grounded on sand, but the very best way to explore Cooloola is definitely by boat. The Noosa River runs deep into the heart of Cooloola, widening out into broad, shallow lakes at intervals and it is easy to hire a canoe or an outboard dinghy from Tewantin or Noosa, at the mouth of the river.

If you choose to drive, be aware that in wet weather the track can become completely impassible to conventional cars. Otherwise, if you head to the villages of Wolvi or Kin-Kin (I'm not making these names up, you know) and look for the road that connects them, you'll find a road that turns off, into the park itself. This is an inexpressibly magical drive – an absolute must if you have your own vehicle. It cuts out a very large and unattractive chunk of the main highway, by cutting through the Cooloola park to Rainbow Beach. In fact, if you so desire, you can dodge the highway all the way to Hervey Bay, starting with this beautiful little stretch of road: there's a road from Rainbow Beach direct to Tin Can Bay and from there to Maryborough and from there to Hervey Bay – all without ever returning to the highway. This diversion comes highly recommended; you'll have at least 1,500km of highway driving ahead of you, if you're headed for Cairns. Why not take the opportunity to try out a couple of scenic back roads while you have the chance?

145

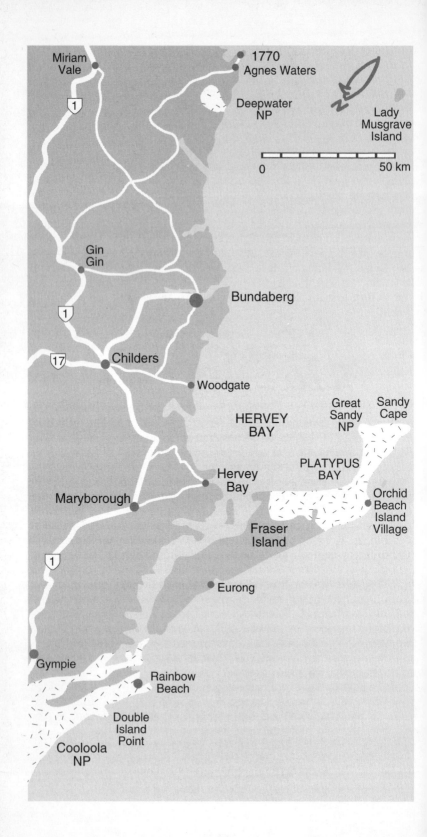

Rainbow Beach to 1770

This covers about 250km of coast. Aside from Fraser Island, accessible from Hervey Bay, Noosa and Rainbow Beach, the region boasts the last of Queensland's broad and beautiful surf beaches. Past 1770, the influence of the Barrier Reef keeps the waves and currents from forming up properly, meaning the beaches are narrower and steeper, with coarser sand and lots of bloody shore-break. On the other hand, the start of the Barrier Reef means you can now really go for the scuba diving and snorkelling thing.

Dirk's Dozen

1. **Fraser Island tour:** either walking, which is strenuous and won't show you a lot of this huge World Heritage sand island, or in a rented 4WD vehicle from Hervey Bay. Don't miss this island.

2. Gorgeous, deserted **Rainbow Beach** itself.

3. **Learn to scuba dive in Bundaberg.** Open-water accreditation for $150. It doesn't get any cheaper anywhere.

4. Chill out for a couple of days at **1770** and **Agnes Waters**.

5. Consider scraping together some bucks and doing a camp on **Masthead Island** – deserted coral cay national park with a brilliant lagoon, snorkelling and diving.

Dirk Dumps On

1. **Gin Gin.**

2. **Miriam Vale.**

3. **Maryborough.**

4. **Hervey Bay**, except for getting to Fraser and whale-watching.

5. **Bert Hinkler** (see below).

Rainbow Beach

If you're looking for a beach sojourn which is off the beaten trail, **Rainbow Beach** is just what you wanted. Going north along the highway, the trick is to turn hard right at Gympie, then follow the road-signs about 75km to the sea. There's not very much to be found at Rainbow Beach.

Follow the beach south and you'll come to coloured sand cliffs for which the area is named. Nearby is the impressive **Carlo Sand Blow** and the northern access to the **Cooloola National Park**. Beyond that, there's a little village, a surf-life-saving club (which is the nearest thing to a pub for nearly 100km) and not a whole lot else.

On the other hand, the beach is gorgeous. It's long, wide, flat and comes equipped with truly magical surf. This is another one of those places where you can basically just pick a stretch of fantastically beautiful deserted beach and have it pretty much all to yourself.

Rainbow Beach has a couple of accommodation options for 'packers. The **Rainbow Beach Backpacker's** (074) 863 288 is at 66 Rainbow Beach Rd – pretty much the first thing you see on your left as you drive in. It's a nice place, with beds under $15 and limited cooking facilities. There's a small pool and a restaurant attached which specialises in Schnitzel. (Would you believe in a place called The Schnitzel Hut? Neither would I. Go and see it for yourself.) Pretty reasonable rates. Very quiet and pleasant, all told.

Rainbow Beach Holiday Village (074) 863 222 is a sort of caravan park, which allows camping and has 'permanent tents' on-site, with cooking facilities. Tent sites under $15, or you can get a bed in one of the 'permanent tents', which sleep three, for under $10. It is also possible to rent on-site vans, should you so desire.

While I personally go to Rainbow Beach for the quiet and for the absolutely stunning beach itself, it is also possible to arrange Fraser Island tours from here. There is a **National Parks** (074) 863 100 at the village if you want to arrange camping permits and you can rent 4WD vehicles for Fraser tours from **Jeep City** (074)863 223, or there are operators who organise day-trips to the island from Rainbow Beach. Costs are pretty much the same as from Hervey Bay and the vehicles drive north along the beach to **Inskip Point**, where they can get a ferry to the island proper.

Maryborough

South of Bundaberg by half an hour or so lies the town of Maryborough. It is touted locally as being of historical interest. The other factor that they try to emphasise is that many of the houses are built in the quintessential 'Queenslander' style of architecture.

Big fucking deal. Keep driving.

Hervey Bay

For some weird reason, Hervey Bay is starting to become a 'destination' in its own right. I can't think why. Truth to tell, the place is a total dive. It's like this huge chain of five whitebread suburbs built along 10km of flat ground next to a big, shallow, muddy bay. Old Australians come here to get older and die in banal subtropical obscurity. Mind you, that does mean the place has the full range of facilities, including banks, auto-tellers, pubs, K-Mart and everything else that goes with the scene.

The swimming in Hervey Bay sucks, sheltered as it is by Fraser Island. The waters of the bay are murky, muddy-bottomed and utterly without surf. And when the tide goes out, it's mud flats as far as the eye can see. The beach itself is narrow and fairly nasty, compared with the utterly marvellous stretches of white sand to the north and the south. The place has only a limited historical interest and it's overall about as exciting as putting your shoes on.

The reasons Hervey Bay started attracting people are obvious, though. Access to Fraser Island is a start. Also, Hervey Bay is famous for its whale-watching industry. Twice a year, the Humpback whales cruise through the bay on their long migration to and from the Antarctic. In the calm waters of the bay, conditions are ideal to zip out in a small boat and have a perv at the huge beasties – so perfect, in fact and so popular, that legislation has been enacted to keep hordes of gawking tourists a decent distance from the whales, for the sake of privacy, or whatever. (What do Humpback whales do in private?)

Beyond these two things, I can conceive of no possible reason to come to Hervey Bay – and no reason at all to linger. When the ice caps melt and the ocean rises, Hervey Bay will go under – and I'll be there to cheer.

Stuff To Do

1. Go and watch the whales. Basically, you front up to your hostel – or any of the various tourist information places – and say 'I wanna see whales.' The season runs between late-ish July and mid-October. Don't bother trying to find a boat at other times of the year; it's not the tour operators who are playing hard to get, it's the whales. You'll be able to get a half-day or a full day on the water, as desired, usually with lunch thrown in, from $40 to about $70.

Whale-watching isn't everyone's cup of tea. Personally, I love 'em, but they don't exactly sing and dance. Well, I suppose Humpbacks do 'sing' – and some of the boats come equipped with hydrophones so you can hear them. Remember that there are fairly strict rules protecting the big creatures; the boats are prevented by law from approaching closer than 100m, but many boat-operators cheat by cutting their engines at the required distance, then letting the whales themselves close the gap. The whales don't seem to mind too much if it's done this way, but the whole scene is getting a little crowded.

Whale-watching is a chancy game. Just because you've laid out your cash and cruised up and down the bay for hours on end, it doesn't follow that you're actually going to see any whales. They use spotter planes, these days, though, so your chances are pretty good. Nonetheless, it takes quite a while to get out to the right spots and even then, there's a lot of chasing back and forth and up and down trying to locate the infernal beasties. On the whole, if you really want to see whales, you're better off doing the full day tour just to give yourself a decent chance.

2. Go to Fraser Island. You can do this in any one of a number of ways. Best bet is probably to hook up with one of the organised overnight tours. If you do it that way, you're not responsible for the vehicle or any costs associated with it and you get the benefit of an experienced guide who will ensure that you get to see all the best bits of Fraser and have a good time in the process.

A typical Fraser day-tour for about $60 will whisk you across **Sandy Strait** to the island, where you get into a large but comfortable 4-wheel-drive bus. They'll cruise the rainforest, stop for a decent swim and take you somewhere for a buffet lunch included in the price. You'll do the obligatory beach drive, visit the coloured sands or the wreck of the **Maheno**, have another swim and return in the evening. Well-organised and pleasant, but you can't choose your fellow-travellers and you have no control over the places you go, or the length of time you spend at each. Mind you, many of the day-tour operators will let you split up the trip, allowing you to take a couple of days and nights on the island before coming back. This is one of the best possible options, giving you an extended stay on the island plus transport and a guided tour.

An overnighter, or two-day tour can be had for about $150. They'll usually feed you – nothing special, but pleasant and filling – and you'll be staying in share accommodation at one of the less flash resorts, such as **Happy Valley**. The rooms are perfectly reasonable and not too crowded, but you'll still have to provide your own sleeping bag. If you were considering an overnighter on Fraser, you might want to consider the next option as well, since it works out only a little more expensive and gives you a lot more time and freedom of action.

Hiring a 4-wheel drive vehicle and driving yourself around the island is not a cheap proposition and is best done with a group of eight or so. This will let you stay on the island a little longer and will give you the choice of where you go and where you camp – but it does mean that you and your party are responsible for the costs of the vehicle.

A typical 4WD group-hire situation will involve about eight 'packers, usually from the same hostel. Base rental cost for a period of about 3 days (2 nights) will be about $100, but this will include all the camping and cooking equipment, with the exception of sleeping bags, return ferry tickets and the appropriate camping and access permits.

On top of this, you'll be paying for fuel and food and there's a bond against the vehicle – about $500 at the current time – which the group will have to come up with. Between food and fuel, you should budget another $30 or so. More, if you're going to stock up on fine wines and delicacies.

Fraser's not big on shops and supplies, so it pays to think long and hard beforehand about what you're taking. Don't forget toilet paper, sunscreen, insect repellent, extra film and swimming equipment. Matches. Cigarettes, too, if that's your vice.

Why go to Fraser Island? I tell you: the place is so totally amazing that it deserves a section all to itself. (See below.)

In And Out

Hervey Bay is down a right-hand turn off the Bruce Highway at any one of a number of places around **Maryborough** – which is itself not on the highway proper. The signs are well-marked, but it's a fair drive down to the Bay and the sprawl of lookalike suburbs at the end is very bloody confusing. Get yourself a decent map and read it carefully; you'll need it. There's an airport at Maryborough, if you're travelling high. Maryborough is also the nearest train access, I'm afraid. If you're doing Hervey Bay on the cheap without a vehicle of your own, it'll have to be by bus. Many of the regular buses between Brisbane and Cairns have a side-track down to Hervey Bay and it's pretty easy to get a bus out of Maryborough too.

Hitching to Hervey Bay in particular is tricky because it is a side-track. Best bet is to ask someone going along the Bruce Highway to drop you off at the turnoff and try again from there.

Shelter

Owing to the popularity of Fraser Island and the whales, there's rather a lot more in the way of 'packer accommodation than one would expect in such an otherwise dire place. Pick of the bunch has to be **Koala Backpacker's** (071) 24 4107 at 408 The Esplanade. This is a big-time party place with bar and entertainment laid on, but to my reckoning, if you're going to be stuck in Hervey Bay on your way to Fraser, you're going to need all the entertaining you can get just to avoid falling into a coma.

Beaches Backpacker's (071) 24 1322 at 195 Torquay Rd in Torquay (one of the five boring suburbs of boring Hervey Bay) is another pleasant, relatively hip sort of place. Nearby is the unnervingly named **The Friendly Hostel** (071) 24 4107 at 182 Torquay Rd. (Where do you suppose The Unfriendly Hostel is? Or The Aggro Hostel? Or The Hostel With Attitude?) It's smaller and quieter, but a little cheaper too. Next door at 184 Torquay Rd is the **Olympus Backpacker's Villas** (071) 24 5331. This place is a bit over the top, being one of the new wave of purpose-built hostels, not simply an older building which has been adapted to a new purpose.

Fraser Island

This is the world's largest sand island, about 120km long, north to south, and covering an area of over 160,000 hectares. The ecosystem is amazing, unlike anything else on earth. Huge patches of desert-like dunes, rainforests, lakes, heathlands, swamps, salt pans, cliffs, beaches that God Himself might envy, mangrove forests – how much can you stuff into one island? And all on nothing more than a bed of accumulated sand, washed into place by the currents of several million years. Fraser Island is a completely amazing place.

It's the sand structure itself that does the trick. Once they were stabilised by vegetation, the dunes started to behave like gigantic sponges or aquifers, storing ungodly amounts of ultra-fresh, sand-filtered water. Thus, where the water table rose to become higher than the dips between some of the dunes, there formed the famous 'window lakes' of superbly fresh water. Other lakes have developed too, perched high on the dune structures, supported by hardened organic layers of decayed vegetation which binds the dunes together.

The Fraser Island lakes contain fresh water of almost magical purity. So uncontaminated is this water that at least one local protection group has raised a fuss about visitors who swim in the lakes and take the opportunity to have a piss. Measuring a few pints of piss in a huge lakeful of water is a pretty tough call, but apparently some of these lakes are so pure that you can do it.

Stuff To Do

Where to start? Let's see. Up the eastern coast of the island is a stretch of broad, white sand called **Seventy-Five Mile Beach**. The name is a bit of an exaggeration – it's actually about 60 miles from Hook Point to Indian Head. Still, think about it for a moment, if you come from any country of the world other than this one: one hundred kilometres of truly beautiful beach, giving onto the rolling blue surf of the Pacific. You won't be the only people on it, of course – but if you can't find a stretch to call your own for a day or so, there's something wrong.

One thing that has become very popular on Fraser is simply driving 4WD vehicles along the beach. And true, it's a lot of fun – tearing along at a great rate with the ocean and the wind and no traffic for miles – but think about it; this is not a smart thing to do, for a large number of reasons.

First reason is that the beach is actually a mapped, registered part of the Australian road system here. This means you drive on the left, give way to pedestrians, obey traffic laws and the speed limit, or you are in fact in breach of law. Not that there's a lot of cops around, but if you piss enough people off, they'll happily inform the authorities and you'll find trouble waiting for you when you get back. Or even when the rangers spot you.

Second reason is pedestrians. Beaches are frequently used for sun-bathing, swimming and playing. It can be very difficult to spot someone lying in a hollow in the beach and the dull thud made by a sunbather going under your tyres at 80kph can put a damper on even the most party-hardy group of travellers. Have some consideration. (Also, if you're planning on sunbathing, keep it up in the soft sand near the top of the beach and make sure you're clearly visible. And look out for traffic when you decide to go for a cooling dip.)

Third reason is the creeks. Many, many little rivulets make their way across the beach down to the sea and usually they cut a little channel in the sand to do it. These channels vary in size and depth and perhaps surprisingly, the larger ones are less hazardous. You can see them well in advance. The smaller ones – say 80cm deep and only a couple of metres across – represent a major hazard if you're stupid enough to hit them at more than 80 kph. We're talking nose-down cartwheeling here.

Fourth reason is the sand itself. Unless you are quite skilled in the techniques of handling a 4WD in loose sand, this can represent quite an obstacle. Many groups of travellers have been surprised and alarmed to find their vehicle just slowly, inexorably falling over because the driver has stupidly taken them into soft, sloped sand.

The moral is this: watch what you're doing and take it easy. Fraser Island is the site of a large number of fairly serious accidents every year just because people are too damned stupid to think about what they're doing. You're a fair way from help out there, should you get into real trouble.

Then, on the other hand, like I said: stupid things kill stupid people. It's just evolution happening.

Because of the sandy composition of the island, travelling Fraser is pretty well limited to 4WD. Motorcycles are discouraged because of the potential they have for going off the marked tracks and tearing up the delicate ecostructure. Walking is a great idea, but don't forget just how fucking big this place is. Try walking more than a couple of kilometres through sand with full pack and camping gear; I guarantee you won't like it.

For the tough nuts and the die-hards, though, hitch-hiking around the island is a real possibility. There are plenty of vehicles and if you're patient and don't look too earnest and overloaded, sooner or later you're bound to find a friendly soul going your way. You'd be well advised not to hitch out to the places on the edge, though. It's a bugger of a walk back to civilisation.

If you do take a 4WD to Fraser, the place just opens up in front of you. Access to the four most well-known of the island's lakes is found about 20-40 km up from the **Hook Point** barge landing site along Seventy-Five Mile Beach. **Lake McKenzie**, a beautiful blue body of water with fine beaches, is a mandatory stop, if only for a walk and a swim. **Lake Boomanjin** is also particularly fine, being completely surrounded by an excellent white-sand beach. It is the largest 'perched lake' in the world. Lake Wabby, the deepest lake on the island, is also found in this area.

Further along Seventy-Five Mile Beach by another 30km or so, **Eli Creek** comes down to the sea. This is a particularly beautiful and interesting area, with boardwalks to allow visitors to follow the course of the creek without causing erosion. It's also a nice place for a bit of a swim; the creek races in a serpentine fashion across the beach down to the sea and it's kind of fun to let yourself get swept down the current with it. Tends to be popular and even a little crowded at times, though.

Past Eli Creek along the beach, you'll come to the wreck of the *Maheno*. It's an impressive old rustbucket, originally displacing over 5,000 tonnes. Originally it was a passenger liner, serving honourably as a hospital ship in WWI. It was sold for scrap in The Great Depression and was being towed to Japan for disassembly when it was blown ashore in 1935. It was used for bombing practice in WWII and it's not the safest of things to climb on, but everyone does it anyway. Have a tetanus shot first, okay?

A few kilometres northwards, the beach 'road' takes you past the famous 'coloured sands' area, with extravagantly colourful sand-cliffs up to twenty-five metres high lining the foreshore. The colour – rich ochres, reds and yellows – comes from organic material in the sand, which helps bind it, giving it the stability to form the high cliffs. At **The Pinnacles** the cliffs have eroded into tortured spires and bizarre shapes. Worth taking a few photographs. You need to be careful if you're going to explore the sand cliffs, though – walking on them or climbing them is out of the question. The formations are extremely delicate and aside from the danger you pose to them, there's a good chance you could pull a few tonnes of sand down on your head if you were stupid.

Fraser Island has had an Aboriginal presence for thousands of years, as shown by place names such as **Corroboree Beach**, further still to the north. At the northern end of Seventy-Five Mile Beach is **Indian Head**, part of the only outcrop of genuine rock on the entire island. Indian Head got its name from Cook, in 1770, when he saw Aborigines there …

aptain's Log, James Cook 1770 World Surf Safari: Saw a totally bodacious expanse of surf beach today, with rollers at least a fathom to the crest. A most stirring sight, which inspired me to immediate action. I had just waxed my stick, however, when Able Seaman Weed sighted indigenes upon the rocks. Given their warlike appearance, it was deemed unlikely that they were surfers and I duly named the place Indian Point. Mr Banks, being the uncool, uptight individual that he is, pointed out that these savages were unlikely to be Indians, as we are nowhere near the Indies. I replied by asking him just who was the navigator on this ship and who was the glorified gardener. As if Banks had any idea where we are! When he further objected to the title of 'glorified gardener', I explained to him he was lucky I did not proceed with my initial impulse and name the place Banks-Is-A-Dweeb Point.'

The beaches around Indian Head and **Waddy Point** are well protected and ideal for swimming. At **Middle Rocks**, between the two, a natural basin in the rocks forms a popular swimming pool at low tide. The sparkling clarity of the waters has given rise to the name **Champagne Pools**.

North of the rocks is **Sandy Cape** and the **lighthouse**. The area north of the rock outcrops is rather isolated and not nearly so heavily frequented as the rest of the island. The interior landscape here is drier, harsher and much less attractive than the southern part of the island. Though there are many lakes shown on the maps, as often as not these are actually shallow marshes. There is a lack of fresh water along the coast and vehicular access to the area is extremely difficult. Unless you were a real 4WD fanatic with more than a week to spend on Fraser, you'd be as well just to skip the area north of the rocky promontories.

The western, or landward coast of Fraser Island is of a different nature altogether to the east, being sheltered from prevailing winds and seas. Beach driving is not really an option here – there's a lot of mangrove and bog south of **Moon Point** and even to the north of Moon Point there are lots of inlets and treacherous areas of soft sand – but there are well-signposted tracks for 4WD vehicles which will take you to the places you want to see. It is also worth having someone get out and walk across first if you're crossing creeks on the West Coast. Fraser Island has it's own peculiar version of 'quicksand' which can look exactly like normal sand, but will bog a 4WD to the door handles. This is very embarrassing.

One of the best West Coast places is **Wanggoolba Creek**, a winding, beautifully clear creek running through exquisite forests down to the sea about 40km north of **Hook Point** on the western shore of the island. Since it flows over sand, the creek is almost completely silent, despite the fact that it is quite rapid-moving. The stillness and beauty of the scene as it passes through the famous **Giant Fern groves** is breath-taking. **Wanggoolba Creek** is also practically your landing place if you come from Hervey Bay.

If you follow the 'road' along the creek, up into the **Pile Valley**, you will be treated to the sight of some truly marvellous forest. Despite the fact that the only thing they've got to support them is sand, there are stands of totally massive Satinay trees here, amongst palms and rainforest. These trees were once the subject of a major logging programme on Fraser Island and it took quite a battle before conservationists were able to put a halt to tree-taking. Satinay timber, it seems, is quite oily and has unequalled resistance to marine borers such as teredo worms and 'gribbles'. As a result, large quantities of Fraser Island's satinay trees were taken to line the Suez Canal, believe it or not. The Pile Valley forest includes some splendid stands of these huge trees and really shouldn't be missed.

Other things to watch for on Fraser Island: There are many interesting creatures living on the island. The Australian wild dog, or Dingo, is found in numbers on the island. In fact, since domestic animals are banned from the island, the Fraser Island population of dingoes represents probably the last group in Australia which have not significantly interbred with domestic species. Don't feed the dingoes; they can be complete bastards and (Lindy Chamberlain aside) they've been known to have a go at small kids on the island.

Lake Bowarrady features a well-known group of tame tortoises. Not only are these not at all poisonous, but they probably won't even bite. Much. The island is also alive with birdlife of all kinds, including dozens of species of migratory seabirds and birds of prey such as the Osprey and the Brahminy Kite.

Special Mention

If you have any interest in Aboriginal culture and heritage, especially concerning Fraser Island, why not contact the **Thoorgine Educational & Cultural Centre** on (071) 244 100? They run camping trips to the island, with a special emphasis on seeing the Aboriginal side of life on the island. For about $90, you'll spend three days and two nights on the island, learning about the way the Aborigines lived. This includes an introduction to local native foods ('bush tucker') and visits to various culturally significant sites and music sessions. You'll need to bring your own bedding, but it's a genuinely different and interesting way of seeing the island.

In And Out

Vehicle ferries operate to **Wanggoolba Creek** from the River Heads site just south of Hervey Bay and to **Moon Point** and **Bogimbah Creek** from the Urangan boat harbour. If it were me, I'd be going from **River Heads**.

Shelter

Although there are quite a number of resorts on the island, they're all pretty expensive by backpacker standards. Furthermore, going to Fraser Island just to submit yourself to the Resort Experience – no matter how eco-aware they may be – is a really stupid idea. If you're going to be staying on Fraser at all, you should be camping.

The southern lakes region has three ex-forestry camp grounds – at **Lake McKenzie**, **Lake Boomanjin** and **Central Station**. All have toilets and water supplies and Central Station even has coin-operated hot showers. Lake Boomanjin and Lake McKenzie campgrounds have suffered from overuse, however. Still, it is as yet not necessary to book for these campsites, so there's something, anyway.

Cathedral Beach – in the Coloured Sands area on the eastern coast – has a private camp-ground with tent sites and on-site vans. The facilities are excellent, but being a private ground, it isn't covered by the island camping fee system. It would be helpful to book in advance here.

In the north, there are campgrounds at **Dundubara** (just east of Lake Bowarraddy), **Waddy Point** and on the western coast, **Wathumba**. All have water supplies, toilets and hot water. You should definitely book sites in advance if your trip coincides with one of the busy periods, such as long weekends or the school holidays.

The **Lake Allom** campsite is less well provided for, being intended mostly for hikers. As a result, though, it is less well-used and might be a good option in busier times. Beach camping is usually allowed if there is already vehicle access to your chosen site on the rest of the island.

Warning

Listen up, pinheads. This is important. Hervey Bay did not start life as a big tourist operation. For years, it was a sort of glorified suburb for retiring Australians. Likewise, Fraser Island hasn't always been super-popular and an awful lot of Queenslanders regard it as a much-loved extension of their own back yard. The end result is this: BACKPACKER'S AREN'T ALL THAT POPULAR WITH THE LOCALS!

How do I know this? I asked. The results were enlightening. Local residents, tour operators, restaurateurs, shopkeepers and even tourist-friendly services were uniformly unimpressed by the standards of behaviour demonstrated by budget travellers. A lot of people taking the whale-watch boats are now starting to ask for services which don't cater to backpackers. Likewise, there is a very, very strong local movement which is trying to restrict the access to and the use of Fraser Island.

There's no suggestion that all backpackers are pea-brained piss-headed lager-swilling Yobs from Hell … but if you don't know at least a dozen backpackers who do fit that description from time to time, you haven't been travelling long, have you? The thing to remember with Hervey Bay is that prior to the influx of budget travellers, it didn't really have a social life. The people there just aren't used to big, toothy, tanned, noisy crowds of near-naked sun-freaks wandering at will in and out of the town's facilities. Chill out a little; keep the serious partying within the confines of the hostel, be polite and friendly outside and wear what the locals do when you're on the beach and you may even be able to come back here next time.

Fraser's a slightly more serious problem. The local 'Preserve Fraser' sentiment is so strong that (I am informed) there is a serious danger of the island becoming inaccessible to budget travellers. You can do an awful lot of good for yourself and for other travellers, then, by reading the section which follows on behaviour and etiquette on Fraser.

Good Times On Fraser

The ecological structure of the island is quite delicate. Sand is particularly poor for anchoring vegetation and the plant-life of the island is easily destroyed. Don't take your vehicle off the marked tracks. Ever. For any reason. Drive at reasonable speeds on the beach. Think about sunbathers, swimmers, small children and other drivers. Beach races are RIGHT FUCKING OUT. Not only are they dangerous to the environment and to other users of the beach, but seeing that you're probably not an expert in sand driving, they're a risk to your own life.

Keep the noise down. That's noise of all sorts, including engines. Plan your campsite and see if you can't stop driving by sunset. Fraser Island is just dripping with peace and quiet, when it isn't being fucked-up by morons with big motors and tiny brains. Boom-boxes and ghetto-blasters are a good way to make yourself very unpopular at a campsite, too. Take heed: locals have been known to quite simply punch out people who refuse to keep their music at a reasonable level in camp.

Stick to minimum impact practices. A lot of campsites forbid wood fires altogether. Others permit them, but you must use the provided wood and fireplaces. If you are at an undeveloped site, the rule is that no fires should be built at all. If you're renting a 4WD through one of the hostels or agents at Hervey Bay, they should provide you with a camp stove or barbecue. USE IT. Fires are lovely, but they get out of control easily. Bushfires in Australia are big-time dangerous. Believe me on this point: you do NOT want to know. Furthermore, fallen wood is very important to the ecosystem. Sand has bugger-all nutrients in it; every fallen leaf that rots helps the whole thing keep going. Don't gather firewood on Fraser.

Carry out your trash. There are bins provided here and there around the island for disposal of rubbish, but think for a moment on the logistics of getting garbage off the island. If you carried it on, you can bloody well carry it off again.

Watch where you crap. This may seem blunt, but it's necessary. In places where toilets have not been provided, you may have to dig your own. Make it at least 15cm deep. Do it at least 100m from any track, trail, or water source, including gullies – even dry ones. Cover it over afterwards. Sanitary pads and tampons should be bagged or wrapped in paper, then carried off the island in plastic bags.

Keep all kinds of muck out of the water. Don't wash with soap in creeks or lakes. Don't rinse dishes or cutlery in the local waterways, either. Try to minimise the use of sunscreen when you're swimming at the lakes. If you're camping in an undeveloped site and you must wash cutlery, brush your teeth, etc, dig a hole to accommodate all the water-waste produced by such activities and cover it over afterwards.

And don't even THINK of bringing dogs or cats or the like to the island.

Childers

Oddly, I kind of like this tiny little town. The highway kinks going through it, turning into a treelined boulevard of sorts. The main street is stuffed with National Trust-listed buildings and the whole place has a kind of laid-back, friendly, small country town ambience about it.

As it's on the highway, you'll probably wind up going through it. If you're looking for work, this is definitely the place to stop. The proprietors of the **Palace Backpacker's Hostel** (071) 262244) specialise in finding work in the local fields. The hostel is a converted two-story hotel nearly a century old and it's a really cool piece of work. Accommodation is very much worker-oriented and the place is pretty full of travelling fruit-pickers most of the year bar February.

It's a good system. Childers is too small to support a decent workforce and the local farmers are glad to have travellers. It's extremely well-run and the hostel owners run a couple of buses to ensure that their charges make it out to the fields on time. The relationship between the farmers and the hostellers is a solid one of mutual trust and both sides have a lot to gain from the situation. As a result, it's all strictly legal and above-board, too. You'll need your work visa, your tax file number and your bank account all at hand, though the hostellers can help you with applying for the TFN or the bank account.

Your accommodation will cost you about $85 a week and you'll be supplying your own meals, but it's an excellent arrangement all round, highly recommended. While you're in Childers, you might check out the **Pharmaceutical Museum**, also in the main street. It's a hoot.

The Spliff

Let's get one thing straight. Marijuana is a very naughty drug and we are most certainly not encouraging anyone to use it. That kind of behaviour is very, very naughty and we think anybody who engages in it should have their wrists firmly slapped and be sent to bed without any supper. However, if we had to say anything about it, we'd have to recommend North Queensland Home-Grown Heads. Sure, the stuff is easier to get on the North Coast of NSW. And even in the Deep North, it's hard to find genuine home-grown, since they get a very nice strain in from New Guinea ... but when you do get hold of a genuine real McCoy home-grown Far North Queensland spliff just chock-full of oozy resinous goodness ... well, consider the experience of Wade, from Seattle.

'I smoked a lot of shit. I've had Hawaiian and Thai and Lebanese Hash and all sorts of skunk from the West Coast. And sure, I've had stronger stuff than I had in Daintree. But not very often.

'I was down on a beach near Cow Bay, just walking and I came across these hippy types. They were sitting around a fire and I smelled that smell, you know. I'd been dry for a week or two and they seemed pretty cool, so I went over and asked them something stupid, you know – like about the tide, or whatever. And sure enough, when that reefer came my way, this guy just passed it to me without a second thought.

'It was smooth. Very tasty. Somebody said there was spearmint in it for flavour. Anyway, we all got really mellow and soon we were good buddies. Somebody with a guitar, singing and everybody's happy. This chick got real friendly with me and I was thinking maybe I was onto a good thing. We had another couple of hits, just her and me, then she pointed out where she was sleeping and went. I was going to follow her. Really I was. That was the plan, I think. Except that I found I couldn't move my fucking legs. Man, I was so completely fucked I couldn't even stand, let alone walk. If I hadn't been so stoned, I might have been worried. As it was, I just flaked out and woke up in the morning with a mouthful of grit and shit like you would not believe. Never again, man.'

Bundaberg

Bundaberg, while it's not exactly a raging storm of delight, has a certain Australian small-town style. Plenty of old buildings, a nice big river running up the guts of it and some decent parks to sit around and get pissed in. It's not too bad a place to take a nice, slow walk around. It's no longer on the Bruce Highway proper, so if you're in your own vehicle it's just as easy to skip it – but the buses stop there, as does the train. It's an easy three to four hour drive from Brisbane, maybe five by bus.

Bundaberg is pretty much held together by sugar and rum. It doesn't have a whole lot of real history, so what it has, it flaunts. The moment you arrive, they start throwing Bert Hinkler at you. He was born in Bundaberg and in 1928, he made the first solo flight from The Old Dart to Oz. Thus, practically anything around Bundaberg that ever had anything to do with old Bert is a bit of a sacred icon. There's his house, of course, which is now the **Hinkler House Memorial Museum**. (Just to show how desperate these guys are: this house was designed and built by Hinkles in bloody Southampton, England, where he lived from 1926 to 1933. The English, quite rightly, didn't give a rat's arse about the place and it was going to be

Flinthart's

Within minutes of hitting this hick burg, I was totally Hinkled out. Looking for almost anything else, I picked up a local tourist rag. It was unhelpful. Between references to Hinkler's Famous Outdoor Toilet and the Site of Hinkler's First Wet Dream, I found articles about the Interesting Water Tower - a masterpiece of brick-laying - and some sort of String Bean Festival. I shuddered.

My current navigator, Gunnar - a huge Norseman from Hel - spotted the sign for the Rum Distillery and wanted to get shitfaced. I said we were meant to be a high-class act and if we were going to get shitfaced, we should do it with dignity. So we went to the local winery instead. Place called Tropical Wines and Sunny Softdrinks, on the highway towards Gin Gin. At least there were no fucking Big Things there.

The couple that ran the place paled when they got a real look at me and Gunnar - 220 kilos of red-eyed bad attitude between us. They laid out the free samples so fast you'd have thought it was raining fruit punch. Pineapple wine, mulberry wine, passionfruit, ginger, strawberry ... even fucking mango wine. The stuff was coming thick and fast;

pulled down – so it was dismantled and fetched to Bundaberg brick by brick in 1983.) Then there's the **Hinkler Glider Museum** in Bourbong St at the Tourist Information Centre. And of course, one mustn't forget his aeroplane, the 'Ibis' is on display in the **Bundaberg & District Histori- cal Museum**. Not to mention **Hinkler Park**, near the Botanic Gardens.

Actually, not a lot has happened to Bundaberg since Bert and there's a lot of people in the city who wish the bastard had just up and flown right back to England again. Especially when some dolt every year trots out the idea that Bundaberg would draw more tourists if it were called 'Hinklerton'.

Stuff To Do

Despite the Hinklermania, there are a couple of useful things to do in and around Bundaberg. Number one, of course, is to work. There's all kinds of picking work in the area, with the season running most of the year except February. Again, it's hot, shitty, thankless work for fairly low pay, but it's there for the taking.

You can do the **Bundaberg Rum Distillery** tour (071) 524 077 for under $5 if that's your bag. Your fee includes tasting and I suppose if

---

Journal

we were set for a real bender.

Then I tasted the stuff. The owners of Tropical Wines are happy to declare that their tropical fruit wines taste nothing like grape wines at all. They're absolutely fucking right. I had no doubt that these were truly excellent Tropical Fruit Wines, but they were nothing at all like grapes.

I like grape wines.

Gunnar tasted the stuff and his face changed colour. He gasped something about pastrami and I checked the bottle. It said 'kiwifruit- loquat-salmonberry'. Pastrami was closer to the mark.

Gunnar was not an easy man to stop, though. The prospect of wasting free booze was too much for him. I took a slow trip around town while he finished what we started. When I got back, he was lying in a pool of his own diges- tive juices, attracting flies and dogs in the front car park. He was clutching a half-empty bottle labelled 'Banana Port'. I figured it served him right. I dropped his pack on the tarmac near his great big square-jawed head and drove off in search of a new navigator. Who could tell? Perhaps Inga was somewhere in town.

you like rum, this could be considered a bargain. Personally, I'd pay more than $5 just to be let back out of a rum distillery. The distillery is a fair way out of town (thank Bog!) on Avenue St to the east, but there're regular buses from **Bourbong St**.

Bundaberg isn't on the coast proper, but you can reach some reasonable beaches within 15 to 20km. You can catch buses from the **Post Office** to **Bargara Beach** and **Moore Park** without straining yourself, at least on weekdays. About 15km northeast of Bundaberg is **Mon Repos** beach. This is famous as a relatively accessible rookery for the sea turtles. The turtles nest between November and January, mostly and the young move out between January and March. Turtle-watching is a very fine thing to do, but it's a definite hazard to the turtles if you don't do it right. Check with Queensland **National Parks & Wildlife** service before you go; they have a centre right there on the beach.

Finally – and this is the reason I'd be stopping at Bundaberg – they've got staggeringly cheap dive courses there. Depending on the season, you can go for full certification in PADI – permitting you to dive in open water – for as little as $150 from **Anglo Diving** (071) 516422, all gear supplied. For the same price, **Bundaberg Aqua Scuba** (071) 535761

The Mud Crab

Justifiably famous the world over, the Mud Crab is the ultimate for seafood connoisseurs. From the inches-thick Mud Crab sandwiches of humble Miriam Vale to Thai Chilli Mud Crab in Noosa, to the simplicity of Mud Crab boiled in salt water in the outback of Cape York, nothing else can prepare you for the treat that awaits.

Why? Well, for starters, Muddies are a decent size. Not like your little bloody spanner crabs and sand crabs and so forth; when you tackle a Muddy you know you've had a meal. Up in the Deep North, they get to be so big they'll take dogs and small children if they get the chance. And that dirty big bone-crunching fighting claw is just packed to the brim with delicious, flaky, delicately flavoured meat.

Here's the proper way to eat Mud Crab: take a team of bearers into the mangroves. You will need them to carry the barbecue, the 44-gallon drum and of course, the esky full of beer and ice. Also the flare pistols, the two-way, the medical kit, the shotgun and the ammunition. And the spare beer.

Plunge straight into the heart of the swamp. Ignore anything you may find around the edges; that's where the tourists and other faint-hearted wimps do their fishing and the best and will work under either PADI or NAUI, supply all gear and even throw in a reef dive. You might also try **Salty's** (071) 526707 – they're only about $20 more expensive and may even get you to one of the islands.

Bundaberg and the **Capricorn Coast** mark the southerly end of the Great Barrier Reef proper, although you certainly do get coral and reefs as far south as Sydney. Scuba diving on the Great Barrier Reef is just as good as it gets – the absolute best in the world for quality, clarity and variety. If you're doing the northward run, you just can't miss this opportunity to gain your certification. The diving may not be as good off Bundaberg as it is further north, but at these prices, who cares? This is $200 less than you'll find in most places and once you've done the course, you can dive without hassles the rest of the way up the coast.

In And Out

Bundaberg is now on a side-road which deviates nearly 50km from the Bruce Highway. The road forks at Gin Gin. You can't miss it – the signposts are everywhere. There is a perfectly reasonable airfield at Bundaberg, with regular flights in and out from both of the main carriers. Also, the relatively modern bus station is situated quite close to the business centre

The Mud Crab

the biggest crabs are elsewhere. Once you're deep in the heart of darkness, shoot your least-valuable bearer and rope him to a decent weight. Throw him in and wait overnight.

In the morning, half your bearers will be have been killed by the mosquitoes and the odd crocodile, but you won't be needing them anyway, since you'll have drunk a lot of the beer. Fill the 44-gallon drum with salt water and set it boiling. At the first light of dawn, use the winch to haul the dead bearer to the surface. Your crab will be trying to have breakfast at this time and will put up considerable resistance to having it's main course hauled away. Have your Sumo wrestler standing ready and as soon as that monster claw breaks the surface of the water, give the signal. If your Sumo takes more than three minutes to get the killer crab from the murky depths into the boiling water, the creature is no longer fresh. Abandon the effort for 24 hours and start again with a new bearer.

Boil your mud-crab for about five minutes and wash it down with all the beer you have left. Shoot the remaining bearers and make your way back to civilisation.

and the railway station is convenient as well. This is the main line, so the usual range of Sunlanders, Queenslanders and Spirits of This and That come through with depressing regularity.

Shelter

The Bundaberg Backpacker's and Traveller's Lodge (071) 52 2080 is easy to get to, on the corner of Targo and Crofton Sts, opposite the bus station. It's big and clean and friendly, if a little worker-oriented and a bed will set you back less than $15. They may be able to help you out with local fruit-picking work, even to the extent of getting you there and back should you be lacking your own transport.

City Centre Backpacker's (071) 51 3501 has been converted from an old hotel at 216 Bourbong St. Again, there's a degree of worker-orientation about the place, but it's still a good bet, with dorm beds coming in around $12. At a pinch, you might also consider the Federal Guesthouse at 221 Bourbong St; the conversion from hotel isn't exactly finished here, so you should expect a solid Australian working-class drinking presence.

There's also the **Finemore Caravan Park** (071) 51 3663 which is conveniently located next to the river about ten blocks from the bus terminal. No tent sites, but they do have a couple of budget options.

Miriam Vale and Gin Gin

Don't. If you do, don't blame me. Miriam Vale does good mudcrab sandwiches, though.

Flinthart's Journal

Miriam Vale: 'Listen, er - what's your name again?'
'Stacey.'
'Stacey, great. Look, don't be alarmed by this, will you? I just need you to answer a question.'
'Mm. Okay, go ahead. Remember I've got a knife, though.'
'Yeah, sure. Umm, Stacey - is that a really Big Mud Crab on top of that service station over there? Don't be afraid to tell me it isn't. I'll just get you to drive for a while.'
'Mm. Well, it's big. Really big. And orange.'
'I can see that.'
'And it's got sort of claws, so I suppose it might be meant to be a Big Mud Crab. It's not very realistic, though, is it?'
'But it is there, isn't it?'
'Uh-huh. Sure. Why do you ask, Dirk?'
'Thank Christ. I thought I might have swallowed the last of the LSD by mistake.'

*C*aptain's Log, James Cook 1770 World Surf Safari: 'Made landfall today at a wooded headland. Most excellent tubes on the exposed Eastern beach. Mr Banks continues to attempt 'Hanging Ten' on the 12ft Malibu Board; I am as yet unable to convince him that this is a bogus practice and he should be using a three-fin thruster to work his cutbacks.

For the completely uncool members of the crew who don't board, the western side of this headland has a totally bodacious enclosed lagoon, where limpid waters pour gently into a sheltered harbour from a truly excellent river. This place is indeed Mondo Cool.

'Unfortunately, not everything is so cool aboard the Endeavour. Last night, Mr Orton, my clerk, got, like, totally smashed. Some of Banks' dudes put the heavy on him and they cut off all his clothing while he was comatose. Then, when he did not awaken, they cut off his earlobes. I mean, barf me out, man!

'This morning, Mr Orton is most egregiously put out, not to mention hard of hearing. I caught him writing 'Bastard Bay' on the charts next to the place where Banks shot the very tasty wild turkey. Now, while I understand his feelings perfectly, for the sake of shipboard relations, we are going to have to record the place as Bustard Bay. Otherwise Mr Banks will lose his limited cool, like, totally.'

These words are as true today as they were when the Great Surfer first recorded them two hundred years ago. In fact, the town of 1770 (yes, that is what they call it. So named because Cook made his first Queensland landfall there in that year) and Agnes Waters (Nobody knows who the hell Agnes was) presented me with a moral dilemma. Do I tell you plebs about this brilliant spot and thereby run the risk of trashing a fantastic little place, or do I cheat you and the publisher alike and keep it for myself?

Tough call. It's a pity I'm such an honest guy, eh?

Okay, here it is. About 50km east of Miriam Vale, or a hundred or so north of Bundaberg lies the township of **1770** and nearby **Agnes Waters**. Currently, it's an ugly drive over a lot of unsealed, pot-holed, corrugated road to get there. There is a bus which leaves the Bundaberg Post Office at 7 am, but it's for people who have booked a trip out to Lady Musgrave Island with the Great Barrier Reef Tours mob. There's certainly no trains. Basically, you turn right (east) off the Bruce Highway at Miriam Vale and keep following the signs.

Why go there? Because it's great.

On the one hand, you've got the surf beach at Agnes Waters. Not as big or as flashy and broad as the ones further south, but a genuine surf beach. And it's the last one as you go North, too. There's not much development here – a pub, a caravan park, some cabins, a few houses … and a petrol station that doubles as a surf shop! – the beach is practically empty. Very nice. You can camp in the caravan park for under $15 per night with your own tent, or try for one of the few on-site vans. Cabins come a little more expensive.

Not far to the south is **Deepwater National Park**. This place is magic – giant waterholes shrouded in beautiful forest which comes right down to the perfect beaches. A very strict national park, access is pretty much limited to foot and some 4WD, which means it's still largely untouched. Camping is limited to the delineated areas. From November to February, sea turtles make their way up the beach to lay their eggs. Observing this totally amazing event is completely cool, so long as you don't fuck with the turtles in any way. Not even by bringing a light to the beach; these poor buggers navigate thousands of kilometres by the stars and the moon. They don't need you screwing up their systems with artificial lights.

About seven kilometres north along the road from Agnes Waters is the tiny 'town' of 1770. There's a marina, a shop or two, a pub and a few places to stay. You can camp next to the beach near the beautifully sheltered lagoon, in a caravan park with full amenities. Or you can stay nearby at the **Captain Cook Holiday Village** (079) 749 219 which has everything from tent sites up to self-contained cabins. Tent sites are about $10 per night ($2.50 extra for each adult past the first). This is probably a pretty good option, as you can get meals, drinks and some supplies here too.

Another excellent reason to come here is for access to **Lady Musgrave Island**. This undeveloped coral cay and lagoon is only two hours away by daily launch and you can get there and back for less than $100. This includes snorkelling gear, buffet lunch, glass-bottom boating, fish-feeding and a total of six hours at the island itself. At the right times of year, there's even a good chance of spotting the Humpback Whales. THIS DOES NOT SUCK. Call **Great Barrier Reef Cruises** (079) 749 077 to arrange bookings.

Now if this weren't enough, pay heed: Lady Musgrave is a national park, which allows camping. You need a permit for this, but the cost is only $3 per night. Permits are to be had from the Gladstone office of the **Dept of Environment and Heritage** – but they can be arranged by phone or fax and the people at Great Barrier Reef Cruises are only too happy to help.

Camping on Lady Musgrave (or **Masthead Island** – that too can be arranged) is a very strictly controlled matter. You'll be given a set of rules to follow, about what you can bring in and what can and cannot be done on the island. FOLLOW THESE RULES. Coral reef cays are very delicately balanced ecological systems. It doesn't take a lot of people messing with them to screw them up permanently.

If you want to go scuba diving, that's a little more tricky. The Reef Cruises people are in the process of arranging their own dive master, but for the moment they need a minimum of five people before they'll bring up a dive master from Bundaberg. Of course, if you're qualified in your own right and you simply want to bring your own gear out, there's a surcharge of $10.

The diving and scenery around Lady Musgrave are easily the equal of Heron Island, or any of the other, more expensive resort islands. Furthermore, there's no fraggin' resort on the island, which is a big bonus, in my opinion.

Another magic thing to do in 1770 is to hire a small boat for about $60 from **1770 Marine Services** (079) 749 227 and explore the **Round Hill Creek** inlet. This is a day rate and the boats seat four, so it can be quite an economical option. They come with a 5hp outboard so you won't wear yourself out. The boats will take you deep into the mangrove maze, to see things you'll never see on foot – or you can cross the creek and head into yet another gorgeous national park – **Eurimbula**. This one is equipped with the usual brilliant beaches and inland it's all wetland and forest. Great stuff.

There's also an environmental tour in a sort of floatable bus. The day trip costs $50 and includes lunch. They cruise all over the area, out to the lighthouse at **Bustard Head**, through Eurimbula, over some excellent sand dune country and up **Round Hill Creek** itself. Pretty good, but needs bookings. Ring (079) 749 227 and inquire about the '**Sir Joseph Banks**'.

The only real drawback to this area is also the thing that makes it so cool: it's undeveloped and hard to get to. Supplies are relatively expensive and facilities are limited. Nonetheless, this chunk of terrain is a real find and if you can manage to get there, it's definitely worth the effort. I'd give it a week, just to wander and chill out. Twice that if you're camping on the islands!

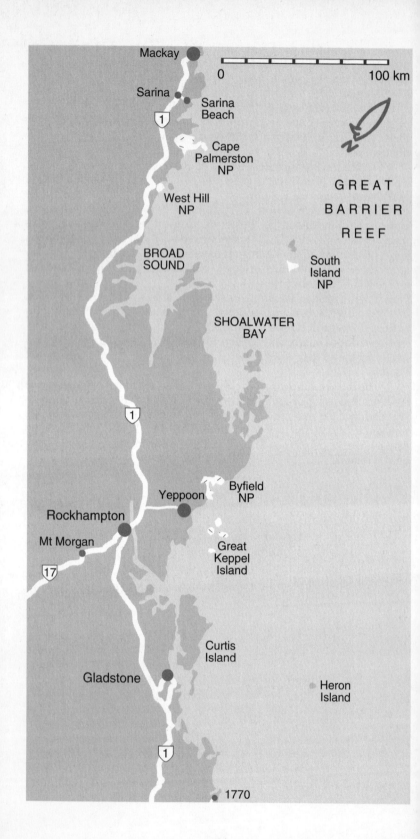

Mackay

Sarina

Sarina Beach

1

Cape Palmerston NP

West Hill NP

BROAD SOUND

SHOALWATER BAY

GREAT

BARRIER

REEF

South Island NP

0   100 km

1

Yeppoon

Byfield NP

Rockhampton

Mt Morgan

17

Great Keppel Island

Curtis Island

Gladstone

Heron Island

1

1770

1770 to Mackay

This is the part of the coast where you don't stop. Just read the guide book as you pass through. Trust me. I live here. That's why I know so much about other places.

From Gympie onwards, the highway runs well in from the sea. You can still get down to the ocean here and there, but access gets downright difficult after Bundaberg. Once you reach Gladstone, though – well, you wouldn't want to go down to the sea anyhow. Major townships are Gladstone and Rockhampton. Gladstone is a little heavy-industry port built on a mangrove swamp. Rockhampton is an ageing beef town. The entire area, running all the way up north to Sarina and Mackay, has very little to recommend it either to the budget traveller, or to anyone else. Great Keppel Island, off Yeppoon, a little way north of Rockhampton, has quite a reputation – but it isn't anything near as pretty as the coastal sites of NSW, or the islands of the Whitsundays.

Dirk's Shortest Dozen

1. Treading heavily on the **gas pedal**.

2. Trying to get from **1770** to **Mackay** in one long run.

3. Lunch stop at **Mt Morgan** to see the Big Hole In The Ground.

Dirk Dumps On

1. See above.

2. **Heron Island** is definitely overpriced, despite very good diving. Save your money and go further north.

Gladstone

I'll keep this short, but let's say your car's broken down and you had to spend a day or two here. Hmm. If you've got the money, you might want to go to **Heron Island**, which is a coral island with some very good diving. Fare is about $110 return. Accommodation is even more brutal, running to roughly $125 per night all found. There are no camping options, no other accommodation possibilities and frankly, there are better places to see the Barrier Reef. Heron Island is the Big Diver's Testosterone scene; it's all by divers, for divers, about divers. You'll even be sharing your expensive lodge room with a bunch of them.

There are two hostels in Gladstone, both in walking distance of bus and train. It's not worth your while trying to camp anywhere, or sleep rough – Gladstone is in the middle of a lot of mangrove swamp and the mosquitoes will drain you dry. The **Harbour Lodge** (079 726 463) is at 16 Roseberry St, an easy five minutes from the train station. Motel-style rooms are currently $20 per person share, or $22 with the (highly recommended) air-con. There's no common room, but the usual range of facilities exist. At 12 Rollo St, closer to the bus drop-off but still within walking distance from the train, you will find the **Gladstone Backpacker's** (079) 725 744. At $15 per night share, ($13 per night after the first) it offers clean, tidy rooms, the usual range of facilities, plus a common kitchen and a nice big back deck for socialising. Unfortunately, due to the number of transient working men who room there, there is a no-alcohol rule in place.

Snapshots

Kieran Goes To Gladstone: I'd been standing outside Gin Gin for hours. Watching rednecks go past, feeling the sun bake the fluids out of me. Nobody was stopping. Finally, some guy in a blue Kingswood pulled over. He asked where I was going and I just said 'North'. We drove off.

He turned out to be one of these big talkers. Wouldn't shut up. Went on and on about the government, the tax rate, the weather, the drought, how you just couldn't catch a decent barra any more, how his ex-wife was screwing him. In self-defence, I went to sleep.

Biggest mistake I ever made. Next thing I know, the guy is nudging me awake. The car has stopped. Where the fuck are we? Gladstone.

Gladstone is town built on mangroves, full of inbreds and mutants spawned by the range of weird chemicals spilled by the ICI plant, the alumina smelter, the giant power station and who knows what else. Nothing happens in Gladstone. There are pubs, but you wouldn't want to go there unless you like watching pinheads in giant hats attempt blind-drunken line dancing. One look and I slunk off to one of the two hostels.

Hitching out was a nightmare. Gladstone is twenty klicks off the main highway and nobody with any reason to go further ever comes down that way. After a full day standing in the sun on the road past the stinking great powerplant, watching the steam rise off the mangroves, I finally gave in and spent $15 on a bus fare to Rockhampton.

Gladstone. I still get nightmares.

For food, try the famous steaks at the **Bellowing Bull** restaurant for a truly amazing amount of dead cow at a very moderate price – about $5 at lunch, $7 at dinner. Further along Goondoon St, you will find **Munchies**, which produces a nice range of mainly Mexican food for around $10. If you're feeling flash, head down to the marina (at the end of Goondoon St) and eat at the **Yacht Club**. Excellent pub fare – steaks, pasta, salads – for about $10-$12.

Rockhampton

This is a dry, elderly cattle town, well inland from the cooling influence of the coast, smack dab on top of the Tropic of Capricorn. The local tourism industry tries to make big points out of this, but who gives a rat's arse anyway? Still, if imaginary lines around the world turn you on, you can always go to the **Tropic of Capricorn Information Centre** on the highway southbound, towards the edge of town. They've even got a big white marker. You can stand with one leg north and one leg south.

The **Fitzroy River** runs through the town, which is nice. And a lot of the buildings are old enough and ugly enough to be on the National Trust register, which means that a half-hour walk around the town centre has some merits. Other than that, the **Botanic Gardens** are big, old and kind of pleasant. Lots of space. There's lots of birdlife, a bit of a zoo and turtles in the lake. A good place for lunch. You can take an **Historic River Cruise**. Costs about $20, but as Rocky hasn't got a whole lot of history, I'd call it overpriced.

Don't get sucked into hanging around for the **Rockhampton Markets**. They're eminently forgettable, compared with places like Kuranda, Eumundi, Brisbane and The Channon.

North of Rocky in the **Berserker Range** there's a couple of limestone cave complexes. There used to be a few more, but a group called Queensland Cement Limited decided we needed concrete more than we needed caves or Ghost Bats. Guided tours of the caves happen at **Olsen's** and at **Cammoo Caves**. I suppose if you've never been caving, it's a pretty interesting sort of expedition and Olsen's will arrange a slightly more strenuous tour for about $22, if you want. If you've any experience with caves, though, you might as well skip it. They're not particularly spectacular and you can't wander off on your own.

There are still some protected Ghost Bat caves at **Mt Etna**, nearby. Since the bat is an endangered species (people keep making car-parks out of its habitat) access is fairly limited. You can do a tour in the wet season (December to February) under ranger guidance, if you like. It's not bad, but as it's timed so as not to disturb the bats at their breeding and nesting, you won't see as much as you might expect.

South of Rocky about 40km is **Mount Morgan**. Worth a visit if you've got time to kill. There really was a mountain here, once. Not a very big one, but a mountain it was. Apparently, the mountain was made mostly out of copper and gold ore and now instead of a mountain, there is a hole in the ground. A really, really big hole in the ground, which you can visit. It's pretty impressive, even though there's frequently a lot of water in it. Mt Morgan the town is a groovy-looking little place full of

more of those gorgeously ugly historical buildings. You can do a tour of the mine from here, which includes the tour of the town and entrance to a man-made cavern where they found dinosaur footprints fossilised in the roof. I like dinosaurs and the dino prints are pretty interesting. Cost you about $20 and they'll throw in afternoon tea. On the whole, a couple of hours spent in Mt Morgan, washed down with a few beers from one of the excessively historic hotels isn't a waste of time and money, especially as Mt Morgan is pretty much on the highway south of Rocky. It's probably not worth a special trip, though.

Shelter

City Heart Backpacker's, 170 East St, (079) 22 2414 is big – cavernous, actually – and clean. Nothing special, costs less than $15 per night for a dorm room. A better bet is the Rockhampton Youth Hostel, 60 MacFarlane St, (079) 27 5288, on the other side of the river, at about $15 for non-members. It's not so central as the other, but they've got cheap evening meals and they're close to the bus terminal. Also, they've got a really good arrangement going for trips to Great Keppel Island and you can book through this YHA to stay at the Keppel YHA. Making such a booking is highly advisable, as the Keppel trip is extremely popular.

Rocky also has a few caravan parks, with campsites available. Try the **Southside Caravan Village** (079) 27 3013, which has vans for backpackers, near the Tropic of Capricorn Information Centre south of town. Closer to the centre, the **Municipal Riverside Caravan Park** (079) 22 3779 has cheap tent sites and it's nicely situated on the river.

Food

Go for steak. This being Mondo Cattle Country, you can get steak of truly excellent quality in most of the larger pubs. The trouble is, nobody seems to know what a rare steak actually looks like; usually, the best you can get is charred and somewhat-less-charred. Still, if you nag and complain and look like you know what you're talking about, you may be able to get a lightly-burnt steak in the less busy periods. The quality of the meat – and it's very low price (about $5 to $9 for a good rib fillet with salad and chips) – makes up for a great deal.

Yeppoon and Great Keppel Island

Yeppoon, a small town on the coast about 40km east of Rockhampton, and **Great Keppel Island** about 13km offshore, make up the region's best known attractions. On the whole, I think Great Keppel is seriously over-rated, but with the huge numbers of people that go there and rave about it, I guess you'll have to make up your own mind.

Yeppoon itself is a nice little town, fairly quiet, reached by taking a well-signed East turn off the highway a little way north of Rocky. If you're not driving, your best bet is to arrange a bus trip through the **Rocky YHA**, which will also help you get to Great Keppel. The coast around Yeppoon is dotted with little coves and beaches, where the swimming is fine. (In winter, of course. Summertime, as usual, one must beware the Dreaded Marine Stingers.) The hinterland of Yeppoon is quite pleasant, especially along the road north to tiny **Byfield**.

Shelter

Look for camping sites in the state forest parks in the area and check out the freshwater swimming holes in **Byfield National Park** and along **Water Park Creek**. There's a nice commercial campsite at **Fern's Hideaway** (079) 351 235 which will let you set up at under $10 per person. It's a good site and you can get hot showers there as well as a swim in the creek.

In Yeppoon proper, you can stay at the **Barrier Reef Backpacker's** (079) 394 702 at 30 Queen St, for about $15. They do pickups from Rocky, which is a big advantage. There are also a number of caravan parks in Yeppoon and in the surrounding region.

Getting to Great Keppel Island itself is done from **Rosslyn Bay Harbour**, about 7km south of Yeppoon along the coast road. There are frequent, regular ferry services to the island, costing $20 to $25 return. Contact **Keppel Tourist Services** (079) 33 6744, to organise the trip. If you're driving your own vehicle, there is an overnight lockup carpark facility available at Rosslyn Bay Harbour.

Great Keppel Island itself is fairly large, rocky and rather dry. It also boasts quite a population of red-back spiders. However, the local waters are relatively clear for inner-reef swimming and there's some reasonable coral around, if you want to go snorkelling or diving. Also, there are a number of secluded beaches which require a good solid walk to reach, so you can do your own thing in relative privacy, if you want.

If you're overnighting, there are a few options open. Ignoring the fairly expensive Qantas-owned resort, you can try the **Great Keppel YHA** (079) 394 341. It's pretty ordinary, but very popular at $15 or therea-bouts for a dorm bed for non-members. Booking in advance is probably a very good idea, if you're determined to do Great Keppel.

It used to be possible to camp next to some of the beaches on the island, pretty much without charge. Owing to the increasing popularity of the place, though, that's not an option any more. In fact, if you're caught trying it, you could be up for a fairly stiff fine. Try **Keppel Haven** (079) 336 744, with semi-permanent on-site tents for about $15. You'll be sharing with up to three others, though.

Food is reasonably priced and easy to come by from a number of outlets on the island, including a pizza place conveniently near the YHA. Groceries, however, are limited and expensive. Bring your own from the mainland if you're on a tight budget.

Great Keppel is a major party island. The resort has a very popular bar and disco scene, which a reasonable number of locals attend as well as the inevitable travellers. The resort promotes the party theme rather heavily; look for a preponderance of 'I Got Wrecked On Great Keppel' t-shirts in the souvenir stands. Anyway, in keeping with the party scene, Great Keppel has the usual range of watersports and activities. You can dive, snorkel, waterski, rent a catamaran, a sailboard or whatever. Some of the boats which ferry you to and from the island do boom-netting runs – where they lower a great big cargo net into the water alongside the boat and drag you through the surf. Fun, sort of.

Bushwalking is also popular on the island, although the terrain is fairly dry, rocky and hostile for most of the year. Nonetheless, a long and strenuous walk on Great Keppel can often be rewarded by a cool swim at a deserted beach, which doesn't suck.

Keppel Tourist Services also organise trips to some of the other islands in the bay, including Middle Island, which boasts a decent under-water observatory and Halfway Island. A number of the other islands are national parks, where camping is permitted. You'll need to take your own supplies and water, but a stint camping rough on a deserted tropical island makes a nice relief from the frenetic party-animal scene on Great Keppel proper. Information and permits from the ranger's office (079) 336 608 in **Rosslyn Bay**.

Flinthart's Journal

Her name was Coralie and she came from Nice. On an island full of pasty Pommies turning piglet pink under the tropical sun, she was a tanned, elegant vision in a white G-string bikini. They say gentlemen prefer blondes. Guess I don't make the grade.

Coralie had been in Australia long enough to know where the Hunter Valley was, so she was properly impressed when I unearthed a bottle of cold chardonnay at the Great Keppel Resort boozerie. In fact, she had a lot of very good things to say about Australian wines. We sat in the shade, drinking from the bottle, watching the beach, talking about the country.

Eventually, she admitted there was one problem for her. The national hang-up about nudity that we inherited from the English made Coralie more than a little uncomfortable. Back in France, she was used to bathing topless pretty much anywhere she wanted. Over here, she said, people stared.

I could understand why. In fact, I wanted to do a lot more than stare.

I asked her to wait on the beach and came back with a little catamaran which was no longer being used by the big blond muscle-boy who'd rented it. Of course, he'd been using it when I found him, but he swam quite well for a European.

Humpy Island was a short, easy 5km away. Coralie took the opportunity to do a little serious sunbathing, which was just fine with me. On the island, with the sail down and the boat drawn up to the treeline, there was nothing to show where we'd gone. It was a nice place, very private.

Nobody stared at all.

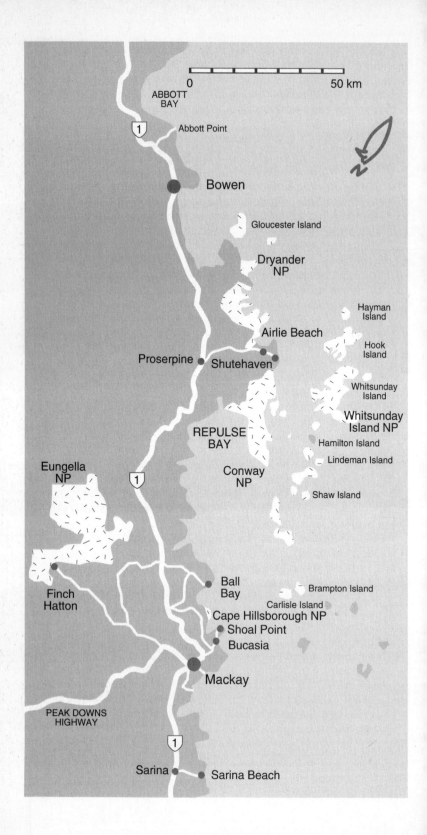

The Whitsunday Coast

This takes you from Mackay to Bowen, the big feature (the Big Feature) being the extremely fantastic Airlie Beach and the Whitsunday Islands. Airlie is a fairly ordinary little 'packer party suburb, over-infested with travellers and hostels, but again, there's some decent rainforest – and those islands! God, those islands!

Near Mackay, the highway finds the seashore again. It's not as wild and windswept and wonderful as it is down south and the surf is laughable, but at least it's there. Mackay is the principal township here, with a look-in from Proserpine. There's some good rainforest in the area of Mackay and since it's not yet a Big Tourist Mecca, it's pretty good.

Dirk's Dozen

1. Anything to do with the **Whitsunday Islands**, particularly boat cruises, camping on the national park islands, snorkelling, diving and rubbernecking at the hideously wealthy on Hamilton Island.

2. Overnighting at **Cape Hillsborough National Park** to watch the wallabies surf.

3. **Conway National Park** near Airlie.

4. Big Party Activities in **Airlie**: drinkin', dancin' and partyin' til ya puke.

5. Platypus-spotting, hiking and camping at **Finch Hatton** and **Eungella National Park**.

6. Camping at **Carlisle Island**, next door to Brampton Island.

Dirk Dumps On

1. **Proserpine**.

2. **Hamilton Island** development.

3. **Brampton Island Resort**.

Mackay

Mackay is self-sufficient, relaxed and, because it has lots of other industries, largely uninterested in the traveller's buck, which makes a nice change. The highway runs pretty much straight through the city, although it shies away from the city heart. Mackay has no decent beaches of its own, but a short way north of the city, any one of a dozen highway exits will get you to the pleasant beaches at **Eimeo**, **Dolphin Heads**, **Black's Beach** and **Harbour Beach**.

The town is on a fairly flat coastal plain, much greener than Townsville or Rockhampton. The centre of the city is laid out in a geometric sort of manner, with nice, wide streets and a slow, easy-going sort of atmosphere. There's not a whole lot of interest to the traveller in the town proper, although there are a few stately old buildings. Nothing to write home about. The hinterland offers a few options, though – enough to make Mackay a useful base from which to venture out sightseeing.

Stuff to Do

The Mackay region has at least three very worthwhile options for travellers. On the mainland, **Cape Hillsborough National Park** is definitely worth visiting and preferably staying overnight, if only to catch the chance of watching the wallabies bathe in the surf at dawn. (Weird. Very weird). The best way to get to Cape Hillsborough is by the road which passes through **Bucasia** from Mackay, as this road also passes through **Mt Jukes National Park**.

The park itself isn't enormous, but it takes in a variety of landscapes, including eucalypt, scrub, rainforest and of course, some excellent beaches.There's a lot of wildlife to be seen here – not just the kangaroos and wallabies, but birds, turtles, sugar gliders and varieties of possum. The park is pretty well off the beaten tourist track, so it makes a very nice layover. You can camp at the **Cape Hillsborough Resort** (079) 590 152 at the end of the Cape Hillsborough Rd for less than $10 and have access to the swimming pool and the laundry, as well as the usual amenities. It's a nice place.

Also on the mainland, **Eungella National Park** and most especially, **Finch Hatton Gorge** are accessible from Mackay. You need to head due west for about 85km and towards the end, the road gets to be steep, narrow and winding. There is fine rainforest here, with excellent walking and swimming and colonies of platypus as well. **Reef Forest Adventure Tours** (079) 554 100 can get you up here on a day trip for under $50 from Mackay. They also do camping drop-offs for a somewhat lesser rate, so if you like, you can stay at the excellent **Platypus Bush Camp** (079) 583 204. This place is close to Finch Hatton Gorge and comes very highly reccommended from everyone who's been there, for peaceful setting, excellent walking and swimming and friendly proprietors. If you can get to Finch Hatton town, a phone call will usually get you a lift to the Platypus Bush Camp.

Eungella is a very special area. It's the southernmost extension of the northern World Heritage listed rainforests. It was saved from the general drying of the region by virtue of the fact that it is situated on a large upland plateau – but in being saved, it was also isolated. As a result, the Eungella region has a number of species of birds and animals found nowhere else in Australia, let alone the world. Consider, if you will, the (now probably extinct) Eungella Gastric Brooding Frog, which keeps its eggs in its stomach and gives live birth to the tadpoles through its mouth.

The town of Eungella itself is a small and pretty mountain village. The **Eungella Hideaway Backpacker's** (079) 584 685 operate nearby and if you go south about 5km of the township, the **Broken River Camp-**

ing Ground features the opportunity to watch platypus in the wild. In fact, they're common enough and familiar enough with humans, that if you come looking at dawn or dusk, you're practically guaranteed to see one of the weird little buggers. This is a chance that should not be missed – the platypus is disappearing from many of its haunts these days, due to habitat destruction and the incursions of exotic species.

The third of the Mackay Hinterland places worth seeing lies off the coast to the north. The **Cumberland Islands** group represents the southernmost extension of the Whitsundays chain. Of these, **Brampton Island** has been developed with a sort of middle-class resort, which is reached from Mackay. You can do day-trips to Brampton for about $45 courtesy of **Roylen Cruises** (079) 553 066, but of more interest is the fact that within spitting distance from Brampton is **Carlisle Island**. Carlisle is completely undeveloped national park, with a couple of camping grounds. Of course, there's no water supply on Carlisle Island and you are advised that you may not obtain water from Brampton Island – but bear in mind that at low tide, you can easily walk from Carlisle to Brampton. And Brampton has a resort, with a café or two and even Cold Beer. Who's going to stop you camping on Carlisle and walking across the sand bar at low tide to eat your meals with the Daytrippers?

Shelter

Naturally, there's not a whole lot. **Larrikin Lodge** (079) 513 278 in 32 Peel St is, despite its name, quiet, laid-back and a little creaky, though wholesomely clean. It's a YHA facility, but true to the North Queensland credo, they don't mind if you want to slide a couple of six-packs into their refrigerator. Outright drunkenness is not accepted, but a few lubricating beers to promote the path of international good will are definitely OK. Less than a block away, practically opposite the bus stop is **Backpacker's Retreat** (079) 511 115 at 21 Peel St. This place is slightly more party-oriented, run by a very friendly Irish lady of indeterminate vintage.

Both places have a pool and barbecue facilities and a simple berth at either comes in at less than $15.

Proserpine

When you get to this town, turn east. You'll reach Airlie Beach in about 25km. Don't look back.

Airlie Beach & The Whitsunday Islands

Airlie Beach is about 25km east from Proserpine. It looks like nothing so much as a modern suburb, strung out along the shore. The actual beach-front section is quite small, perhaps three blocks long, but it is in this area that the real brunt of the 'packer action occurs. And quite a brunt it is, too. Other than Cairns, Airlie Beach is without a doubt the most jam-packed Action Packer Mecca on the whole of the coast.

Now, as Airlie Beach itself is quite small and the beach is very ordinary, to say the least, there must be some sort of a reason for this kind of 'packermania, right? And that reason is, of course, the **Whitsunday Islands**. I don't want to come across all gushing and touristy here, so I'll try understatement. If there's a spot on the planet closer to God's original blueprints for Heaven than the Whitsundays, I've never seen it. We're talking seventy-odd continental islands of varying size, covered in primal rainforests and fringed by pristine, extravagantly beautiful coral reefs. This place is nothing short of amazing.

Snapshots

Dave and Lorraine Gush Nauseatingly: Oh my God, weren't the Whitsunday Islands just the most beautiful place in the whole world? Oh, wow. I mean, gee, how gorgeous! All those beautiful little islands, with the reef and the coral all around them? We must have seen about a million fish. It was just amazing. Isn't scuba diving just the most amazing thing? You have been diving, haven't you? Oh, of course you have. Oh, my God, I don't know how we ever lived without it. And that cute little Airlie Beach. Wasn't it the sweetest place? All the people were really nice to us, especially the ones on the boat. That was just a blast. We had the best time out on the boat. And I got tanned all over, too! Because most of those little islands, right, well, nobody lives there. So you can get put down for a day and be all on your own. Isn't that just the most amazing thing? Of course, you have to carry food and water, because there's nothing there, which is a shame. But some of the islands had the most gorgeous little resorts on them. Oh, they were so pretty!

What's that? Oh, yes, of course Dave and I are going to come back. My God, how could you go back to Michigan after something like that? I mean, it's winter there right now, you know. With snow and everything. Have you ever seen snow? I mean real snow? Oh, of course you have. Dave and I are going to apply for citizenship. I can get a job as a teacher and he can just keep working as a programmer. Does the Internet reach the Whitsunday Islands? You do know about the Internet here, don't you? Of course you do.

What a total waste of beer.

The waters of the islands are safe from jellyfish and other evils all year round, remaining pretty uniformly crystal-clear no matter what the weather. And the islands themselves provide quite a barrier against the vicissitudes of the wind and the elements. Even quite inexperienced sailors drift around these sheltered waters with impunity. And the fishing … and the snorkelling … the diving … the swimming …

Actually, I'm not too sure why I bothered to leave.

Stuff To Do

Okay, let's get the bullshit out of the way. Being a 'packer mecca, Airlie has the usual range of stuff they think 'packers like to do. Skydiving, drinking, parasailing, partying, horseback riding, drinking, bungy jumping, getting laid, biplane rides, drinking, jet-skis, ultra-light planes, abseiling, rock-climbing, yattata yattata yattata … Where do these people come from? Don't they have homes to go to? If you want to try any of these things, just talk to any of the local hostels, or practically any of the businesses on the main street.

One fairly unusual local attraction is 'land-sailing'. This involves getting onto a sort of three-legged skateboard with a triangular sail and rocketing along **Conway Beach**, when the tide is out. It'll cost you about $35, but it's a different sort of experience. Experienced sailors and windsurfers take note: a land-based sailing craft doesn't handle quite the same way that you're used to. Take it easy until you know how to turn without going over!

Local rainforest tours are available. This is a nice option; the **Conway Park forests** are in particularly good condition. You can either book yourself into one of the half-day tours to **Cedar Creek** for about $35, or if you have your own vehicle, you can drive around that way and do your own walking. Drive back along the road to Proserpine and look for a left hand turn about 5km short of the main highway. The road goes to **Bonavista** and Conway. About 10km along that road, another left hand turn into a much more dubious road will take you back to Cedar Creek and the falls. Definitely worth the trip.

Also worth mentioning is the local zoo, **Eden Fauna Park**. It's on Shute Harbour Rd in Cannonvale, short of Airlie proper. The park is quite large, very well run and extremely informative. If you're heading northwards, this is a good opportunity to get a look at some of the wildlife you may encounter before it gets a look at you. Check out the crocodile feeding sessions!

Scuba diving in the Airlie Beach/Whitsunday region is a particularly fine option. It's not too expensive here – less than $300 for full PADI certification – and you will find that there are a lot of extras thrown in. **True Blue Dive**, for instance, currently provide accommodation and some feeding during the length of the course. Most importantly, though, all the local courses and even simple introductory dives, will get you out onto the Whitsunday reefs, which are simply world-class brilliant.

One particularly interesting option is a so-called 'dry dive'. Basically, they give you a short lecture on the effects of compression and nitrogen narcosis, then they put you in a big tank and turn up the pressure. Gradually, as nitrogen narcosis, or 'rapture of the depths' sets in, you and your companions will begin acting like a bunch of drunks. It's a lot of fun and there's no hangover. It's also a great way to learn about the phenomenon and since the sessions are videotaped, you get another big laugh afterwards watching yourselves behave like a bunch of drunken fools.

Of course, the main thing to do in Airlie Beach is to get the hell on out to the Whitsunday Islands. This can be managed in a number of ways.

Snapshots

'Robinson Kiwi', by Crackers of Melbourne: This is a true story. Only the names have been changed to protect the extremely guilty …

We wanted to go bareboating in the Whitsundays. Me and three other blokes, we checked the hostel and found a couple of others to come with us. Six in all, so we could cut costs to the bone.

One bloke pulled out at the last moment and we had to replace him on short notice, which is how Mike the Kiwi came aboard. He seemed alright back in Airlie, but after a couple of hours on a boat with him, we were ready to kill the prick.

He was one of these blokes who's always got to be one up on you. Been there, done that, seen better, ate the t-shirt. You know the kind. Plus, of course, he was big and blonde and tanned and he looked the part, which none of us skinny pale bastards did. Worst thing was, though, he was a real ape-shit drunk. We were going out five days all up and he packed five fucking bottles of cheap scotch. The first night, we had a real party and it was pretty funny, but Mike got really horribly drunk, staggering around the boat, puking his guts and bellowing about all the women he'd fucked. It was a nightmare.

The hangover kept him quiet the next morning, but sure enough, next night out came another bottle and he was off again. We managed to avoid the worst of it this time, because we were moored at one of the resorts, but he still managed to spew all over the gangway and pass out in a puddle of his own vomit.

Something had to give.

Next evening, we decided to have our party on one of the little deserted islands. We moored the boat and the six of us got into the dinghy and made for shore. It was a pretty little place, with a beach and lots of forest. We waited until Mike got ratshit drunk again, then we pissed off back to the boat. Left him with enough food and water for a few days, figuring we'd be back to get him.

Fishing Charters: a day trip fishing on the outer reefs. Costs about $65 and until you've been fishing on the Barrier Reef, you've never been fishing at all. Now naturally, this doesn't get you into the islands much, but if you've got limited time or money, it's worth a thought.

Snapshots

We took his scotch, though. Served him right, we thought.

The next couple of days were really great. Having the extra space on the boat made it all so much nicer. Finally, we sailed back to the place where we'd left him – and wouldn't you know it, the bastard was gone!

We searched that little island one end to the other. Fucking 'cooee!' until our lungs fell out. In the end, we just had to give up. We figured he'd managed to flag someone, of course, but there was a nagging worry there that maybe he'd done some stupid bloky thing like trying to swim for the mainland. He was dumb enough.

We shouldn't have worried. Kiwi Mike was back at the harbour waiting for us, with a great big shit-eating grin and half-a-dozen women clustered around him. When he was sure we'd all seen him, he gave one of the women a big tonguey and strolled over like we were best mates.

Seems he'd been 'rescued' shortly after he woke up the next day. It didn't take him long to work out we'd ditched him, so when this boatload of Canadian and American women went past, he had his story all worked out. How his girlfriend had died in a car accident and he'd got stuck into the booze 'to dull the pain'. How he decided to quit and went to live on a deserted island, going cold turkey until he was dry. How some of his mates came around periodically and kept him in food and water. How he'd been there for weeks, wrestling with his alcoholism.

They lapped it up. An hour after he was aboard, they thought he was Crocodile Dundee, Tarzan and Robinson Crusoe all rolled into one.

The other blokes just walked off in disgust when they found out what had come of our ditching him. Me, I did what I reckon any reasonable bloke would do under the circumstances: offered to back up his bullshit story for him if he'd introduce me to the brunette with the big tits.

Bareboat charters: This is a very popular option. It will take a bunch of you together to swing it, but it does give quite a lot of freedom of action. Essentially, you and your group will rent a small yacht, without crew or skipper. You'll get some basic instructions and then be turned loose for the duration of your hire.

Cook described the Whitsunday Islands as being one gigantic safe harbour, but then, he was in a dirty big ocean-going vessel. In actual fact, the almost maze-like nature of the islands can make for some tricky winds and currents, especially when the tide is running. On the whole though, the place is safe enough for even the most hamfisted of landlubbers to pootle around.

Bareboating isn't cheap. There's a $500 or so security deposit, to begin with. Some charter groups may accept a receipt from your credit card for this, to be cashed when and if you actually trash their boat. On the other hand, you'll still be paying between $80 and $110 per person, per day, in rental fees for the boat itself. Usually, you must hire for a minimum of five days, although this may be negotiable in the off-season. (By the way, it's not a good idea to 'overload' the boat past the number of berths available. Contravenes safety regulations, amongst other things.) You'll also need to provide your own supplies.

On the credit side, though, bareboating means that you and yours go where and when you like. It's true that seasoned skippers who know the region can find the very best places to go, but the Whitsundays as a whole are so outrageously beautiful that it's hard to imagine finding somewhere you wouldn't want to be.

Another point in the favour of bareboating is the fact that some of the resorts permit yachts to moor for a fairly minimal sort of rate. Once you've coughed up the cash, you're then permitted the use of resort facilities, like pools, bars, discotheques, spas, watersports gear, or whatever. A five day bareboat jaunt through the Whitsundays ought to cost you personally about $600 – but it may well be the best $600 you've ever spent.

Sailing Cruises: In this case, what you're paying for is a berth on a vessel which has a skipper, plus perhaps some crew. At the moment, you'll get about three days and two nights out amongst the islands for $250-$300. Food is provided and the skipper's experience will ensure that the vessel gets to all the very best spots around the islands.

This option is a little lazier than the bareboats, but it doesn't leave you holding the bag if anything goes wrong. Having an experienced skipper aboard is a very reassuring thing, believe me. Hostel-owners and tour operators suggest that this is a better way to do the Whitsundays than bareboating. I don't know about that. It doesn't have the same potential for disaster, admittedly – but then, there's something very seductive about the freedom of a bareboat cruise. Work it out for yourself.

Daytripping: There's about half a dozen different resorts amongst the islands. Boats leave pretty much all the time from **Shute Harbour**, going out that way. A return trip will cost you less than $50 and depending on which resort isle you choose, you may find that the use of some resort facilities is included. If you've got only a little time or money, this is the way to go. It doesn't really give you a very good look at the Whitsundays, though.

Paddleskis: This is a really nifty idea, but only for the very fit. From Shute Harbour, the nearest of the Whitsunday Islands are less than 5km away and camping is permitted on many of them. An interesting and challenging trip through the nearer isles is easy to put together, but your time will be limited by the need to carry drinking water.

Camping: Many of the islands have national park camping grounds. Permits are available from the local **National Parks office** and cost only $2 per night. Typically, you can arrange to be dropped off and picked up again by any of the multitude of daytrip operators and charter boats for about $50 – $70. Most of the islands don't have drinking water. Make sure you find out from the National Parks service about the place you're planning to go.

If you do follow this option, it pays to remember the Rule of 'P': Proper Planning and Preparation Prevent Piss-Poor Performance. Check the list in the introduction of this book where it discusses 'Accommodation and Camping' and make sure you've brought everything you're going to need.

Now, the easiest way to arrange any or all of these options is through your hostel in Airlie, or through any one of the prolific tourist information joints lining the main street. Everyone – and I mean everyone – in Airlie has a sideline in getting people out to the islands. If you want to make a few preliminary inquiries, though, you might contact any of the following: **Whitsunday Visitors Information** (079) 466 673; **Airlie Tourist Information** (079) 466 665; **H.B. Cruises** (1 800 677 119); **Mollo Australia** (008 075 006); **ProSail** (1 800 810 116); **Destination Whitsundays** (1 800 644 563); **I Love Whitsunday Cruises** (1 800 577 119); **Whitsunday Connections** (008 0750127); and **Airlie/Shute National Parks and Wildlife** (079) 467 022.

In And Out

Airlie Beach is really only road accessible for the budget traveller. There is a small airfield, but it mostly covers traffic to and from the islands. If you haven't got a car, then, you're pretty much limited to bus. This isn't really a problem, though. Airlie is so popular that buses from both long-distance lines happily make the detour from Proserpine. Find out before you board your bus whether it is actually going to Airlie, though – about fifty percent of the buses go straight on through Proserpine on their way north or south, skipping Airlie and Shute Harbour. Not to worry, though: there are frequent local bus services from Proserpine to Airlie.

Airlie to Brisbane by bus is about 16-19 hours and costs around $100. Airlie to Cairns is about eight hours and costs about $50. All the long-distance buses stop in a car-park halfway along **Shute Harbour Rd**, behind the shops. If you're trying to get out, practically every store and every hostel in the central part of Airlie can book you a ticket away.

Shelter

Airlie is crawling with 'packer accommodation, most of which has all mod cons and features, with beds generally below $14 per night, sharing four or six to a room. If you shop around in the off season, you may find that competition has brought beds down below $10 per night.

On your way into Airlie, about a kilometre from the beach stretch proper, you will find **Bush Village Backpacker's** (079) 466 177 at St Martins St, just off the main road. Facilities are excellent and the proprietors are very helpful. Accommodation is in four-bed cabins, which are airy and light, quite spacious in comparison with most 'packer places. The cabins have cooking facilities too, and the place sports a small pool. The Bush Village people can organise many different tours for you and help out with the hire of boats, mopeds, bikes, scooters, or whatever. A top spot, despite being a little away from the centre of the action.

Also out of Airlie in this direction is **Beach House** (079) 466 306 which overlooks **Shingley Beach**, on Shute Harbour Rd. This is a set of units with a pool and optional air-conditioning, which can be a lifesaver in summer.

Reef Oceania Village (079) 466 137 at 147 Shute Harbour Rd, is actually a minor sort of family resort, which has an area set aside for 'packers. Fairly cheap, with good facilities.

In the centre proper, the **Whitsunday Village Resort** (079) 466 266 on Shute Harbour Rd is very attractively laid out. Two pools, tropical garden sort of theme – but the emphasis is on Big-Time Partying. They've got their own restaurant and bar and the place tends to be more than a little wild. Accommodation is in six-bed or four-bed units.

Club 13 (079) 467 376 at 13 Begley St is positively ridiculous. The place is set on a hill overlooking the town and the bay and it looks exactly like a multi-level apartment complex – which it is. Complete with pool, spa, undercover parking and bodacious views from the verandahs. Christ, why would you bother with Club Med?

Beaches Backpacker's (079) 466 244 is another Big Party zone. Restaurant, bar, pool – the place was once a motel and the accommodation itself is still quite good. Also equipped with a full booking agency who can arrange practically anything short of international air tickets for you. Party, party, party: forget sleep and prepare to Rage Unto Extremity.

Nearby is **True Blue Backpacker's** (079) 466662 which is smaller, more basic and a touch cheaper. It's not so well set out for the party scene, but being in the town centre, it's close enough to the action. A good compromise if you decide you want to actually go somewhere and sleep once you're partied out. Also, **True Blue Dive** operate from this place, so you can easily arrange all your scuba excursions from here.

Still near the centre of the action, **Blue Waters** (079) 466 182 is another block of units dedicated to 'packers. What, no pool?

Out towards the Shute Harbour end of town, the **YHA Club Habitat** (079) 466 312 is another converted motel, quite large and comfortable. Lots of atmosphere, good facilities including a pool and although the YHA organisation isn't so big on the party scene, they're pretty laid back here in Airlie Beach.

Further out towards Shute Harbour proper is **Backpacker's By The Bay** (079) 467 267 in Hermitage Drive. A little smaller, a little quieter than the action-vortex places in the town centre, it's a groovy, friendly sort of place.

With all these cheap, well-appointed hostels, you'd want to be a little masochistic to be camping around Airlie. I mean, tent sites are only marginally cheaper than beds – if at all – and not nearly so comfortable or so near the action. If you must, try the road between Airlie and Shute Harbour. There are at least four caravan parks along the way, plus a national park camping ground about 6km eastward, in the **Conway National Park**.

The Islands

Most of the Whitsundays are national park. This is a good thing, because it means that poverty-stricken 'packers can legitimately camp there, without having to fork out megabucks to resort owners. Unfortunately, it makes fishing a little weird. They've got some kind of a crazed zoning system whereby Zone A means you can fish a little bit and Zone B means not at all, except when you're not in a Marine Park, whereat Zone A and Zone B have different meanings again, unless it's a Sunday or a public holiday other than Easter. Rather than try to explain the situation in depth, I suggest that you contact the local office of **National Parks and Wildlife** (079) 467 022 between Airlie and Shute and get exact details of what you can and cannot do from them.

The Whitsundays are continental islands, being the tops of mountains once connected to the Conways during the last ice age, when the sea level was a lot lower than it is now. (I wonder if Neanderthals worried about Global Warming? I can see it now: 'Stop, Thak, stop! Mustn't use fire! Ice will melt! Sea will cover everything!') As a result, they've got quite a range of forest cover, although there's not a lot of permanent water out there. Despite being continental islands, many of them have excellent fringing coral reefs and the diving and snorkelling amongst the Whitsundays is superb.

Whitsunday Island proper is the largest of the chain. There is no resort on the island, but there are at least four national park campsites scattered around. **Whitehaven Beach** in the south-east corner is probably the best beach of the whole island chain and the campsite there is correspondingly popular. There's excellent snorkelling and diving to be had at the north end of the island. There's fresh water on the island too, during the summer rainy season.

Next largest of the islands is **Hook**, which is just north of Whitsunday itself. There is a resort on Hook, which has the distinction of being the only one on the islands within cost-reach of budget travellers. It is also the oldest of the resorts and the least over-blown. In fact, there's not much more than accommodation, food and a bit of souvenir shopping there. Basic water-sports facilities are available, but nothing like as complex and showy as elsewhere.

There are camping areas on Hook, including a couple right next to the resort, which have access to showers and toilets. Hook is therefore a fairly easy proposition for a relatively lengthy stay and as a result, it's quite popular with budget travellers.

Third largest island is **Shaw Island**, in the Lindeman group. It has a campsite and some fine reefs on the east and west coasts, in the south.

Near Shaw Island is **Lindeman**. In 1992, Australia's first Club Med went up here and the place has festered ever since. Despite the fact that most of the island is national park, there are no camping facilities here

Captain's Log, James Cook 1770 World Surf Safari: 'Still no decent surf. Confound this mondo uncool reef! The ship has just entered a veritable host of attractive islands not far from the mainland. Seeing as it is Whitsunday, I have left off brown-nosing the Admiralty and opted to suck up to the Church for a change, in naming the isles for this holy festival.

'Banks, as usual, insisted upon having the last word. The dude is such a geek, it's a wonder his personality hasn't imploded. He says that today is not Whitsunday. In vain, I showed him the calendar and the series of scratches on the wall next to Ponsonby in the brig – Banks would have none of it. He continues to rave about something called the International Date Line. According to him, by sailing around the world in a westerly direction, we have lost a day. Utterly bogus! How can one possibly lose a day? Where would it go? Banks is most definitely an utter Melvin.'

and unless you want to spend at least $170 a night to be dealt with by the Club Med Fun Police, you might as well resign yourself to at best daytripping to Lindeman. Not to worry; there's plenty of others.

Just to the south of Whitsunday Island is **Hamilton Island**, a place with a typically Queensland story. See, once upon a time there was a Fat Bastard named Keith Williams, who knew a good thing when he saw one. And the good thing was the incredibly corrupt National Party Government of Queensland in the seventies and most of the eighties. So Keith took himself out a lease on Hamilton Island for the purpose of farming deer. The deer-farming lease miraculously became a 'bulldoze the shit out of the whole island and create and enormous fucking resort-complex' lease! Those were the magic days in Queensland, they were. You could hardly turn around without discovering that another chunk of irreplaceable coastline had been mugged by a dodgy resort complex, owned by friends and relatives of the Nationals …

In a word, Hamilton Island sucks. They've converted the place to a suburb of the Gold Coast, complete with high-rise apartment blocks. The place is so fucking commercial that in defiance of the rest of Queensland, it operates on daylight saving time. Now in the tropics, Daylight Saving is about as useful as a chainsaw up the backside and nearly as comfortable. Nonetheless, by virtue of operating on daylight savings time, Hamilton Island manages to stay in synch with the Big Business zones of the Deep South. Probably a good thing for stressed executives who can't bear to be away from the business for too long, but it sure makes life difficult for random daytrippers from the coast. Be sure to check arrival and departure times carefully if you plan a daytrip to Hamilton.

Hamilton has no national park. Hamilton has no camping. In fact, Hamilton has a 'No Poor People' rule, near enough. If you want, though, you might consider mooring a bare-boat here and seeing what use you can get out of the local facilities, just to piss off the swarms of wealthy sunsuckers who are avoiding the lower classes.

There are a bunch of other resorts out there – **South Molle**, **Daydream** and **Long Island** all have them. They're pretty much of a muchness – out of the price range of most of us budget travellers and sporting nothing out of the ordinary in terms of facilities and entertainment. Hayman Island has one too, but huge bucks have been thrown at it to make it the excessive height of elegance, sophistication, style, luxury and expense. This is another place where it's fun to come ashore and go slumming for a while amongst the painfully wealthy.

The Mango

If you have the good fortune to be in Queensland at the right time of year, you will be blessed by the discovery of The Mango. Now it's true that there are those who say The Mango is just a piece of fruit - but these are the same people who claim that beer is not one of the five food groups. They are the deluded, the weird, the deeply geeky clingers around the unwiped butthole of life.

The truth is that The Mango is to fruit what total, animal sex is to aerobic exercise.

Mango. The word itself has a kind of tangy, juicy, tropical flavour in the mouth. The Queensland Mango is beyond my meagre powers of description. When you cross the border from the Dark Lands into God's Own Country, you must march immediately to the very first fruit vendor you discover and there you must say in a loud voice, 'I demand a large, ripe Bowen Mango be given to me immediately and damn the expense.'

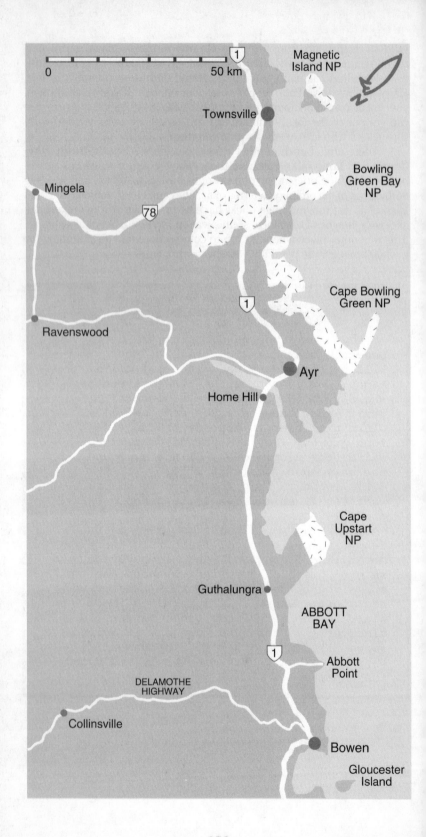

Bowen to Townsville

This is another area you should hurry through. Things get ugly around here. The townships are small and loaded with country-town prejudices. The landscape is unappealing, the coast is inaccessible and where you can find it, it's not particularly attractive. Major township is Townsville, which you'll probably wind up overnighting in simply because it's a bastard of a drive to push on much further.

There's a lot of agriculture in the area, though. Try looking for picking work around Bowen and in the Burdekin Region.

Dirk's Dozen

1.   A trip out to **Ravenswood** from Townsville.

2.   A day-trip to **Magnetic Island**, if you need a break from travelling.

Dirk Dumps On

1.   Practically everything else in the region, including **Bowen**, **Ayr**, **Home Hill**, **Guthalungra** and most everything else.

Bowen

South of Townsville about 200km, there is a blot on the coastal landscape called Bowen. These days, it's about a dozen blocks square and boasts a population of about 8,500, but in the early days of Queensland's history, it came damned close to being selected as the Big Noise of the North. Of course, the fact that it was situated on a sort of mud flat near a flood-prone river didn't help very much.

These days, there's a fair bit of fruit and veg growing around Bowen and if you were desperate, you might look for work in the area between April and November. Bowen is also the home of the luscious **Bowen Mango**, which you might be able to pick during December. There's a salt-producing facility too, but they don't do a lot of hiring.

Bowen isn't particularly attractive, nor is it near anything which is really outstanding. It's got a couple of decent beaches not too far away, but as per usual, you can write them off during the stinking hot summer months. As the highway passes pretty much through the town, the bus lines come through Bowen, so getting in and out is pretty easy. The train stops at a siding a fair way out of town, though, so if you're travelling by track, you'll need a cab to the town proper. Such as it is.

There's a couple of hostels in town, dealing mainly with transient workers. Try **Barnacle's Backpacker's** (077) 861 245 or **Bowen Backpacker's** (077) 863 433 if you really need somewhere to stay. Barnacle's is probably the more comfortable of the two.

Other than work and maybe the mango orgy of a lifetime during December, there really is no conceivable reason to be stuck in Bowen.

Ayr & Home Hill

The Burdekin Region: See if you can sleep through this bit.

Townsville

Townsville reminds me of a scabby, dysenteric dog, skulking around the edge of the pack, scavenging for scraps. And I mean that in the nicest possible way. First off, it's a military town. Army base, Air Force base, fuel and supply depot and all that kind of thing. This means that what little night life you may find is jammed up by beefy guys with short hair and long attitudes. Not that I've got anything against the military, Oh no – not me. Some of my best friends are military, yessir.

Then there's the terrain. Aside from **Castle Rock** sticking up like a gigantic inflamed zit in the middle of it, Townsville is flat as a cheap spare tyre. Flatter, even. Sure, there's mountains to the north, south and west – but the town itself is flat and dry and butt-ugly. Nothing much grows in Townsville, not even marijuana – at least not the way it does in the real North Queensland. If Cairns and thereabouts mark the place where the rainforest comes down to the sea, then Townsville is the place where the Red Centre makes a bid for freedom.

You can reach the reef from Townsville, of course – but not nearly so cheaply nor thoroughly as you can from, say, the Whitsunday Passage, or Cairns. And there's **Magnetic Island**, naturally enough – but it's a large, hot, dry, mainland island without a whole lot to recommend it and on the whole, the locals would probably be happier if you'd just shove off and let them get on with impregnating their sisters.

Get the idea I'm down on Townsville? I'm not, really: it's a nice enough town in its own right. It's just that there's nothing there to interest

a traveller. The casino? Big deal. Everybody's got a casino these days. It's no more exciting to lose your money in Townsville than anywhere else. You see, Townsville's real problem is simply that it's dry and ugly and the rest of coastal North Queensland is lush and beautiful, both north and south of Townsville itself. So why waste the time and money on Townsville?

Stuff To Do, If You Have To

Ummm, well – you can go to the **Great Barrier Reef Wonderland** at the casino end of Flinders St – they've got the inevitable **IMAX Theatre** and an enormous walk-through **marine aquarium** which is damned impressive. Cost you about $25 to do both of those and the museum as well, or you can pick which ones you want to see and pay separately. It's an impressive and well-managed complex, very educational and interesting, but there's better ways to see the reef. And once you've done **Undersea World**, you've just about exhausted Townsville. The **Perc Tucker Art Gallery** in the Flinders Mall carries some interesting local work from time to time and it's free. You can lose some money at the Casino. Or you can day trip to **Magnetic Island**, where it's hot and dry and you can wonder where the beaches are. (There are some – but don't expect surf, or anything like that. Plus during stinger season you're advised to swim in the stinger-proof enclosure.)

Actually, Magnetic Island has a pretty good koala sanctuary and yet another oceanarium with sharks in pools and stuff. There's some good bushwalking too, although the words 'hot' and 'dry' continue to play a major part in the experience. On the whole, Maggie makes a decent day trip, if you're not expecting too much. Should you decide to overnight on the island, there are a number of hostels and backpacker's places, including **Geoff's Place** at Horseshoe Bay (077) 78 5577) which also offers camping facilities, the most excellent **Magnetic Island Resort** (077) 78 5955 in Nelly Bay (almost an excuse for coming to the island in itself) and the very good **Hideaway Hostel** (077) 78 5110 in Picnic Bay. Magnetic Island, being quite close to the mainland and supporting a decent-sized population of its own, also has pubs, restaurants, cafés and a few shops, so you can get what you need for a reasonably extended stay if you want. I still don't see the attraction, myself. You can get to Magnetic Island and back for around $20 from the **Hayles wharf** on Flinders St, about a block past the casino end of the Mall. Ferries leave quite regularly, all day long.

There is some good diving to be had through Townsville. The wreck of the *Yongala* is one of the most famous and interesting dives on the Barrier Reef, but it's under at least 30m of water and wants a certain amount of experience before you go. The *Yongala* was a passenger craft that went down in a cyclone back around 1910 and nobody knew what the fuck had happened to it for a long time. (Pretty stupid, losing a large ship in a major cyclone and then saying 'Gosh, I wonder whatever happened to the old *Yongala*?')? Anyway, they finally found it again in WWII, but by then it was too bloody late, wasn't it? It's a totally awesome dive, though. Most of the Townsville dive schools can arrange a trip out here for you. A full certificate dive course around Townsville will cost you somewhere between $250 to $400.

Shelter

There's a couple of outsized places in **Palmer St**, not far from the **Transit Centre**. **Adventurer's Resort YHA** (077) 21 1522 is big, cheap (dorm beds less than $15) and a bit anonymous. On top of the the transit centre itself is **Andy's Backpacker's** (077) 21 2322, with similarly low prices. It also boasts its own bar and restaurant. But who wants to stay above a bus station? Slightly cheaper and a little more fun is the **Globetrotters** (077) 71 3242, also in Palmer St. **Civic House** in Walker St (077) 71 5381 comes well recommended and there's a new place called **Nomads** (077) 71 4316 which will have just opened at the time of writing this, opposite the Transit Centre in McIlwraith St. There's a few more scattered around the place, but who cares? You're not going to be staying in Townsville anyway.

Camping is vaguely possible at the two caravan parks – but with a tent site costing what a bed does in the hostels, why give yourself the grief? There's certainly nothing special about the caravan parks or the scenery nearby!

Food

Cruise the eastern (casino) end of Flinders St. What with the Transit Centre opening there, and the Reef Wonderland and all the 'packers places, this is the Restaurant Zone for Townsville. Such as it is. You can find Thai, Japanese, Mexican, Chinese, Malaysian and a few others in the general area, if you ask. Prices are reasonable on the whole and some of the food is getting to be quite good. Try the famous **Hog's Breath Café** steaks, or chase vegetarian dishes at the **Thai International**. Local seafood is reasonably good, as well. One thing, though: Barramundi is a much overrated fish. Sure, it's pretty good eating, but you'll pay a mint for it and often it has been frozen for storage or transit. Better off with Sweetlip, Red Emperor or Coral Trout, so far as I'm concerned. Mind you, if you're not too worried about mercury build-up from the canefield run-off, even flake (shark) can be good eating.

Flinthart's Diary

Had to stop for petrol in Townsville. A
bit of a miscalculation on my part – I
should have arranged it so I could just
shoot straight on through without stopping.

The petrol station on the way out of town
was full of desperate sorts with huge
backpacks, futilely trying every possible
means of getting out of the place. Strong
men were crying and pleading; women were
brazenly offering themselves against the
promise of passage out of Townsville.

It was no use. Every vehicle was full.
I'd picked up two travellers in Ingham,
going to Airlie. They stood guard over the
Red Terror, using sticks to beat off inter-
lopers while I paid up for the fuel.

We left Townsville behind in a blue cloud
of vapourised rubber. Everyone in the car
was silent. I remember thinking: Truly,
this is a place abandoned by God.

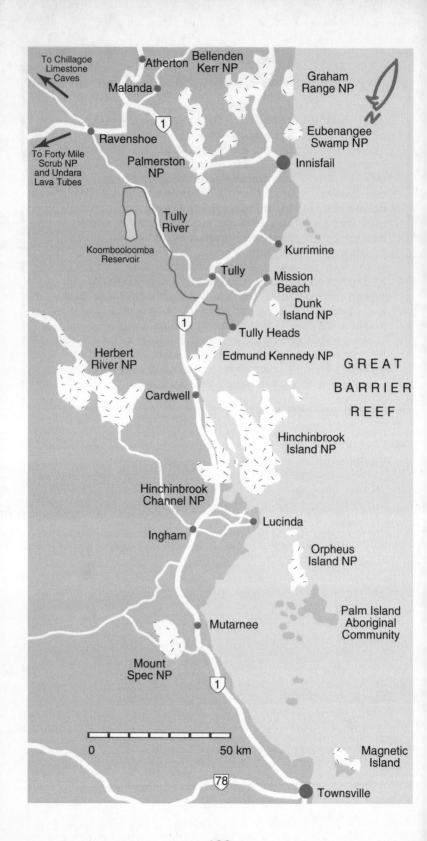

To Chillagoe
Limestone
Caves

Atherton

Bellenden
Kerr NP

Graham
Range NP

Malanda

To Forty Mile
Scrub NP
and Undara
Lava Tubes

Ravenshoe

① 1

Palmerston
NP

Eubenangee
Swamp NP

Innisfail

Tully
River

Kurrimine

Koombooloomba
Reservoir

Tully

Mission
Beach

Dunk
Island NP

① 1

Tully Heads

Herbert
River NP

Edmund Kennedy NP

G R E A T

B A R R I E R

R E E F

Cardwell

Hinchinbrook
Island NP

Hinchinbrook
Channel NP

Lucinda

Ingham

Orpheus
Island NP

Palm Island
Aboriginal
Community

Mutarnee

Mount
Spec NP

① 1

0   50 km

78

Magnetic
Island

Townsville

Ingham to Innisfail

Here the highway runs quite close to the ocean, often alongside of World Heritage listed rainforests. None of the little towns here – Ingham, Cardwell, Tully and Innisfail – have yet exploded into a tourist frenzy like Cairns has, which makes a few days spent around these parts quite rewarding.

The landscape is utterly without compromise. If it's not forest – frequently deep rainforest – then it's cleared agricultural land, or foreshore. That's all. This is a great area to explore on foot with a pack on your back and a tent close by. Good picking work to be had through Cardwell, local fishing is excellent, lots of waterfalls and swimming holes.

Dirk's Dozen

1. Walking the **Thorsborne Track** on Hinchinbrook Island.

2. Walking at least part of the **Dalrymple Track** leading inland.

3. Driving around the South Johnstone River Valley in search of **Paronella Park.**

4. Camping on **Dunk Island**, off Mission Beach.

5. White-water rafting through World Heritage forests on the **Tully River**.

6. Camping on **Orpheus Island**.

7. Driving up the **Palmerstone Range** from Innisfail to the Atherton Tableland.

8. Walking through **Cassowary Territory** at Mission Beach.

Dirk Dumps On

1. Hanging around **Innisfail**.

2. Staying overnight in **Tully**.

3. **Dunk Island** resort.

4. **Orpheus Island** resort.

Ingham

About an hour and a half north of Townville on the Bruce Highway is a pleasant little sugar-cane town which seems to speak mostly Italian. This is **Ingham**. There's no backpacker's places here as such, but you can get cheap, decent accommodation from some of the pubs – notably the **Hinchinbrook Hotel** and the rather more basic **Royal Hotel**, both in Lannercost St (the main street).

Ingham itself isn't worth much more than a lunch break, but the surrounding countryside hides a few pleasant surprises. Check out the following:

Paluma: closer to Townsville than Ingham, to the west of the highway in the mountains is a pleasant little village. The drive to get there is picturesque as all hell and there's some fine walking tracks along the way. Not far from the town itself is **Paluma Dam**, which is nice for swimming and walking.

Mt Spec National Park: actually sort of surrounds Paluma. Good swimming, walking and camping, especially at **Paradise Waterhole**. Very pretty area, with terrain varying from open eucalypt through to pockets of rainforest.

Jourama Falls National Park: about 40 km south of Ingham. Camping is okay, with permits required, but you can self-register on-site. Good walking, waterfalls and swimming.

Wallaman Falls National Park: 50km inland from Ingham, the 300-odd metre waterfall constitutes the longest single-drop falls in Australia. Runs all year, which is a bonus in this country, but it's most spectacular in the Wet Season, of course. The road to it is unpaved, but can be handled by conventional vehicles. Swimming and national park camping permitted close by.

Lucinda: a funny little village with most bodacious fishing. Lucinda is about 30km off the highway to the northeast of Ingham. Aside from being the access point to the southern end of Hinchinbrook, you should see the totally gigantic jetty used to load sugar. Waters are shallow around here; the damned thing had to be 6km long to allow loading of decent-sized ships. Six kilometres of wharf? You've got to see it to believe it.

Orpheus Island: this is one of the Palm Islands, most of which are Aboriginal reservations, which can be visited only by special permission. Orpheus, however, is national park. There is a hideously expensive resort on Orpheus, but as with so many of these places, you can skate around the edges with your camping permit. Orpheus is a continental island, but it has really excellent reefs around it, perfect for snorkelling. You'll need your own gear, though; the Orpheus resort is expensive and exclusive enough that it has no need to be kind or accommodating to dirt-poor backpackers and campers. Fresh water is another limiting factor; you'll need to bring your own drinking water.

The usual way of getting to Orpheus is by air, which is damned expensive – about $250 return from Townsville and even more from Cairns. Your best bet is to take a boat from **Dungeness**, near Lucinda. This should cost you about $130 return.

While Orpheus is a very pretty island, with excellent reefs, the expense of getting there, plus the fact that there is a resort development and the lack of fresh water or facilities, makes it a less attractive option than the **Franklands**, for example.

Cardwell/Hinchinbrook

Cardwell's this weeny little town about halfway between Cairns and Townsville on the coastal highway. Takes about an hour and a half to get there by road from either of the two cities. The train line runs through it and it's a regular bus stop, but it has no airport. It doesn't look like much

Great King Rat!!

Seeing that you have to carry your food into Hinchinbrook, it would be a shame to let someone else eat it, right? You will need to consider securing your provisions against the Dreaded North Queensland White-Tailed Rat, if that is the case.

This evil bastard is actually a native, found up and down the coast, especially around rainforested areas. (Big problems on Cape Tribulation, too!) Unlike most rats, they don't give a damn about the usual methods of food security, such as metal boxes (they'll chew through them in very short order), hanging from branches (these things just love to climb ropes and eat through bags), or even eating tinned food (yep, tins and all, down the hatch. Yum yum!). Given time, these rats have been known to chew through concrete, metal, wood, plastic and just about every other substance on the planet.

The approved method for securing your food is to run a wire between two trees. In the middle of the wire, suspend your food bag from another wire, so it hangs about a metre off the ground. At either end of the cross-wire, you should have a plastic bottle with the bottom cut out, to act as a loose 'collar', preventing the rats from climbing to your food. Make sure the bottles are loose and free to rotate, as it is this which dumps Ratty to the ground.

Otherwise, be prepared to share generously.

as you zoom through – a couple of caravan parks, a few petrol stations, some houses – but if you want to step off the 'packer treadmill for a while, there are far worse places to do it.

Stuff To Do, Apart From Work

The Cardwell Ranges: This is another area of heritage-listed rainforest with an interesting history to it. About a century or so ago, there was a lot of gold-mining and logging going on hereabouts and the Cardwell Ranges had some important access tracks cut through them. As a result, there is some utterly brilliant walking to be had in the area, with waterfalls, pristine rainforest stands, historic bridges and tracks, cassowaries, Aboriginal middens and scores of other points of interest. Of special note is the **Dalrymple Gap Walk**, which takes you along what was once a stock route, across a 120 year old stone bridge (hey – in Australia, that's pretty historic, okay?) to the **Valley of Lagoons**. Guided walks are available through the local ranger and the hostel, but it's a lot more fun simply to get a map from these people and to strike out on your own.

The Kennedy

In the Cardwell region, you'll come across lots of parks, places and plaques dedicated to a bloke called Edmund Kennedy. This is pretty weird, as by and large, he is one of the Great Failures of Australian exploration.

Now, Back in 1848, North Queensland was pretty much the End of the World. Down south, there was a lot of interest in the unclaimed territory. What with the rest of Australia practically bleeding gold and cropland, they figured there were a few bucks to be had in the North as well.

So in goes Kennedy. The man is reputedly an experienced explorer. Despite this, he screwed the pooch in royal style in North Queensland. He loaded up his expedition with 100 sheep, plus three carts full of supplies, with over 300kg of shit in each cart. Then the stupid fucker made landfall at Rockingham Bay, in the mangroves near present-day Cardwell.

Naturally, herding all those sheep and dragging those massive carts through the mangroves turned into a complete clusterfuck in no time at all. Nonetheless, Kennedy was nothing if not determined. He and his party literally hacked

Hinchinbrook Island: This is a large, mountainous, rainforested island separated from the mainland by no more than a narrow, mangrove-choked strait. To date, it is almost completely untouched and in fact, is largely unexplored in any formal sense. Hinchinbrook is a national park and it is possible to hike and camp most of the way around it. In fact, the **Thorsborne Trail** is one of the most magic experiences available in the deep north. Basically, it's a track of about 32km length which pretty much follows the coastal side of the island. This means that on one side, you've got virgin rainforest, full of waterfalls and streams and swimming pools and on the other, you've got beach and the sea.

This is a rough and rugged track and you should allot at least four days to make the journey. Camping equipment will be necessary and of course you'll have to carry all your food with you. The camping is minimalist, aimed at the 'no-trace' level of impact and only 40 people are given permits to be on the track at any one time. Clean, fresh water is available pretty much year-round from the various streams that cross the track. Care should be taken in crossing these creeks; where this happens down by the sea, you should certainly wait until low tide in case of croco-

Factor

their way north to the Mitchell River region, then as far as the Palmer River, shedding sheep and supplies and carts every which way as they went.

Eventually, though, they realised that there was no way they were going to make rendezvous with the ship which was supposed to collect them, as laden as they were. Bright boy Kennedy immediately split the party up, leaving most of them at the mouth of the Pascoe River under William Carron, with all of their geological samples and the remaining sheep. Kennedy himself went north, taking his faithful black guide 'Jacky-jacky' and three others. Their object was to reach the 'Ariel' – their pickup ship, landing up at Cape York.

The rest is pretty much history. There was an encounter with hostile Aborigines at Escape River and Kennedy was speared, along with the other three. Jacky-jacky made it out, though, and a rescue was duly sent to the Pascoe River. Unfortunately, due to disease and shortage of supplies, there were only two survivors there. All in all, it was a bit of a fuckup.

dile attack. Also, in summer it should be remembered that there will be box jellyfish in the sea here. Likewise, summer brings the monsoon rains and the occasional tropical cyclone. If you decide to take the **Hinchinbrook Track** in summer, be certain to inform the local ranger that you are doing so.

Acquiring maps and permits to Hinchinbrook can be done through the **Rainforest and Reef Centre**, 79 Victoria St, Cardwell, (070) 66 8601.

Fishing: Being lodged amongst the mangroves on the coast, Cardwell also has brilliant fishing. If you are going to spend a little time in the area, you might enjoy having a go. Fishing gear can be had from the YHA hostel and the hostel owner can clue you in on the best places to throw in a line, as well as Stuff To Do with your fish once you've caught them.

Shelter and Work

To date, Cardwell has only two backpacker's hostels, the **Cardwell Backpacker's Hostel** (070) 66 8014 at 178 Bowen St towards the north end of town and the **YHA Hinchinbrook Hostel** at 175 Bruce Highway, a little north of the town centre proper, (070) 66 8648. The caravan parks cater to the 'packer trade as well.

The YHA hostel offers a camping facility, whereby 'packers can use the facilities for a very low rate (under $10) if they have their own tent. They also have a good range of gear for use or hire and can help organise your Hinchinbrook expedition, including camping gear. The chap who runs the Cardwell hostel knows the area thoroughly and can arrange for you to take all the best walks and trips. Better still, he also knows the local farmers and can arrange for you to find work in the thriving fruit-picking industry. They grow all kinds of things up that neck of the woods; you may find yourself picking lychees or mangostines, or simple, prosaic green beans. The work is demanding, but the pay is adequate.

Tully/Mission Beach

The Tully River: Raft It Before They Dam It. The World Heritage-listed Tully River, easily one of the most beautiful and exciting spots in Australia, has been hanging under the on-again, off-again threat of being turned into a hydroelectric project for several years now. Local raft operators are dead-set against the idea, as one might expect and conservationists are right behind them. Various state governments, though, have had different opinions.

I did some research into the Electricity Commission's investigations of the project and amongst the thousands of pages of garbage, I found a couple of interesting things. Firstly, there was the question of whether the electricity was actually needed. At the moment, the National/Liberal government of Queensland has backed out of joining that state to the national electricity grid, which would certainly have removed the need for the Tully Dam project. Why?

Then there was the cost of the project: three potential sites were selected, at Burdekin River (where a dam exists already), at Herbert River and of course, at the Tully River. The State Electricity Commission were claiming five years or so ago that they could set the whole system up for about $500 million – which they said was 'around the lowest cost' for any of the three sites. What the fuck do you suppose 'around the lowest cost' means when you're selecting from only three sites?

There is a possible reason behind the seemingly expensive and potentially unnecessary Tully Dam, though. You see, the nearest town to the dam site would be Ravenshoe, which once lived on timber-cutting. Then, when the World Heritage listings came through and logging was banned in the region, Ravenshoe copped it in the teeth. There were huge protests from timber-cutters and loggers and a lot of bad blood all round.

Now, reading those thousands of pages of bullshit from the Electricity Commission, I found that they had a special, environmentally-sound plan in place. Y'see, to do the Tully River properly, they proposed not one dam, but seven. And they expected to flood quite a lot of forest region. Now, says the Electricity Commission, trees left to decay underwater produce methane, which as everyone knows, is a naughty Greenhouse Gas. Can't have that, can we? So of course, what they suggest is that the trees which will be flooded should be logged first. By local contractors. And guess which town full of disgruntled, unemployed timber workers would be closest to the scene?

Tully has the distinction of being the wettest inhabited spot in Australia. We're talking a yearly rainfall in excess of 3 metres. I don't know what the local record for a single day of rain might be, but I've personally been stuck in the area when it received nearly a metre in 24 hours. This is NOT your average sun-shower.

Tully itself is a straggling little township a bit more than an hour south of Cairns on the Bruce Highway. There's not a lot of interest there and the word is that the local backpacker's hostel should be avoided if possible. If you do wind up stuck in Tully, definitely go to the caravan park and book yourself a van or a cabin; by all accounts the hostel is very much a last resort.

The **Tully River** is the main source of interest in the area. White-water rafting the Tully through **Raging Thunder** or one of the other groups is a remarkable experience. It'll set you back about $110, but for that you'll spend a day rafting through World Heritage-listed rainforests, in cool, crystal-clear water of the sort of purity that only North Queensland seems to produce any more. If you plan to do any rafting at all while you're in Australia, the Tully River should be your choice.

The other matter which might tempt you to stay in Tully for a while is the availability of banana-picking work. The local hostel can help you out with finding the work, but you'd probably be just as well off to simply ask down the pub. It's a small community and everybody knows who's hiring. Banana picking is particularly demanding work, involving lots of contact with snakes and spiders and huge cane rats and prolonged back-breaking effort in the fiendish tropical heat and humidity. Being such crappy work, there's usually a few jobs to be had. For my money, picking bananas is a mug's game; I'd even prefer to pick pineapples first. Still, it pays.

Mission Beach, which can be reached by **Greyhound Pioneer** and **McCafferty's** buses, is a different kettle of fish. It's quite a pleasant place – scattered settlements along 12km of beach to explore and rainforest running right down to the foreshore. Coconut palms, lapping surf, sunshine – all the best North Queensland ambience, without the frenetic bullshit of Cairns or the over-hype of Cape Trib. Mission Beach is also the way to get to Dunk Island, which is well worth the effort.

If you're travelling by road, the way to Mission Beach is found by turning east from the Bruce Highway either at **Tully**, or further north at **El Arish**. Both turnoffs are well signposted and easy to find. If you're coming in from El Arish, you may wish to stay at the **Treehouse Hostel**, in Frizelle Rd at Bingal Bay, (070) 68 7137; under $15. The Treehouse Hostel specialises in the peace-and-quiet nature experience kind of backpacking and comes highly recommended for its atmosphere and layout.

In Mission Beach proper, **Scotty's Backpacker's** (167 Reid Rd, Wongaling Beach (070) 68 8676; under $15) is a lively and well-organised place to stay, with excellent budget facilities and a very pleasant atmosphere. The Scott family who run the show are as friendly and decent a bunch as you could wish for, willing to help in any way possible and prepared to go out of their way to make your stay fun and interesting.

Accommodation can also be had at the **Mission Beach Backpacker's Lodge** (28 Wongaling Beach Rd, Wongaling Beach (070) 68 8317. Under $15), which is clean and well-run, but perhaps less inviting than the other two.

There's plenty to do in Mission Beach. It's possible to organise your whitewater rafting trip down the Tully River from here, which is probably a much better way to go than hanging around in Tully. The guided rainforest walks are a good bet, being shepherded by local Clump Mountain Aboriginal people. Chances are pretty good that you'll see one of the rare cassowaries here. It's also possible to go horse-riding through the forests, should you so desire. One thing about horse-riding in rainforest: there's this lovely local vine, called 'wait-a-while' by the locals. It hangs little green tendrils down over practically every trail and clearing and these surprisingly strong tendrils, nearly invisible against the green of the forest, are covered in needle-sharp backwards-curving spines. Personally, I would never, ever, ride at any speed at all through a North Queensland rainforest, but it's your holiday, right? Just leave enough money to cover the plastic surgery bill when one of those little bastard plants tears half your face off as you gallop past …

Boating, fishing, scuba and reef trips are all available from Mission Beach. A PADI course here will cost you under $350, leading to open water certification. Reef diving is excellent in the area and it is possible to take day-trips to deserted cays on the Barrier Reef. For a real win, though, get yourself a national parks camping permit and take a quick water-taxi ride for less than $20 (return) to marvellous **Dunk Island**.

Dunk is a mainland island mantled by excellent rainforest. It has quite a history, due to the efforts of a chap called Banfield, who wrote the famous *Beachcomber* books about his time on Dunk from 1897 to 1923. He's buried there too. Lived independently on a little farm, in harmony with nature and all that good eco-hippie bullshit right up until his appendix gave way. It's a pity the back-to-nature lifestyle didn't include a doctor.

The island is only 5km from the coast, so it's an easy ride and though it would cost you over $150 per night to stay at the resort, you can camp in the national park there for less than $5 per night. You're supposed to get your permit from the **National Parks & Wildlife** office in Cardwell, but the Mission Beach hostels can help you get one without having to make the extra trip. The campsite has toilets, tables, fireplaces and for an outlay of about $25 for a resort pass, you can use the facilities of the resort, including swimming pool, sports gear, drinking water and showers. There is, however, a maximum of about 30 campers at any time and a maximum stay of three days. Coupled with the fact that the resort will only handle about 400 people at once, Dunk never seems to get too crowded.

Food can be had from one of the two restaurants associated with the resort, so long as you buy that resort pass. It's expensive, but the food is good and quite interesting, from all accounts. There's also a fast-food and snacks joint down by the Jetty, if you're day-tripping or camping. Prices there are pretty reasonable, but the food is nothing out of the ordinary. Might save you hauling a truckload of food to the island, though.

Dunk Island has an artist's colony on it, which is a pretty quaint idea these days. Visitors are accepted for $4 twice a week – Tuesday and Friday mornings, I think – and it's worth a look in. Must be tough, living on a rainforest island producing artworks for a living …

Aside from visiting the artist's colony and poking around the famous gardens, Dunk's got quite a bit more going for it. For starters, it's an island. I love islands. The sense of weird isolation you get is just excellent. Then there's the swimming, snorkelling and diving. If you're not carrying your own gear, the resort will rent snorkelling equipment to you at a very moderate rate – about $5 for four hours or so – and you can dive the fringe reefs from the various beaches. It's not great diving, though; shallow and visibility is not as good as elsewhere on the reef proper.

Best of the lot is probably just walking. Dunk has about 13km of walking tracks, which take in the peak in the centre of the island and the decaying WWII radar installation there. The rainforest is stuffed with birdlife and the famous Dunk Island butterflies, notably the Cairns Birdwing and the Ulysses. There's a good view from the top and the walk isn't too strenuous, especially if you allow for swim breaks at the various beaches. There's quite a number of little streams running through the forest as well, should you want to take a quick dip in some fresh water. All things considered, Dunk Island is a great way to get off the backpacker trail for a few days and relax.

Innisfail

South of Cairns by about 100km, this is an ugly little town, propped up by sugar cane and property development. Unfortunately, it lies smack in the middle of some utterly gorgeous scenery. If you get here, you absolutely must drive back into the maze of little roads in the **South Johnstone River Valley** – very beautiful. Look for **Paronella Park** – a bizarre monument to one Spaniard's homesickness, set in rainforest next to a beautiful waterfall and rock pool. Paronella Park features a somewhat dilapidated Spanish castle/hacienda, complete with exotic gardens, birds, butterflies and enormous fish. The place is beautiful, weird, cheap to get into and definitely worth the visit. You can only get there by private transport, though. In its heyday, when it had a tennis court and a working cinema, it was right on the highway. Unfortunately, the road got moved. Then there was a flood. Or was it two floods? And a fire. The present owners are busily restoring the site and it is truly a valiant effort – but one has to wonder how long it will be until another huge flood washes them away too. See it while you can.

Innisfail itself is right on the Bruce Highway, accessible by bus or train, about an hour south of Cairns. There's a couple of hostels there: **Backpacker's Innisfail**, in Rankin St (070) 612 284 gets much of its business from itinerant workers and pickers. You might also try **The Endeavour** at 31 Glady St (070) 616 610, which is close to the main street and the bus stop.

Not far from Innisfail is Queensland's highest mountain, **Bartle Frere** which isn't saying much in terms of height, but it's a hell of a walk through heavy rainforest to the top from the nearby village of **Babinda**. This is a great walk to do, if you're a serious walker; challenging, interesting and scenic as all hell. A good, solid, full-day trip starting early in the morning – or you can carry a daypack and consider overnighting up there somewhere. Not much in the way of facilities, mind you. You can check out **Josephine Falls** on the way, too – a truly breathtaking place.

Babinda itself is a tiny little place, about ten minutes north on the highway from Innisfail, but the walk up the mountain and the nearby Josephine Falls and **Babinda Boulders** make it worth a stop. The Boulders are particularly interesting; the water races between gigantic granite rocks and quite a number of people have drowned here over the years. Local Aboriginal legend holds that a young woman, wronged by a man,

drowned herself here and her ghost lures young men to their deaths. It's a pretty neat place to visit, but if you're going to swim, it's best to stick to the more placid waterhole nearby. The Boulders themselves are every bit as treacherous as the legend makes out.

Also in the area is the **Oolana Gallery** – one of the better places to acquire Aboriginal artifacts. You can even watch the pieces being created in the open workshops, if you like. Oolana Gallery is in Munro St in Babinda (070) 671 679.

Another excellent area for walking and swimming is the **Wooroonooran National Park**, next to the Palmerston Highway, which runs from Innisfail to **Millaa Millaa** at the southern end of the **Atherton Tableland**. (This is a neat drive to take in any case, if you have the chance. I actually saw a wild cassowary here once, years ago.) There's about 17km of track through various degrees of rainforest, with half a dozen waterfalls scattered around. Great to do if you've got a couple of days to just poke around in beautiful rainforests and there's a free camping area at **Henrietta Creek** if you decide to make it an overnight stay.

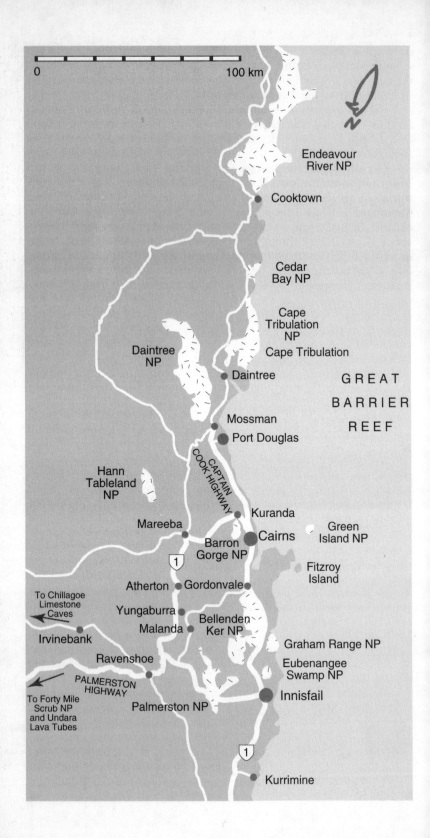

0   100 km

Endeavour
River NP

Cooktown

Cedar
Bay NP

Cape
Tribulation
NP

Cape Tribulation

Daintree
NP

Daintree

GREAT

BARRIER

REEF

Mossman

Port Douglas

Hann
Tableland
NP

CAPTAIN
COOK HIGHWAY

Kuranda

Mareeba

Green
Island NP

Cairns

Barron
Gorge NP

1

Fitzroy
Island

Atherton   Gordonvale

To Chillagoe
Limestone
Caves

Yungaburra

Malanda

Bellenden
Ker NP

Graham Range NP

Irvinebank

Eubenangee
Swamp NP

Ravenshoe

PALMERSTON
HIGHWAY

Innisfail

To Forty Mile
Scrub NP
and Undara
Lava Tubes

Palmerston NP

1

Kurrimine

Innisfail to Cooktown

Centering on Cairns and including Port Douglas, Cape Tribulation and Cooktown at the north end, this area has received enormous hype internationally. And why not? There're the World Heritage-listed tropical rainforests, the secluded and beautiful forests and beaches of Cape Tribulation, access to some of the best scuba diving on the planet, a thriving artistic community and a whole range of other things.

The trouble is, everybody knows about Cairns now. The place is rampant. It's not really a trekker's place at all, any more. Once you arrive here, prepare to be swept off your feet and whisked through the full gamut of attractions and excitements.

Oh well, someone's got to do it.

If you've just flown in from a Northern Hemisphere winter, give yourself a few days to acclimatise. Otherwise you might die from excitement.

Dirk's Dozen

1. Diving the **Barrier Reef**.

2. Walking or mountain-cycling the **rainforest**.

3. Swimming in the tropical **rainforest creeks**.

4. Visiting the **Undara Lava Caves** at the back of the tableland.

5. A trip to **Cooktown**, preferably by way of the Cape Tribulation road.

6. A stay at **Cape Tribulation.**

7. Visiting **Kuranda** for the markets and the scenery and the cable-car trip.

8. **Surfing**! (See the section on Surfing The Edge and Planet Beach.)

9. Camping on the **Frankland Islands**.

10. Cruising round the **Atherton Tableland**.

11. Visiting **Chillagoe Caves**.

12. Actually there isn't a twelfth recommendation, but don't whinge. Readers who've been paying attention will have noticed this is the first of Dirk's Dozens to make it even to *eleven* recommendations. In

other words, this will probably be the best part of your trip, so allow some time.

Dirk Dumps On Strenuously

1. **Green Island**.

2. **Port Douglas**.

3. The super-heavy-duty **Cairns hostel party scene**.

4. Expensive, trendy **shops**.

5. **Rampant development**, including subdivisions in the Daintree and Cape Tribulation rainforests, hydroelectric schemes on the Tully River up on the Tablelands and the skyrocketing land prices which are starting to prevent locals from being able to continue living in the area.

Cairns/Atherton Tableland

I grew up in Cairns. The place had some character back then, in the seventies. The old hipsters had fled to the region to hide out and lick their wounds after the collapse of the Great Aquarian Love-In Revolution and the local miners and cane-farmers didn't know what the fuck to make of all these long-haired dope-smoking weirdos. The uneasy truce between the two groups made for some fascinating developments and the place is still crawling with world-class artists and craftsmen. And women.

Unfortunately, Bjelke-Petersen and his bully-boys let the Yuppie Motherfuckers loose once they figured out there was money to be made in the stunningly beautiful north. Bad scene.

Cairns used to exist as a last-stop port for the Northern seaboard. It was a sleepy little town in the Deep North, where flooding still washed the occasional crocodile into the lobby of the best hotel. There was only half a television station and air conditioning was largely a rumour, but the sleepy little town sat smack in the middle of some of the most gorgeous terrain on the face of the earth.

With that kind of a setup, word eventually gets around. Cairns is still there, of course, but these days it's nothing like the sleepy little township of twenty years back, where a big night out was a feed of KFC down on the Esplanade above the mud-flats and a flick at the Rex with its canvas-backed chairs. A place like Cairns used to be draws developers and money the way shit draws flies.

Developers are a special breed of noxious creature you can't find words enough to insult. The kind of gaping, suppurating asshole who will turn a beautiful little town like Port Douglas into a plastic life-support system for a Marina Mirage complex, then run off to fucking Majorca for the rest of his unnatural life. The sort of person who will plough a private access road through ten kilometres of heritage forest, choke a river with fallen trees so that he can build a dam and then turn around and force the government to cover the cost of putting tarmac on his road.

It was funny, when I first came down to Brisbane from the Deep North. Down there, people kept saying how bad Russ Hinze and demented old Joh Bjelke-Petersen were – and I guess they were right. Trouble is, these people had never met Martin Tenni, the local member for my home region. His grip on reality was so tenuous, he actually tried to convince us that it was a good idea to plow a road through the Daintree wilderness in order to cut down on the white slave trade. And he even expected people to believe him.

That's North Queensland for you. If you've got the money, it doesn't matter what sort of big, ugly lie you front with: the place is yours. And so, for twenty years, the money has poured in. Yakuza golf-course cash. Japanese tourist-abbatoir developments. Rainforest parcelled up into suburbs and sold. Whole towns traded back and forth like television station shares back in the Eighties.

It's kind of tough, coming back into something like that. I mean, this is where I grew up. Right here, along the beach, right up that crystal-clear creek into the mountains – this is where I was a boy, where most everything that made me into what I am got started. And they have sold it all, developed it, and turned it into marketable shit.

Dirk's Dozen

1. **Surfing The Edge:** At the **Planet Beach** surf shop in the Smithfield Campus shopping centre (roughly 10km north of Cairns proper), you can make arrangements to be taken out to the far edge of the reef, where the monster waves roll in off the Pacific. Three metres and more to the foaming crest. These trips last a day and you'll get lunch, snorkelling (of course) and real live surf, way to hellangone out of sight of land for $130. Now that may seem a little expensive compared to the more usual reef daytrip price of about $50, but think about it: just you, your board and the boat out in the middle of the big blue. Maximum heavy shit.

    Thing is, when you come in on those tubes, you're going to be speeding towards savage, jagged coral reefs. Now your $130 does in fact include insurance – but I wouldn't take this trip if I wasn't a confident, competent surfer. At the moment, Planet Beach are the only people who can make the arrangements for you, although **Rosie's Backpacker's** on the Esplanade is supposed to be getting in on the act. If you surf, you owe it to yourself to Surf The Edge.

2. **Rainforest By Night:** Not many people are aware that even the blackest night in a tropical rainforest is awash with light. The decay of all that leaf mould gives rise to the most remarkable fungi and moulds, many of which glow with an eerie blue light in the darkness. I have picked up an entire leaf skeleton, perfect in every detail, beautifully illumined by this strange, magical glow. Many different groups offer guided rainforest walks. While you're in Cairns, you should make every effort to get with one of the groups that goes by night. There's more creatures to see and the darkness adds a wonderful atmosphere of creepy mystery to the whole experience. And

when that moment comes and the lights are switched off and slowly you become aware that everything – every last little piece of the place – is glowing faintly, it's like stepping into another world. The Cairns region is best for this on the simple grounds that even by night, it's fairly warm, whereas, taking a night walk through damp rainforests elsewhere can be a little chilly. Don't miss it.

3.   **Mountain bike tours of the rainforest.** Requires a certain amount of fitness, stamina and possibly even insanity – but it's a really cool way to see some of the forest and if you like rough-riding or mountain-tracking at all, this is really intense fun. A full day ride will cost about $100, with pickup, setdown and lunch. You'll probably get to swim in a mountain pool during the process and the ride is guaranteed to be challenging and entertaining. Contact either your hostel, or **Dan's Tours** (070) 33 0128.

Stuff To Do

Cairns has a lot of things for the traveller. I mean, a *real* lot of things. For starters, there's the usual gamut of bungy, skydiving, water-skiing, paragliding, catamaran/small boat hire, canoe hire, mountain bike hire, horse-back riding, rap jumping/abseiling, Tiger Moth Biplane rides and all the other stuff that goes with the tourist hot-spots. You want it, you got it. Quite a lot of it doesn't occur in Cairns proper – which has only a muddy, shallow harbour frontage and no beach or surf swimming at all – but at the beach suburbs, about twenty kilometres to the north. The buses leave regularly from Sheridan St, though, and it's easy to get to the beach and back in the space of a day.

Swimming at the local beaches isn't particularly exciting. The string of coves up the coast – **Machans Beach**, **Holloways Beach**, **Yorkey's Knob**, **Trinity Beach**, **Kewarra Beach**, **Clifton Beach** and **Palm Cove** – provide reasonable beaches with fairly murky water and no real surf. Naturally, during the summer months the threat of Box Jellyfish makes swimming at any of these beaches a poor idea. Each of these areas, though, is fairly well developed with a range of other amusements and facilities.

Further north, past Buchans Point, the beaches are fewer and farther between and far less developed. The swimming is much more pleasant too, on the whole. **Ellis Beach** has an unofficial nude beach at the southern end and beyond that, along the winding coast road as far as **Wangetti Beach**, the shore is dotted with nameless little beach coves. Nice, often relatively secluded, lined with coconut palms – but still no surf to speak of and the jellyfish will keep you at bay during the summer months.

Fortunately, during those self-same sweat-soaked summer months, there are plenty of local freshwater swimming sites which make a pleasant day's outing. You can go to **Mossman Gorge** – Coral Coaches leaves Cairns several times a day – where the water is clear and beautiful and the rainforest is well-tracked and safe. Closer to Cairns there's **Lake Placid**, on the Barron River. Further up the Barron, a long walk past the hydrostation, there are a couple of really huge freshwater swimming holes, which are extremely picturesque. Down the Barron from Lake Placid is the **Kamerunga Crossing**, which has reasonable river swimming. You can also paddle at the popular **Freshwater Swimming Hole**, or jump from the cliffs at the extremely popular (read 'crowded as hell') **Crystal Cascades**.

There is also an adrenalin-charged nightlife in Cairns. There are any number of clubs and nightspots which stay open most of the night through, many of which cater almost exclusively to backpackers. You'll have no trouble finding them, as they're all in the city central district, easily reached on foot. More to the point, practically every different hostel has a deal going with one or another of the nightclubs whereby you get a free meal and discounted drinks if you can show you're from the hostel in question. The food is generally reasonable – things like pasta, lasagna, fish & chips, nachos and whatnot – and who's going to argue with a free meal, anyway? Try places like **Samuel's**, **The Woolshed**, **The End Of The World Nightclub** and the **Fox & Firkin** just to name a few prominent places which cater heavily to 'packers.

Take note: Cairns by night is not a place to seek peace and quiet, or tropical atmosphere. It is a wallowing flesh-dive that makes an evening on the Gold Coast look tame as Bingo at the local church hall. Cairns clubs, especially in the wee hours, are crowded as the adulterer's circle of Hell, even in the off season on a quiet night and the atmosphere is frenetic. Loud music, competitions, indoor games and cheap booze poured down your throat until dawn. Cairns has got to be regarded as a kind of 'packers sex mecca. My own personal suspicion is that if you can't get laid in Cairns, you might as well give up trying.

Sex & parties aside, the really big drawcards to the Cairns region are of course, the **Barrier Reef** and the **rainforest**. Your hostel will most certainly have more information than you could possibly want regarding a myriad of trips to either or both of these. Be wary, though – intense competition has led to a degree of pressuring from various hostels and agents and you can be sure that there's plenty of under-the-table kickback money flowing from the tour groups to the hostels. Therefore you should shop around before you decide which tour or trek to take.

Nonetheless, you'd be mad to miss the reef if you've come this far north. Should you have your own scuba ticket, you ought to contact one of the dive groups directly – they're all in the Yellow Pages. A day trip to the reef, including equipment, lunch and a decent day's diving should cost on the order of $40-$60 for certified divers. This is an absolute bargain, especially as the reefs in the Cairns region are generally just fantastic, especially the outer reefs. It's worth finding out before you sign on just how far out the trip will go, as the difference between the outer reefs and the inner reefs is quite marked.

It's entirely possible to do full dive courses leading to certification around Cairns and with the local scenery, such a course is a real pleasure to do. On the other hand, you will pay upwards of $350 for a five-day course. Longer dive trips can also be arranged for certified divers, to some of the more distant and exotic locations like Lizard Island, Cod Hole and the Ribbon Reefs, but these tend to be pretty expensive, going well past the $500 mark. Best left to the real scuba-freaks, in my opinion.

If your budget doesn't stretch that far, it's still possible to get in some genuine reef diving. Novice and introductory dives, supervised by a dive master, are available through most of the reef operators as well. The

prices are usually pretty much the same as those on offer to certified divers, but you don't get nearly as much time in the water and of course, you're limited as to what you can do and how deep you can go. Still, just to make the point clear: you'd be fuckin' daft to come all this way and then not lay out the $50 for a totally magic day on the most amazing dive-paradise in the world. It's so easy in Cairns! Most of the tour operators will even do a complimentary pickup and return, on top of supplying all food and equipment. At the very least, if medical reasons prevent you going the scuba scene proper, you should strap on a mask and snorkel and take one of the day trips to the edge.

The rainforests in the Cairns region include the World Heritage-listed areas of the **Daintree**, **Cape Tribulation** and the **Bellenden Ker/ South Johnstone** sites. Although there was considerable logging over the last century – and some logging is still going on around the Mt Windsor region – there are still areas of rainforest which have been left pristine. The local rainforests are just about the oldest on the face of the earth; they may, in fact, represent a real live example of the Gondwana forests that once stretched across the planet in warmer, more humid times.

Again, there are a dizzying number of operators cashing in on the rainforest thing in the Cairns area and the same warning holds regarding pressure from over-eager hostel-operators who may have a fiscal interest in promoting particular groups. Shop around! It may be no more than taking a brief walk along the Esplanade, talking to different hostel operators, but it could make a lot of difference to the kind of trip you take.

Even if you have your own vehicle, a guided tour through the rainforest is probably a better idea than taking off on your own. Most of the rainforest fauna is nocturnal and there are more than a few creepy-crawlies at large in the undergrowth. Local knowledge goes a long way; a well-informed tour guide will ensure that you get to see the best there is in the forest, without causing too much damage, either to the delicate environment or to yourself.

A visit to the rainforest is every bit as mandatory as a visit to the reef. The place is fantastic. There are few things more exquisite than swimming in pure, cool water running over giant granite boulders in a forest more wild and gorgeous than Hollywood could ever devise. I've seen pools so clear you could count the grains of sand on the bottom five metres down. The North Queensland rainforests are indescribable – visiting and walking through them will recharge and revitalise the most jaded of souls, even in the worst of weather. Daytripping through the forest, lunch, pickup and set-down included, should be about $40-$60. Longer expeditions are definitely possible, including overnight trips with nocturnal walks, which are a blast.

Once you've done the mandatory reef and rainforest things, there's still a host of great stuff to do in the Cairns region. There is, for example, quite a strong local Aboriginal culture, although it is made somewhat confused by the fact that white intervention has mixed and matched Aborigines from all over the country to new areas. Still, if you can afford it, a trip through **Quinkan Country** – especially with **Trezise Bush Guides** (070) 521 552 – will give you the chance to see Aboriginal art galleries thousands of years old, as well as introducing you to some of the most beautiful, most raw and challenging country you will ever see in your life.

Just a note in passing: why Trezise Guides in particular? Because Percy Trezise from the tiny outback township of **Laura** has been actively rediscovering and helping promote and preserve Aboriginal culture in the region for decades. The man has aided and assisted Aboriginal artists, lobbied loud and long for the listing and preservation of Aboriginal sites and probably knows more about the local Aboriginal culture than most of the Aborigines themselves do. A two-day trek with this lot will cost you close to $300, but it's the real thing that you'll be seeing.

Also on the Aboriginal culture front: you might consider doing a tour with the **Aboriginal Tribal Tours Group** (070) 312 912. They run day trips through local forest areas, guided by Bama Aborigines. You'll get the opportunity to sample **bush tucker** (native foods) including crocodile and kangaroo, watch Aboriginal artefacts being created in the traditional manner, trek the forests, swim, and get a handle on the culture of the rainforest people.

In Cairns itself, there are a number of places dealing in Aboriginal instruments and artefacts. The local **Art Gallery** is a mine of information on Aboriginal art and is well worth the visit, as the Cairns and regional arts community is particularly strong and vibrant. You can even get didgeridoo lessons through a group called **Sounds Aboriginal**.

More To Do

If you've done all the above things and find you just can't leave, here are a few more things to do.

Gunslinger Tours (070) 41 2085 or the **Cairns Shooting Centre** (070) 321 722 if you've ever wanted to practise your Clint Eastwood impression with live ammunition. Live firing on a shooting range under the instruction of a range officer, for about $90-$120.

Rusty's Markets offer a wide range of food, produce and off-beat souvenirs, including a lot of stuff brought in quasi-legally from Indonesia.

Several of the **bungy places** will let you jump free if you jump nude.

Rusty's Tavern hosts the infamous Far North Qld Drag Follies, notably the Priscilla, Queen of the Daintree shows.

Check the interesting, informative and well-signed mangrove boardwalk within spitting distance of the **airport**.

One very popular distraction involves day tripping to **Kuranda** by the famous Kuranda Railway, or riding the new **Skyrail** through the rainforest treetops. Skyrail is a remarkable piece of work: half an hour of hanging gondola ride through nearly ten kilometres of rainforest treetop, with a couple of interesting and educational stops on the way. Fantastic views of the mountains and the gorge, as well. As anyone who knows the rainforest will tell you, the treetop level is the most varied, interesting and colourful. The supports for Skyrail were lifted in by helicopter and the whole construction was done in a manner to utterly minimise impact on the environment. And why not? After all, the whole point of the ride is the chance to float over world heritage-class rainforests. If the company had fucked up those rainforests, everybody would still be riding the Kuranda Train.

Skyrail can be boarded at the base of the mountains in Caravonica, north of Cairns, or near the train terminal in Kuranda. A regular bus runs between Cairns and Caravonica, costing about $5. The cost of the ticket itself is currently under $25 one way, or just under $40 return. A more interesting option is to mix the Skyrail journey with the older Kuranda Train, one up, one down. This option costs under $60 and takes much longer, but the train journey with its many tunnels and winding mountain path is almost as interesting as Skyrail.

One point to note is that the Skyrail people aren't happy to let you take dirty big backpacks aboard their little six-person gondolas. If you're thinking of an extended stay in Kuranda, don't go by Skyrail. Daypacks are okay, though, so if you figure you can get by with a few changes of underpants and your toothbrush, by all means go ahead.

In And Out

Cairns is tucked into a niche in the mountains, coming down to a shallow, muddy estuarine bay. The busy central area is relatively small, easily travelled by foot or bicycle. Southbound, the Bruce Highway eventually runs back towards what passes for civilisation. Northbound, the Captain Cook Highway goes … well, it goes as far as **Mossman**.

The hinterland to the immediate north of Cairns is rather pretty and heavily populated. There's a string of little suburb/villages which have grown up along the beaches, which are fairly nice on the whole, but a little unexciting after the beautiful, broad beaches of the south. Also, unfortunately, most of the accommodation in a reasonable price range is in the city proper.

Cairns is sort of the End Of The Line for a lot of things. The regular passenger train route, for example. Long distance bus routes, for another example. And it has one of the busiest airports in Australia. As a result, you can go directly from Cairns to almost anywhere you really want to.

The airport is up the north end of town, about five minutes by cab from the business centre. Regular domestic flights go several times a day,

Beware The Rip-offs

In Australia today the indigenous arts industry is worth millions of dollars. Wherever you turn, there are shops selling t-shirts, posters, boomerangs, didgeridoo etc. Aboriginal artistic motifs are used on everything from wine bottles to carpets. Despite this, there is relatively little return to the artists and craftspeople who are creating the work being reproduced.

The popularity of the art of Australia's original inhabitants may be based upon romantic ideas of primitive peoples, being politically correct or the very real attraction of a truly unique artform.

Aboriginal artists often are the traditional holders of stories or dreamings which have been passed down from generation to generation and as a result are the only people permitted to reproduce their designs, a right which has only recently been affirmed by Australian law. Traditional law could often demand harsh penalties for artists whose work has been degraded through improper use; artists from traditional communities have been known to be so affected at the sight of their work on a tea towel or t-shirt that they have been unable to paint for months or years.

Merchandise is the area which has the worst offenders - t-shirt manufacturers, carpet manufacturers and other producers of products which have ripped-off Aboriginal designs have been successfully taken to court and forced to pay damages to the artists whose work they have used.

If you want to enjoy Australia's indigenous culture beware of shops which are full of Aboriginal designs but don't have any Aboriginal people to be seen, markets where English backpackers try to sell didgeridoo and cheap mass-produced imitations. There is an increasing number of Aboriginal owned and run enterprises where your money will go towards the people who really are creating the artwork. They are the ones who need it the most.

all the way down the coast, stopping at Townsville, Mackay, Bundaberg, Brisbane, Gold Coast, Sydney, Melbourne and so forth. Brisbane one-way is usually about $350, Sydney $500, Townsville $150, Darwin $400 and Perth about $600. These prices vary seasonally and you'll get a much better deal if you book them from overseas. International flights come and go to Papua New Guinea, New Zealand, USA, Japan, Indonesia, Malaysia and a few other places.

The **long-distance bus line** is down near the wharfs, on (wait for it) **Wharf St**. It's an easy walk from there to the nearest hostels, on the Esplanade, only two blocks distant. All the usual bus lines operate in and out of Cairns. **McCafferty's** and **Greyhound Pioneer** run services down the coast just as far as you could want. Book all the way to Perth, should you so desire. By bus, it's about five hours to Townsville, ten to Mackay, fifteen to Rockhampton and about twenty-two to twenty-six hours, depending on the route, the condition of the road and the nature of your bus driver, to go to Brisbane. The full Brisbane run is about $130; Rockhampton about $90; Townville about $40.

Locally, **Coral Coaches** run to useful places like Port Douglas, Mossman, Cape Trib/Daintree and Cooktown. It's about $15 to get to Port Douglas or Mossman. You can also get on a coach service for Karumba from Cairns, but you'd have to be mad. There's not a lot out Karumba way.

The train station is at the junction of **McLeod** and **Shields Sts**, close to the central business district. The trip to Brisbane will cost you about $130 minimum and will probably take you 36 hours or more. The journey is mostly bland and dull – scenery bits are minimal. Stops are available at most of the coastal centres as far south as Gladstone. Then things get a bit wacky and the train goes inland for a while. Don't expect to get a train to Hervey Bay, for example. Personally, I really hate travelling by Queensland Rail and I wouldn't recommend it to my worst enemy.

Shelter

Cairns is just berserk with backpacker's places. It's beyond belief. Not only that, but most of them run near-full pretty much all the time. Nonetheless, the sheer number of players in the market means that the overall standards of service and accommodation available to the Cairns backpacker is very high. You should expect the following from your hostel.

1. Bed will be between $10 and $15, for accommodation in a dorm of four to eight.

2. Share kitchen facilities, secure lockup, common room area and often a pool will be available.

3. The hostel will be able to rent bicycles, snorkelling or surfing equipment to you at a cheap rate.

4. The hostel will be a locally accredited travel agent, able to hook you and book you on all local tours and practically any travel short of flight bookings.

5. Your evening meal will come free (or very cheaply) when you show your hostel docket to one of the various city night spots.

This is pretty much a typical Cairns hostel setup. You'll also find that it is quite crowded and noisy, with people coming and going all the time and a sort of party/carnival atmosphere at all hours. You may find that some places trade off one set of facilities against another, or offer a quieter, more peaceful atmosphere instead of a pool, but if you nose around, you'll find what you want.

Hostels in Cairns can be loosely divided according to geography. There's the **Esplanade hostels** and the **non-Esplanade hostels**. The Esplanade is the long, wide street that parallels the waterfront and where it nears the city proper, it is jam-packed with backpacker's places. These tend to be the liveliest, the fastest, the most crowded and the noisiest, but by virtue of their proximity to the city centre, the wharfs and the bus terminal, they are also among the most popular. Don't expect to get a lot of room or sleep if you decide to stay here, but you are pretty much guaranteed a 24 hour party.

Hostels in this area include **YHA on the Esplanade** (070) 311 919, **Hostel 89** (070) 317 477, **The Bellview Hostel** (070) 314 377, **Jimmy's** (070) 317 477, **Caravella's 77** (070) 512 159 and **The International Hostel** (070) 311 424. They're all only two blocks from the wharfs and the bus station, right in the heart of the city. About three blocks further along the Esplanade is another cluster of hostels – slightly more laid-back than the city-centre Esplanade hostels, but still very lively indeed. This group includes the well-regarded **Bel-Air Hostel** (070) 314 790,

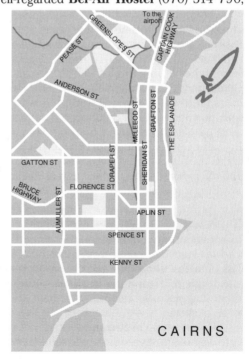

the friendly and helpful **Rosie's Backpacker's** (070) 510 235 and **Caravella's 149** (070) 512 431.

Once you leave the Esplanade, things get a little quieter – but not always and not a lot. On 204-212 Sheridan St, on the way into town from the Airport, you'll see a truly monumental concrete statue of Captain Cook. That marks the enormous **Captain Cook Backpacker's Hostel** (070) 516 811, a converted motel. This one boasts two pools, as well as free evening meals in the in-house restaurant. Also on 191 Sheridan St is **Rick's Place** (070) 412 184 which advertises free cable TV ... as if you need it in Cairns. **U2 Hostel** (070) 314 077 is also up this end of town, at 77 McLeod St, but it's a little dark and basic. At 11-13 Charles St, quite near the big Captain Cook, is **JJ's Hostel** (070) 517 642, which is pretty standard for Cairns. Also nearby is **Castaways** (070) 511 238, at 207 Sheridan St, which is a bit quieter than most.

Back towards the centre of town, the **Parkview Backpacker's** (070) 513 700 at 174 Grafton St is a nice relaxed sort of place. About a block away on 141-143 Sheridan St is **Inn The Tropics** (070) 311 088 and close by at the corner of Grafton and Minnie Sts is **Tracks Hostel** (070) 311 474, which is big and cheap.

Opposite the railway station is the **YHA McLeod St** (070) 510 772. They give preference to YHA members and won't take bookings from non-members, but they do have an arrangement whereby you can stay, if there's a bed, for another $2 on top of their prices. Also near the railway station is the **Coconut Palms Hostel** (070) 516 946 at 69 Spence St. Just a couple of blocks west of the railway station at 274 Draper St is the **Gone Walkabout Hostel** (070) 516 160) which is a little smaller and a lot quieter than most. Nice if you want to chill while in Cairns. Further still to the west, past the Cairns Showgrounds at 164-170 Spence St is the **Uptop Downunder Hostel** (070) 513 636. This one is a fair way out and lies towards what could be unkindly termed the rougher stretch of town, but it's a cool place.

This list is not complete and comprehensive and it will probably change without warning. Cairns is a fast-moving sort of place in terms of tourism and backpackers. Besides the huge hostel scene, there are also a number of cheap, pleasant guest-houses. If you're camping, or driving a sleeper-van, you might want to consider a caravan park. There are about a dozen, although none are really close to the city centre.

Around Cairns: If the city pace doesn't suit you, try heading a few kilometres north to one of the beach suburbs. Yorkey's Knob has the closest beachfront campsites to Cairns at the **Yorkey's Knob Beachfront Van Park** (070) 557 201. Trinity Beach offers cheap lodging at the **Sundowner Motor Inn** (070) 556 194 on the Trinity Beach Esplanade. Clifton Beach has a caravan park: **The Paradise Gardens** (070) 553 712 next to the highway. Palm Cove, which is otherwise fairly boring, upmarket and expensive (although it has one of the better beaches in the area), has the **Palm Cove Camping Area** (070) 553 824 which lies on the Palm Cove Esplanade. (They're not real inventive with names for streets up in this part of the world.) The **Palm Cove Retreat** (070) 553 636 offers horse-riding as well as reasonable and cheap accommodation, providing a real alternative to the crowded Cairns scene.

Food

I don't know why I'm bothering with this. Chances are, most of you will scarf up your free meals from a hostel/nightclub deal, sink lots of piss, miss breakfast altogether and choose McDonald's for lunch. Still, should you decide to escape the treadmill, Cairns has a really good range of interesting places to eat. Many of them are even cheap enough to welcome 'packers.

When you're in **Kuranda**, check out the markets for food. There's a growing range of very authentic south-east Asian food popping up there.

I had the best mee goreng I've had outside Malaysia for under $5

Down in Cairns proper, there's a sort of food hall in Aplin St, near Abbott St, called **The Meeting Place**. It does about a dozen different sorts of Asian cuisine, including some very fine Japanese (go for the sushi), passably good Thai and decent Chinese. Also Italian. It's a big, busy place, very reminiscent of a Singapore or Malaysian food court. Made me kind of nostalgic, actually.

The exotically-named **Elissar, Queen of the Sea** on the Esplanade in the heart of 'packer heaven makes extremely fine Lebanese food, including the ubiquitous kebab and the all-conquering felafel. Nearby, at the corner of Asplin St, **Licks** is a great place for designer ice cream and sherbets. Or should that be sorbets? Whatever – they're cold, tasty and perfect for the steaming tropics.

The **Tandoori Oven** in the Mainstreet Arcade, off Lake St – near Hides Hotel – is reputed to do a seriously fine tandoori, with a sideline in killer curries. **Café Zuzu** in Grafton St opposite Rusty's Market has fine food and very enthusiastic proprietors who are probably worth a visit in their own right. Plenty of ambience here. Also quite near to Rusty's Market is **The Cake**, owned and operated by an escaped French pastry chef seeking asylum here in Australia. And finally, for vegetarians, try **Tiny's** on Grafton St. They also do an amusing line in therapeutic juices. (No, I will not explain. Go and find out for yourself.)

Kuranda & The Tablelands

Kuranda itself is a funny little mountain village, much cooler and more pleasant than sweltering coastal Cairns. The place is absolutely sodden with crafts, markets, arts and Aboriginal culture. Of late it has become more than a little crowded and commercial, but it's still worth the effort. The markets are famous for their colour and variety and works from artists of international standing can be found in local businesses. At this time, there is still a hostel in Kuranda – **Mrs Miller's** (070) 937 355 – but as it is up for sale, things may change. It's a nice old place, though, with a pleasant atmosphere and none of the 'party fever' which grips Cairns. A good base to work the Tablelands from, at least for a few days.

For a very different accommodation experience, consider the newly-opened **Tentative Nests** (070) 939 555 at the back of town. Not your usual 'packers place, it provides quality, comfortable, permanent tent-style accommodation (including food) on platforms high up in the trees in a section of rainforest at the back of the town, off Barron Falls Rd near Jumrum Creek. It's a pretty good set-up, although a bit on the New Age side and prices were quoted at about $80 overnight. If you've got the money, this is a very interesting way to spend a night just about as close to the rainforest as you could get.

Aside from the markets, Kuranda boasts some good walking and a couple of interesting attractions. There's a walk-though butterfly sanctuary, said to be the largest in the world. The tropics produce some spectacularly beautiful insects, notably the Cairns Birdwing butterfly and the

Ulysses, otherwise called the Mountain Blue. The **Kuranda Wildlife Noctarium** has a setup in which they've reversed the day-night cycle on a small clump of enclosed rainforest environment. That means you get the opportunity to see the critters which ordinarily don't come out until nightfall. This is an interesting arrangement if you're just passing through, but for my money, if you've got the time, you're better off taking one of the night-time rainforest spotlighting walks which can be had pretty much all over the region.

If you're going to explore the region around Cairns, you shouldn't miss the opportunity to go road-tripping around the **Atherton Tableland**. Access by bus is possible, of course, but doing the journey slowly and thoroughly, with your own vehicle to explore all the by-ways, is a real treat. The area up there, centred around the townships of **Atherton**, **Yungaburra**, **Tinaroo**, **Millaa Millaa** and **Malanda** is cool and green, like something pilfered wholesale from the English countryside.

The place abounds with fantastic walks and waterfalls, pretty little towns, lakes and pockets of rainforest. **Lake Eacham** and **Lake Barrine**, near the top of the **Gillies Range**, are natural volcanic crater lakes surrounded by rainforest. They have excellent swimming facilities and very good (relatively easy) walking tracks. Check out the two **Giant Kauri Pines** – these things are enormous, maybe eight metres through the base and pushing ten times that for height. Gives you some idea of what the place was like before the loggers came and pillaged it.

Also worth a stop, if you're in your own vehicle, is the **Giant Curtain Fig Tree** and **The Crater National Park**. **Millaa Millaa** and **Malanda** are practically besieged by waterfalls, almost all of which come with their own glorious swimming holes. In fact, it's probably worth devoting a few days to simply trekking around the Tablelands, if you can. Budget accommodation can be had in most of the little towns and there are a number of caravan parks and campsites available too. The highly regarded **On The Wallaby** (070) 510 889 hostel in Yungaburra does pickups from Cairns for free and allows camping as well as dorm accommodation. It's pretty centrally located and makes a good base for exploring the Tablelands.

Worth mentioning is the **Peeramon Hotel** (070) 965 873 in minute Peeramon (between Malanda and Yungaburra) which provides cheap accommodation in an old-style pub with truly marvellous atmosphere. Malanda proper comes with the **Malanda Falls Caravan Park** (070) 965 314 which is right next to the excellent swimming provided by Malanda Falls. Look out for possums and brush turkeys raiding your tent site for food, though. **The Malanda Hotel** (070) 965 101, in the town centre, also has budget accommodation and has a reputation for excellent food in large quantities at a very low price.

Near Malanda is the **Platypus Forest Resort** (070) 965 926. This is a quiet and very pleasant place set in rainforest, with lots of wildlife and good local swimming and walking. It's a really good way to dodge the high-energy crap of Cairns for a few days, if you need to shake off your hangover.

Atherton itself isn't really all that interesting to the traveller. Most of these other little places have the odd museum, historical site, park, waterfall or walkway. Atherton is really all about managing the business of the

Atherton Tableland. It does have a backpacker's, though – the **Atherton Backpacker's** (070) 913 552) near the centre of the town, at 37 Alice St. The interesting Herberton Historic Railway leaves from Atherton as well. It's a neat trip, if you're a rail buff.

Tinaroo is a tiny township situated at the base of the Tinaroo Dam, a whacking great complex set up for the Barron Falls Hydroelectric scheme. You can hire all kinds of watersports equipment here and there's a really excellent circuit drive that goes around the lake proper through an old pocket of rainforest. **Tinaroo Pines Caravan Park** (070) 958 232 is a reasonable place to stay if you want to spend a day or two on the lake. Also, if you follow that road around the lake, you'll come across a number of free lakeside camping grounds maintained by the Department of Primary Industries ... probably trying to score points for the logging industry, the bastards.

If you drive out west of Mareeba, past the Atherton Tableland, you come to the dry, jagged country around **Chillagoe**. It's an old mining town, which pulled practically every possible mineral and metal out of the ground at one time or another – gold, silver, lead, copper, wolfram (tungsten) – there's even some local tin. Chillagoe also produces what may be the world's finest marble, now that Carrera in Italy is pretty much played out. Chillagoe marble comes in all the colours of the rainbow and there's more of it up there in that mountain range than perhaps ever there was in all of Greece and Italy together.

Chillagoe also has a pretty extensive **limestone cave system** nearby. The caves are almost entirely above-ground, being inside large limestone outcrops, which means that they're easy to get around in. Not too wet and dank, except in the monsoon season, when they're prone to sudden closure. There are at least three local cave systems with guided tours and if you talk to the rangers at the **National Parks & Wildlife Service** office in Chillagoe, you'll find out about other cave walks which are self-guided, needing only a good electric torch to see you through.

Personally, I love caves and caving: I reckon Chillagoe is worth a look-in on that account alone, despite the fact that it's a bastard of a drive over a lot of dirt road to get there. There is some budget accommodation in Chillagoe, so if you get there, you won't have to turn around immediately and drive all the way back. Check the **Chillagoe Tourist Village** (070) 947 177 for campsites, or the **Post Office Hotel** (070) 947 119 for cheap beds. You may also want to check out the **Chillagoe Bush Camp & Ecolodge** (070) 947 155 for more familiar, if somewhat basic, 'packer lodgings.

South of Chillagoe – but on a completely different road, running out through Ravenshoe to the Gulf of Carpentaria – you'll find access to the wholly remarkable **Undara Lava Tubes**. This is a really amazing place and should probably be on the 'must-see' list if you have any eco-tourist in your bloodstream at all. The lava tubes themselves are situated in evil, forbidding, dry and jagged country and they're accessible only by guided tour from the Information Centre at Undara. Fortunately, there's plenty of these tours arranged from, and originating in, Cairns and Townsville. Check with your hostel for details on getting there.

A fairly useful tourist facility has been built in the national park complex here and camping facilities are available. The tubes themselves are gigantic tunnels formed in lava rock about 200,000 years ago, give or take a few millennia. Essentially, there was a truly colossal eruption and a bunch of lava flows headed for the sea. As they went, the surface rock cooled and set, but the lava in the interior just kept on flowing underneath the crust, so that eventually, these huge pipelines of basalt were left behind. The whole thing is spooky and amazing and certainly worth the time and effort involved in getting there and back.

Port Douglas

Along the coast north of Cairns about an hour's drive, you come across the turnoff to Port Douglas. This used to be a beautiful sleepy little village locally famous for its excellent pies and for the lovely **Four-Mile Beach**. Unfortunately, a blood-maddened developer named Christopher Skase found it in the '80s and proceeded to blow the budget of half the country in 'upgrading' it. As a result, Port Douglas is now a sleepy little village with a huge marina and several extravagant, over-priced, nauseatingly luxurious big-money resorts. And Australia has an extremely large foreign debt.

Skase was a remarkable sort of creep. Had a development company and sank jumbo bucks of other people's money into all sorts of shady real estate, not least of which was his monumentally extravagant redevelopment of Port Douglas. Then, when the Reagan Years ended and everyone realised somebody had to foot the bill, Skase and his wife Pixie pissed off to Majorca, leaving about a billion and a half in bad debts. They claimed they were bankrupt but a week later the family cats followed them, by air.

Naturally, Australia applied for extradition, but somehow Skase's health just quit on him and he couldn't travel back to face the charges. Emphysema, apparently. During all the court proceedings in Majorca, you never saw the man except that he was in a wheelchair, gasping like an ugly grey carp into a very ostentatious oxygen mask. 'Subtlety' and 'underplaying' were never part of his vocabulary.

Of course, once the Spanish courts ruled that he was far too sick to travel and would never have to face the extradition process again, Skase made a truly miraculous recovery. Gee, those Spanish courts … These days he's fit as a fiddle and keeps talking about schemes to make the Majorcans hate him almost as much as the Australians do.

Still, where does that leave Port Douglas? It's worth a visit, I suppose. It's a good base from which to explore the northern end of the Cairns region, with at least as many reef and rainforest tour operators as Cairns itself. The little town itself is still quite pretty, with a very nice Sunday market operating. Four Mile Beach is right there, next to the town, which is a big step up from Cairns' unpleasant mud-flat vistas. Still no surf, though, and the inevitable box jellyfish set in during summer. There's also a cutesy steam-train to ride – the **Bally Hooley Railway** which orbits the town – and a paddle-wheeler which cruises the local creek. You can do a combination of the two rides for a reasonable price. The excitement's not exactly mind-blowing, but it's pleasant enough.

Port Douglas is the main point of departure for the **Low Isles**. This is a nice little coral cay with a beautifully-kept old lighthouse on it. Good snorkelling, pleasant beaches and most of the boats provide lunch and/or boom-net riding. Low Isles trips are pretty popular and often quite heavily booked. Probably you should save your money for one of the less heavily trafficked destinations.

Another point worth mentioning is that the food is notably good in Port Douglas, as might be expected with the mass of upmarket resorts in the area. In general it's not exactly cheap, but if you poke around, you can get some excellent seafood for around $20.

If you're going to stay in Port Douglas, try the **Port O' Call Lodge** (070) 995 422 in Port St. It's a YHA affiliate, well-kept and well-run with excellent facilities, though it's a little more expensive than most of the Cairns places ($15-$20 range). The place is exceedingly popular and it pays to call in advance. Failing that, you might try the **Pandanus Caravan Park** (070) 995 944 in 111 Davidson St. Well south of the town proper is **Four-Mile Beach Caravan Park** (070) 985 281 which is nicely situated right next to the beach.

The Islands

The Cairns region has a number of islands nearby which are popular with daytrippers. A big one to avoid is **Green Island**, which has been the major reef destination of the region for day-tour victims for decades now. It's only a little island and the local reef and vegetation are most certainly showing the wear and tear of a truly massive flow of tourists. (Three or four boatloads per day, with a couple of hundred per boat, most every day of the year.) Used to be that you could walk away from most of the tourist bullshit by just strolling around the island, but these days Japanese corporate megabastards Daikyo have dumped a fucking great luxury resort on the little island and the place is pretty much a dead loss so far as the 'coral island experience' goes.

Green Island has the usual – scuba, snorkelling, sunbaking, fish observatory and glass-bottomed boats. There's also a fairly interesting zoo/aquarium/museum called **Marineland Melanesia**, which has an odd array of Papuan and Melanesian artworks, lots of fish and a genuinely daunting saltwater crocodile reputed to be the largest in captivity. It's fuckin' huge. On the whole, Green Island qualifies as a nice day out, but only if you haven't the time or resources to check out somewhere less touristed.

About 30km from Cairns, mostly to the south, is **Fitzroy Island**. It's a big one with daytrippers too, but it has some good points. Fitzroy is a continental island, not a coral island, so it's considerably larger than Green Island. The beaches aren't so hot, though – they're composed mostly of broken coral and shellgrit. There's good snorkelling in the area and a couple of very decent walking tracks around the island as well.

Fitzroy has a minor part in North Queensland history. During the Palmer Goldfield rush period in the 1870s, the large numbers of Chinese diggers who turned up became very unpopular with the Europeans. (Although reputedly, the local Aborigines preferred to eat the Chinese diggers to the Europeans … something to do with the largely vegetarian diet of the Chinese, perhaps.) Anyhow, Fitzroy got made into a quarantine station to hold incoming Chinese until it was certain they weren't carrying smallpox, or any other really depressing diseases. Naturally, once there were about 3,000 Chinese stuffed onto tiny Fitzroy island with insufficient fresh water and appalling sanitation, there was a bit of an uproar. Scuffles and disease broke out. A lot of Chinese died. You can still see the graves.

The **Fitzroy Resort** – run by Great Adventures, who are (surprise!) owned by Daikyo – has the usual range of watersports equipment for hire. You can rent catamarans, paddleskis, canoes and snorkelling equipment at fairly moderate rates. Dive courses are available and the usual introductory dive for about $60 can be had for persons without prior scuba experience. If Giant Clams are your thing, there's some sort of a clam farm on the island, which is open to visitors. They call it Reefarm. It's supposed to be moderately interesting and informative, but my interest in giant clams without an appropriate sauce is very, very limited. There's also some fine walking to be had, with a long track which runs to the rather unattractive lighthouse and back.

If you decide you want to stay overnight, the Resort has four-share bunkrooms at about $25 per night. Camping is also an option, as the island has a national parks campground. Sites will cost you $10. Supplies can be bought from a sort of shop near the bunkrooms and there's a kiosk where you can get greasy take-aways.

A nicer option would be the much-less developed **Frankland Islands**, well to the south of Cairns. These are continental islands, but they have long been national parks and there has been no development. They have beautiful forests, great beaches and diving and you can camp there for the cost of a permit from **National Parks & Wildlife** in Cairns. Mind you, since there's nothing there, you need to carry all your own food, water and shelter. A return trip to camp on any of the Franklands will cost you about $100 through **Frankland Islands Cruise & Dive** (070) 316 300, who will bus you from Cairns to the take-off point on the Mulgrave River. Remember, though, that if you have the stamina and the supplies, that $100 could see you there for a week or so. Fancy a week on a deserted tropical island?

Buying A Car In Cairns

For those who start their journey in the Deep North, Cairns is a logical place to look for a car. Unfortunately, there are some problems. Firstly, it's not exactly a buyer's market. Cairns is a boomtown and prices tend to reflect that. Secondly, the boom is in tourism and as every good hick con-man knows, tourists have far too much money and not nearly enough sense.

Cairns has epically high rainfall. Upwards of three metres a year, in normal times, which leads to an almighty rust problem in local vehicles. Of course, you're not going to be overly concerned about rust if you're only keeping the thing for six months or so – but it will certainly make it harder to re-sell if the car is held together by sticky tape and bog and you need to be certain that the rust is within official road safety limits.

If you are going to buy a car in Cairns, stay away from the dealers around the Esplanade. They love nothing more than making rich little foreign 'packers squee-eeal like a pig. There are some perfectly respectable used-car dealers elsewhere in town; see them first.

If you know anything about cars, you should definitely consider buying from a 'packer. You'll find any number of adverts stuck up on the boards in all the hostels. Advantages here are that 1) the vehicles for sale tend to be the sorts best adapted to backpackers, like vans and wagons and 2) the owners have a vested interest in getting rid of the things so they can leave the country. You may be able to drive a bargain.

The downside is, of course, that 'packer vehicles tend to be poorly maintained and driven hard. (You know what those backpacker bastards are like). Your bargain may well turn out to be a disaster, if you're not careful. One way of insuring against this is to arrange for a vehicle inspection. Now in Queensland, any vehicle being sold must have a roadworthy certificate from a recognised mechanic, dated within thirty days of the transfer of title. Nonetheless, bodgy mechanics are pretty easy to find and you'll find that the $50 or so it costs to have the vehicle roadworthied by the Royal Auto Club of Queensland or RACQ, the major consumer vehicle organisation in Queensland with offices in most every city – main office (07) 3361 2444 – may save you a lot of time and money.

The bottom line is this: finding a cheap, reliable vehicle in Cairns requires patience and a generous dose of good luck. Unless you know cars and engines quite well, or have someone onside who does, you should have the car inspectd by the RACQ.

Daintree/Cape Tribulation

This area has a hell of a reputation to live up to and for my money, it doesn't quite make it. Don't get me wrong – I love the place, with its heavy mantle of rainforest which stretches quite literally down to the secluded beaches and the crystalline creeks that wend their way down through the mountains to the sea. It's just that everybody knows about

Cape Trib and Daintree and everybody comes expecting so much more. It's still good, but there's plenty of other good stuff on the east coast of Australia and a lot of it will be pleasantly unexpected. As I hope you've found out by now.

Cape Trib and Daintree lack the party-animal freneticism of Cairns and surrounds, which I think is a good thing, myself. Daintree is this tiny little village well up a meandering river valley, with some blatantly tourist-oriented businesses and a bunch of cows. Mind you, since a lot of it burned down in 1995 and then washed away in 1996, I suspect there's been some remodelling. The Cape Trib settlements consist of a whole bunch of different resorts – mostly eco-based, thank Bog; no Bastard Club Med here yet – and some suburban developments plonked down in between, on a meandering one-lane road that varies from shitty to im-passable.

On the whole, it's expensive to visit, with supplies costing a mint since the locals know they've got you over a barrel. And even though the two backpacker's places are fine for accommodation, Cape Trib is the kind of place you come to in order to get away from crowds of noisy backpackers, not hang out with them. At least, that's the way I feel about it.

Stuff To Do

Check out the rainforest, the beaches and the reef. Also some horse-riding and kayaking. Definitely for the eco-packer, not the surf-rat. Personal recommendation: grab a day-pack and follow the road to a decent-sized creek. Then follow the creek up into the rainforest. The water will be cool and crystal-clear, running over smooth granite boulders. There will be birds and fish, ferns and moss, ancient trees, waterfalls, swimming holes – and best of all, there won't be another person around all day. Wanna do the walk nude? Nobody's going to care except the mosquitoes.

One particularly worthwhile exercise in this area is a 4-wheel drive safari. Although the Cape Tribulation All-Weather road is actually completely

> Captain's Log, James Cook 1770 World Surf Safari:
> 'Having a particularly shitty time navigating this endless reef. When will I see a decent tube again? In order to make myself feel better, I have named a bit of land that sticks out into the sea. Banks has been nagging me to name something after his mother, so I have called the place Cape Tribulation. It's only fair after that Bastard Bay business, I feel.'

Snapshots

Jens from Hamburg Meets The Feral Pig: I was staying at Cape Tribulation. It is very beautiful there. I did not have much money left and I did not want to go with many other people on the tours, so I walked into the rainforests by myself.

It was easy. I took some bread and some cheese and I walked on the road until I found a small river. Then I walked along the river into the mountains. After an hour, perhaps, I found a small trail and I walked away from the river.

The trail was very winding and I walked for an hour or more, but I don't know how far. Then I heard a sound and there was a little pig beside the trail. It was very small and pretty and I wanted to take a photograph. Just then, the much bigger pig came running from the trees towards me. It was very angry and made a noise like I have never heard a pig make before. I was like you say: shit-scared.

I ran into the forest as fast as I could. I thought I could hear the pig behind me. The small vines with the thorns – you know? The 'wait-a-while' vines? They cut me, on my hands and my face and tore my shirt, but I did not stop running until I could not breathe. Then I fell down and lay in the dirt.

It was very quiet. There was no pig. There also was no trail. There was nothing but trees and birds. I tried to follow my footmarkings back to the little trail, but I could not do it. All the time, I was afraid the pig would come back. I wandered for a very long time and there was nothing but forest. It was like no people ever had come there before. Although I was frightened of the pig, it was very beautiful to be walking in this forest, where there were no people at all.

After a long time, I found a small creek. I walked along the creek the same way the water went and soon it joined a big creek. I followed the big creek for a long way, over rocks. Once I had to climb down a waterfall. At last, the creek crossed the road and then I could find my way back to the hostel. It was very exciting.

useless to conventional vehicles, it makes an utterly brilliant excursion in a rough-terrain car. The road winds along the rainforest coast for over a hundred kilometres, punctuated by crystal-clear mountain streams. You can follow the road all the way up to Cooktown and be back in only a couple of days. There are plenty of companies in Cairns who can arrange a safari for you and the price will be under $180, fed, watered and catered. It's a great drive and if you really wanted to see Cooktown, it's an excellent way to do that as well.

In And Out

This is dead easy. If you're driving, get on the coast road out of Cairns and go north. Past **Mossman**, you start following the signs and it can't be missed. Literally – there's nowhere else to go, once you're up there. It's about an hour and a half by road from Cairns.

Cape Trib and Daintree are such big pullers that everybody and

Macho Bullshit

This little aside is especially for the hardcore Pepsi Max suckers amongst you: the guys who are jaded with bungying into gorges full of rabid tigers, or hang-gliding naked through Bosnia in winter, or whatever it is that used to get you off. Northern Queensland boasts one pastime which is to date completely untouched by tourism and which calls for a greater degree of machismo than practically anything else I know.

Back in 1770, Cook – like a complete dickhead – released a couple of pigs onto Cape York, reasoning that they'd breed and provide a food source for future mariners and the like. He was right – but unfortunately, the little bastards went completely feral as well. To this day, the feral pigs are one of the biggest ecological disasters in Australia. Tough, intelligent, dangerous and utterly omnivorous, they rove the rural north like so many miniature bulldozers. Wherever they go, they tear up the ground, eating whatever they can find – eggs, snakes, roots, plants … practically anything at all.

Queenslanders have responded to this in time-honoured fashion: they head bush with packs of ugly, brutal dogs, large, brutal guns and beer. Pig-hunting in Queensland is one of the few ecologically sound blood-sports in the world. And as practised by Queenslanders and by the their dog has a trip arranged there. **Coral Coaches** run a regular bus to Daintree proper and to Cape Trib as well. Most of the hostels in Cairns operate safaris to the Cape, or at the very least can connect you with them. The best bet is private transport, as always. You need to be careful of the Cape Trib road if you're in a conventional vehicle and in the Big Wet, even a 4WD will serve to do nothing but get you killed. Just this year, a particularly heavy flood washed away just about everything along the Daintree River, including the vehicular ferry …

Shelter

PK's Jungle Village (070) 98 0040 is a full-on 'packers hostel, with the party-animal spirit in abundance. About $15 per night. **Crocodylus** (070) 98 9166 is the name of the local YHA, but it doesn't suffer from the perennial YHA uptightness. Actually, Crocodylus is probably the best of the lot if you're there to see the Cape properly, not just notch up another

'Packers Take Note

feral pigs, it is also one of the most danger-ous. A full-grown bush pig can weigh in at more than two hundred kg of lean pork. They come equipped with a skin that will turn most axes and a set of razor-sharp tusks. They are also fast, smart and enormously strong.

Getting onto a pig safari is not easy for a visitor. Long gone are the days when big-game hunting was fashionable and pig-hunting never had the glamour that lions or rhinos or any-thing else close to extinction had. If you want to really get under the skin of rural Queensland, though, going bush with a bunch of pig-hunters will give you one of the most pri-mal experiences you could desire. It'll get you deep into the real bush, far off the beaten track, in the company of seriously weird local people.

Finding pig-hunters isn't really a problem. Pick any medium-sized rural Queensland town and go to the blue-collar, working-class pubs. Ask the bar staff to point out any of the regulars who do any shooting. It's up to you, after that; tact, diplomacy, enthusiasm and a willingness to purchase several rounds of drinks will stand you in very good stead. A word of caution, though: pig-shooters tend to be almost as rough and hairy a mob as the pigs themselves.

night of beer and bonking. It's well laid out, with interesting architecture aimed at fitting into the environment. Great facilities, too. Both of the hostels have regular bus services and if you phone them in advance, they can help you arrange your way there from Cairns, Port Douglas, Mossman, Daintree or wherever.

Cooktown & Places North

Cooktown has little going for it other than history. A little history. It was a big place, once – second biggest town in Queensland during the Gold Rush days of the 1870s, when the Palmer River fields were drawing diggers in their thousands. Once the gold ran out, though, Cooktown declined as well. These days it's really just a backwater.

The **Cooktown Museum**, now unfortunately open only three or four days a week, is a rather interesting place, despite the fact that it's out in the arse-end of the world. Check out the account of the Lizard Island Escape of October 1881, in which Mary Watson, the wife of a beche-de-mer fisher on Lizard Island put out to sea with her baby and one Chinese servant in a very large iron cauldron. The cauldron itself, unfortunately, is in Townsville – God and the National Party alone knowing why – but the story behind it is fascinating. It seems there was a bit of trouble with a party of Aborigines who arrived on Lizard Island and knocked off one of the two Chinese servants. Two days later, they speared the other servant in four places, and in a panic Mary Watson, her baby and the servant set off for the mainland. Iron cauldrons are hell to navigate, though, and the end result was that they all drifted around the reef for about ten days until they died of thirst. The three of them were found on one of the Howick Islands in January the next year. They were still in their big iron cauldron, which ironically had filled with rainwater in the interim. A punitive expedition was mounted immediately and succeeded in killing a

whole lot of Aborigines who had absolutely nothing to do with the event. Mary Watson's tombstone is still in Cooktown, but her diaries which record the whole depressing saga are now in the Oxley Memorial Library in Brisbane.

The whole Cook thing is very big here, as might be imagined. They have a largish festival every year in which everybody gets staggeringly drunk and a lot of boozed-up blokes in dubious costumes re-enact the Cook landing. If you wander down Charlotte St to the riverfront, you will find that practically everything there is labelled with a dedication or a plaque of some sort. There's one for Edmund Kennedy, a couple for Cook, one for the *Young Endeavour* (a replica of the original *Endeavour*

Flinthart's Journal

Cooktown: Kevin and I brought raging hangovers and the Red Terror here to the desolate arse-end of Queensland in pursuit of Inga, the Famous Mythical Legendary Nymphomaniac Swedish Blonde Backpacker. It was a hell of a drive. Nearly 300km and I think we saw two cars.

Cooktown died years ago. The flies are still settling. We checked into our hostel, had a beer, then walked the main street to the wharf to throw stones at the crocodiles. Then we walked back again. Inga was nowhere in sight.

Passing the Cooktown Bowls club, a certain disgusting fascination gripped the pit of my stomach when I saw that it was Wednesday evening – the club was open to the public. No white uniforms required, bowls provided. Come on in and chuck a few down.

We did. The clubhouse was only a shed, but there was beer. The locals were pretty affable on the whole. A couple of the older ones resented Kevin's shot-put style of bowling, on the grounds that it left craters on the green, but they quieted pretty quickly when I threw the bar-keeper at them.

On the way back, Kevin bet me that I could put my trousers on my head and walk starkers through the main street back to the hostel without anyone noticing. Nobody noticed. I hope it was just because it was too dark to see.

Still no Inga. We're leaving tomorrow, if the cyclone holds off. I'd really hate to be stuck here for a week.

crewed by a lot of under-age sorts as a history/publicity scam) and even one, stuck to what appears to be a very large water-filled hole in the ground, for Russell Cooper, an odious man who is still involved with the Queensland National Party.

Even the **Botanic Gardens** are steeped in history. Left pretty much untended from about 1918 to the early 1980s, there are still trees and stuff there as reported by Joseph Banks back in 1770. Back along Charlotte St, you'll see a large iron cannon, cast in Scotland in the last century. This cannon, three cannon-balls, one officer and a couple of rifles were the sum total of the arsenal sent north in the early part of this century to thwart a feared Russian invasion. (Same one that got the sea-forts built around Sydney Harbour.)

If you're not interested in history, Cooktown could pall quickly. You can arrange for a couple of different safari trips to various inland sites. Or you can get into the fishing, which is pretty good. Or you can drink. The locals do a lot of that. Be careful, though – Cooktown is a peculiar place. There's two pubs on the main street. One – nearer the wharf end of Charlotte St – is accepted as a mostly Aboriginal drinking joint. Whites drink at the pub a block or so further up. Now obviously, there's no law that says where you're going to drink, but you may well draw hostile reactions if you do the wrong thing, especially if the locals are well-advanced in their consumption at the time.

In And Out

Flight West operates twice per week from Cairns. About $100 one way and frankly, there's not much point in hanging around, hoping for a fare reduction. **Coral Coaches** (070) 98 2600 costs about $45, takes over six hours and happens only three days a week. Leaves from the **Cairns Coach Terminal**, down by the wharfs.

Best bet is an arranged tour or expedition, leaving from Cairns. Contact your hostel, or a local travel agent to arrange the details. You'll get a night or so in Cooktown, plus travel there and back, accommodation and a feed for under $200. Or you can arrange a day-trip safari for under $100. This is a good thing, as it saves a lot of wear on your own vehicle, if you have one. The road to Cooktown is a complete fucking disaster. You can choose from the inland route, from Mareeba through Mount Molloy and onwards, or the coastal route along the infamous Cape Tribulation All-Weather Road.

Unless you're in a four-wheel drive, don't mess with the Cape Trib road. Kevin and I, in the Red Terror, crawled in low gear about 10km past the Cape itself before we came to a deep creek full of dirty great sump-rending rocks. The RACQ road reports that day indicated that the road was open to conventional vehicles. I don't know what the RACQ considers to be a conventional vehicle, but it certainly doesn't include the Mitsubishi Colt.

The inland route is much better kept, being fully tarred for all but the last 90km or so. That last stretch can be a bastard, though. Loose gravel, bulldust, stray cattle all over the place and absolutely nobody around to call for help. Not only that, but in the wet, the myriads of low-lying floodways on the road can fill up awfully fast and you could find yourself stuck for some time, waiting for the flood to recede. One impor-

Captain's Log, James Cook 1770 World Surf Safari: 'Most bogus event occurred last night. Mr Midshipman Garth, being ripped off his tits on the local skunk, like, totally bombed out on piloting the boat. It was, like, wipe-out city. We hit this way huge piece of, like, coral, man and it was just, you know, utter water emergency. We even had to, like, ditch the cannons, dude. Just to stay afloat. Wow, the Admiralty are going to be really uncool about that, I bet.

'Anyway, we were kind of lucky because a big chunk of that coral stuck in the boat and kept the water out long enough to sling a canvas patch. Then we headed in shore and up this, like, river. The local natives are pretty cool, with most excellent tans, but they know nothing of surfing. Mr Banks and I have been trying to show them a thing or two while the boat-dudes patch the hole, but like, with the reef out there and all, the waves are totally bogus. It's all beach-break, nothing bigger than three or four feet ... I hope we can get out of here in time to catch the return season in Hawaii!

'There is one totally tubular side to this otherwise major downer, however. Mr Banks has been ashore to gather, like, Botanical Samples. This is a most excellent thing, as supplies were getting dangerously low. In fact, I caught Bosun Everding, like, drinking the bong water the other day. Fortunately, the locals cultivate a variety of plant which is most bodaciously effective, dude.

'We saw a most funky animal today. As tall as a short dude, with the ears of a rabbit, the head of a deer, a great big fat tail and huge industrial-economy sized hind legs for boinging about upon. I found it most amusing and suggested it be named the Elefunken-rhinospringer, but Mr Banks declined and noted it down as the Kangaroo. Tho' I objected most strenuously, he pointed out that as navigator and Captain, I got to name all the geographical features. Thus, he said, it was only fair that as Science Officer he got to name all the plants and animals. I said there were mondo many plants and animals and that Kangaroo was a really bogus sort of name and what about Bastard Bay, but Banks got really uncool about it all and went off in a sulk. He is a complete geek about some things.'

tant piece of advice concerning the road to Cooktown: DO NOT TRY TO HITCH-HIKE. It's a long, long way between lifts.

On the road to Cooktown, it's well worthwhile stopping at the **Black Rock Mountains National Park**, about 15km short of Cooktown itself. This place is too weird for words; it looks for all the world as though when God made the world, there were two or three handfuls of giant black rocks left over and He just put them down in the most out-of-the-way place He could find. The formations here are quite literally small mountains composed entirely of black granite boulders, ranging in size from a refrigerator to a large caravan. They are bleak, mysterious, moody and very impressive and they have an extremely evil reputation with locals of all colours.

If you have the time, a stop at the **Annan River** about 20km short of Cooktown is a top place for a swim – and after nearly eighty kilometres of dirt road, a swim is going to seem like a great idea. There's a couple of fine waterholes, a very nice waterfall and a pretty gorge. Although there's no official campsite here, it's an extremely well-known unofficial place for travellers to stop.

About 18km short of Cooktown is a turnoff which is signposted **'Lion's Den Hotel'**. This is the place where the coast road joins the inland route. The Lion's Den is one of the most colourful outback pubs you will ever encounter, well worth the detour if you're going to stay for a beer or two. Camping is possible here as well.

Cooktown itself redefines the term 'sleepy'. Actually, it's a lot closer to 'comatose'. There's one main street, one parallel street worth noticing and a few cross-streets. Two pubs. A couple of hotels. A handful of shops. A small wharf, with a scattered collection of boats of various sizes and a big dose of history. Cooktown is not for the Adventure Packer – but it is an interesting day trip, well off the beaten track.

Shelter

Cooktown Backpacker's (070) 69 5166 is less than $15. Corner Charlotte & Boundary Sts. Cool, relaxed, with a pleasant common room, although the facilities have a kind of sports-camp feel to them. **Cooktown Motor Inn** also caters to 'packers at under $15, but it's a little darker and more enclosed than the other. Mind you, the bus drops you practically on the doorstep, which is a real bonus; carrying your pack the four blocks to Boundary St can be a complete bastard in the summer.

Food

Pub food is about the limit. It's not bad, reportedly. You can also get the usual range of hamburgers, fish'n'chips and so forth. The **Sovereign Hotel** boasts a (gasp!) a la carte menu and the **Endeavour Hotel/Motel/Restaurant** pushes its steaks. I ate at a perfectly reasonable corner chippie called **The Galley** and was quite pleased with the result.

THE END

Index

Notes